SET FOR LIFE
SOCIAL EMOTIONAL TOOLS FOR LIFE

AN EARLY CHILDHOOD
TEACHER'S GUIDE
TO SUPPORTING
STRONG EMOTIONAL
FOUNDATIONS AND
SUCCESSFUL SOCIAL
RELATIONSHIPS

©2014 Michelle M. Forrester and Kay M. Albrecht
Printed in South Korea by WeSP through Four Colour Group
Innovations in ECE Press
3733 Westheimer Rd, Suite 1, PMB 715, Houston, TX 77027
832.717.5349

Visit us on the web at www.innovationsinecepress.com and
www.SocialEmotionalToolsforLife.com for more information.

All rights reserved.
No part of this publication may be reproduced (except as noted on individual pages), stored in a retrieval system or transmitted in any form by any means, electronic, mechanical, photocopying, recording, or otherwise without prior permission of the publisher.

II | SET FOR LIFE

Forrester, Michelle M.
   SET for life : an early childhood teacher's guide to
   supporting strong emotional foundations and successful
   social relationships / Michelle M. Forrester, Kay M.
   Albrecht.
      pages cm
      Includes bibliographical references and index.
      LCCN 2013910197
      ISBN 97809859299-1-6

      1. Teaching--Methodology. 2. Emotions in children.
      3. Interpersonal relations in children. 4. Social
      skills in children.   I. Albrecht, Kay M. II. Title.

      LB1025.3.F67 2014   371.102
                      QBI14-600030

Design: Doug Gobel, GobelDesign.com

Cover Photographs: Ashley Edwards, Masami Mizukami, and
Cynthia Oualline

Photographs: Jennifer Fiechtner, Masami Mizukami, Michelle
M. Forrester; Kay M. Albrecht, Ashley Edwards, Linda Padovani,
Cynthia Oualline, Mary M. Sliman

MICHELLE'S DEDICATION

To my best teachers—

Emma

Mom and Dad

The following people, for being the support that makes life workable and who are an integral part of our village: the Padovanis, "Mimi" (Cynthia Oualline), the Russells, Marilyn Caul, the Taylors, the Boswells, the Stephens-Chawlas, the Liddi-Browns, the McDonalds, Maureen Maillet, and Kathryn Eaker.

KAY'S DEDICATION

To early childhood teachers, regardless of setting, who are making a difference today in the emotional lives of young children.

"I've come to a frightening conclusion that I am the decisive element in the classroom. It's my personal approach that creates the climate. It's my daily mood that makes the weather. As a teacher, I possess a tremendous power to make a child's life miserable or joyous. I can be a tool of torture or an instrument of inspiration. I can humiliate or heal. In all situations, it is my response that decides whether a crisis will be escalated or de-escalated and a child humanized or dehumanized."

Haim G. Ginott

ACKNOWLEDGEMENTS

Jennifer Fiechtner whose expert editing made this book a reality.

Doug Gobel whose design brought the book to life.

Masami Mizukami and the beautiful children and families of
Small Steps Nurturing Center who shared the wonderful images
you will see throughout this book.

Additional photographs were provided by Jennifer Fiechtner,
Cynthia Oualline, Ashley Edwards, and Linda Padovani.
A big thank you to all!

Diane Barghi, Nancy Gibbs, Danielle Tschirhart,
Christina Navarro and all the interns and families at
Michelle M. Forrester, Ph.D., PC.

The BAG ladies, Jill, Lynn, Teddie, Shea, Lynn, and Lori, who
started this **SET for Life** journey before we knew what it was.

Ellen Pearlman, Ellen Reinstein, and all the past and present team
of Cheerful Helpers, where it all began for Michelle.

SET FOR LIFE
TABLE OF CONTENTS

CHAPTER 10: CREATE A CLASSROOM WITH A SUPPORTIVE ENVIRONMENT 237

FOREWORD

Social Emotional Tools for Life: An Early Childhood Teacher's Guide to Supporting Strong Emotional Foundations and Successful Social Relationships is a wonderful contribution and an invaluable resource. This book will serve as a guide not only for teachers, but also for parents, therapists, and all those concerned with helping children establish the social and emotional foundations necessary for learning. *Social Emotional Tools for Life* also provides real world strategies to help children relate to each other and to adults, and to cope with life both inside and outside of the classroom.

Turn to any point in this book, and you will learn how to encourage each child to feel competent, aware of his or her feelings, and able to evaluate both challenges and solutions. Each page is compelling; not only in its beautiful presentation, but in guiding readers' understanding of the stepping stones to helping children develop age appropriate capacities for self-regulation, self-control, and self-awareness; as well as for relating, thinking, and learning.

You will no longer have to ask yourself, "How do I say that?" *Social Emotional Tools for Life* provides practical language to use with children, and guides you seamlessly as you learn to focus on strengthening relationships with children, and then use the context of that connection to help children learn to identify and analyze challenges, communicate with each other, and problem solve. Excellent real life examples can be found alongside each strategy, showing you what *SET for Life* looks like in action, and helping you to apply what you learn in your own work with children.

. . . .

Although the authors indicate this book is for teachers, you can be sure all those who teach and care for children —parents, teachers, and, of course, early childhood educators— will find useful, expert guidance that will help them to feel successful and rewarded in this role. I really appreciate this book and so will you!

Serena Wieder, PhD
Co-Developer of the DIR Model
Clinical Director, Profectum Foundation
Mendham, NJ

www.profectum.org

Co-Author of *The Child with Special Needs; Engaging Autism; Infant and Early Childhood Mental Health;* and *Visual Spatial Portals to Thinking, Feeling and Movement.*

INTRODUCTION

SET FOR LIFE:
AN EARLY CHILDHOOD TEACHER'S GUIDE TO SUPPORTING STRONG EMOTIONAL FOUNDATIONS AND SUCCESSFUL SOCIAL RELATIONSHIPS

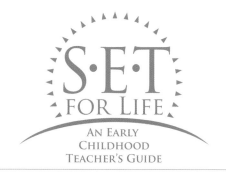

INTRODUCTION TO SET FOR LIFE

If you are reading this book, the well-being and development of children is already important to you. If you are an early childhood educator, you are also aware that as family structure continues to change, with more children living in single-parent families and in families where both parents work out of the home, children are spending more and more of their lives in out-of-home childcare settings. For many children, the hours they spend in the care of teachers and other caregivers exceed their hours spent at home.

When you spend many hours a day with a young child, you are much more than just a substitute for his or her parents. You become an integral adult in the child's life, and what you do in your classroom can impact the course of a child's entire social, emotional, and academic life. In short, the way you interact with children matters a great deal, and for some children, it can make all the difference in the world.

Why SET for Life?

Taking deliberate care to meet emotional needs and teach social skills will help you create classrooms that run more smoothly, and give children the opportunity to grow, thrive, and become well prepared to achieve their full potential.

Learning to deal with emotions and operate in the social world are vital life skills. Children learn them through their interactions and experiences along side caring and supportive adults. Some of these skills must be taught—they aren't learned through routine interactions with others. The classroom is an ideal environment to introduce, model, and support the development of these skills. Because many young children spend so many of their waking hours in a classroom setting, it is important that teachers embrace the role of social and emotional educators, as well as academic teachers.

The purpose of **SET for Life** is to give you the tools you need to address the many and varied emotional needs of children in your care, and also to give you a new lens to look through as you deal with young children's inevitable challenging behaviors. Taking deliberate care to meet emotional needs and teach social skills will help you create classrooms that run more smoothly, and give children the opportunity to grow, thrive, and become well prepared to achieve their full potential.

ABOUT THE AUTHORS

Michelle M. Forrester, Ph.D., is a licensed psychologist who has been in private practice in Houston, Texas for 10 years. For 8 years prior, she directed a program she created at Texas Children's Hospital to address the needs of children with a wide range of difficulties, including autism, ADHD, anxiety disorders, behavior disorders, and depression. She realized that there were real limitations to confining therapeutic intervention only to mental health settings. For children with challenges to really thrive, they would need extra support in all areas of their lives, including at home and in school.

Kay M. Albrecht, Ph.D., is an early childhood education specialist. For 16 years, she directed HeartsHome Early Learning Center in Houston, Texas, and she has spent her entire career working with young children and in teacher education. Over her years working with a wide variety of children, Kay encountered some children who simply did not respond to good teaching strategies — there was something missing in their experiences, and they could not participate and learn, even in an excellent classroom environment with highly skilled teachers and a well-designed curriculum.

The authors paths crossed when Michelle visited HeartsHome to observe a child who was having great difficulty in school and whom she was seeing therapeutically. Michelle introduced new techniques to the teachers at HeartsHome. When they tried these new strategies, they found that not only did the children with difficulties benefit — all of the children in the classroom did.

Giving just a little extra support to children without significant challenging behaviors showed great promise. Equipping all children with the skills they need to manage became the primary goal of our collaborative work. A second goal was to develop a system that would help teachers create stronger and richer relationships with children, and decrease behavioral difficulties in early childhood classrooms. We began this book with the intention of meeting both goals.

We call this approach Social Emotional Tools for Life, or **SET for Life** because it is in the social and emotional realms that children develop and learn the skills and abilities they need to navigate in the rapidly changing world around them. Further, we know that emotional health and well-being is a prerequisite for later success in life. We drafted techniques and asked teachers to try our strategies in real classrooms to be sure we'd hit the mark. After hundreds of real experiences in play therapy groups and classrooms, we synthesized these techniques into the chapters that follow. We include vignettes to help you see what **SET for Life** looks like in action (changing names and details to protect the privacy of children and families involved), and we provide language that you can use to put the **SET for Life** philosophy in motion in your classroom.

As you shift your focus as a teacher towards the emotional and social well-being of the children you work with, you will not only find yourself in a classroom where you spend less time managing challenging behaviors, but you will be able to devote much more time to the more satisfying work of helping children develop and learn. We hope yours is as rewarding a journey as ours was to write it down for you.

WHAT IS SOCIAL EMOTIONAL TOOLS FOR LIFE?

AN EARLY CHILDHOOD TEACHER'S GUIDE TO SUPPORTING STRONG EMOTIONAL FOUNDATIONS AND SUCCESSFUL SOCIAL RELATIONSHIPS

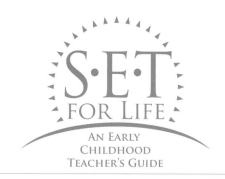

S·E·T
FOR LIFE
AN EARLY
CHILDHOOD
TEACHER'S GUIDE

Social Emotional Tools for Life is an approach to the way children and the significant adults in their lives interact. Designed to build strong emotional and social skills, this approach recognizes and validates the vital role that early childhood educators play in the emotional health of young children. These important skills—ones you can teach in your classroom—enhance the present and improve the future for young children.

SET for Life requires no fancy teaching materials, no particular education or background, and no special classroom supplies or equipment. Your understanding of how children develop and learn, and a few new ideas about how and what to do to specifically support emotional and social development, are the only things you need to implement SET for Life.

Warm, sensitive, caring relationships are the key to optimal development for all children. This book is designed to help you develop the kind of relationships with the children in your classroom that recognize every child as amazing, unique, and entirely worthy of your time and attention.

> "All labor that uplifts humanity has dignity and importance and should be undertaken with painstaking excellence."
>
> MARTIN LUTHER KING, JR.

Warm, sensitive, caring relationships are the key to all children's optimal development.

WHAT'S IN IT FOR YOU AND WHAT YOU WILL LEARN

SET for Life is designed to make your life in the classroom easier. It will help you learn some very specific teaching strategies and teacher talk that increase the chances your interactions and interventions with young children will work. And, SET for Life teaching strategies benefit children by supporting their emotional and social development, resulting in a more harmonious classroom.

As you read this book, you will learn about child growth and development during the early childhood period, and particularly about how children mature emotionally and socially. You will also learn specific teaching strategies that, over time, support children's emotional and social growth. Finally, you will learn the language to use along with these teaching strategies, so that what you say and how you say it supports emerging emotional and social skill development. **SET for Life** provides a new lens to look through when dealing with both normal and challenging behaviors.

It is important to note that the teaching techniques included in this book are educational, rather than therapeutic. Anyone working with young children can study, learn, practice, and implement them. They can ease tensions, help children be more cooperative, and assist children in developing appropriate emotional and social interactions. As a result, children will reach middle childhood prepared and ready to tackle the academic and social learning that is slated for this next period.

Some of the strategies will not be new to you, particularly if you are an experienced early childhood teacher. Others will be more unfamiliar. Some may sound familiar but are used in a slightly different way. When a strategy is offered, ideas and examples of the language to use are provided. These strategies are the "action" part of **SET for Life**. They are built on the foundation of a positive state of mind and intentional teaching to support children's emotional and social development.

A teacher's most important job is building healthy relationships.

What You Will Learn

- How young children develop emotional and social skills during the early childhood years.

- Specific, easy to implement teaching strategies that support emotional and social growth.

- Language to use to communicate effectively with children and support emerging self-regulation of emotion and behavior.

These teaching strategies are not a quick fix, magic, or the only answer to all problematic situations in the classroom environment. They are tools to help teachers invest in the children in their classrooms now, and although they take time to yield returns, they may ultimately increase children's successful outcomes.

PRINCIPLES OF SET FOR LIFE

SET for Life is organized around five principles. Taken together, these principles lay the foundation for **SET for Life**.

> ## Five Principles of SET for Life:
> 1. **Build Positive Relationships with Young Children**
> 2. **Understand and Support Emotional and Social Development**
> 3. **Support Development and Learning**
> 4. **Manage Normal and Challenging Behavior in the Classroom**
> 5. **Partner with Families**

WHY THESE PRINCIPLES MATTER

Early Childhood Period: *The period of development and learning from birth to age eight.*

Children are born into this world totally dependent on their caregivers to survive. As they learn to communicate their needs, they begin a lifelong process of growing, developing, and learning. This process takes place across four areas of development—physical, intellectual (cognitive and language), emotional, and social. During the early childhood period, from birth to age eight, the social and emotional domains of development are closely linked, providing the foundation for future growth, development, and learning in other areas.

CHILDREN NEED TO HAVE THE RIGHT EXPERIENCES AT THE RIGHT TIME

Neuroscience suggests that there are several important windows of opportunity for brain development—periods during which the brain is primed and ready to develop neural connections for particular skills, abilities, and knowledge. Some of these periods occur during infancy and toddlerhood, others during the remaining years of the early childhood period. Not surprisingly, many of these optimal moments for development are related to the emotional and social domains. During each of these optimal times, brain development is influenced by the type and quality of the interactions children have with the important adults in their lives.

WINDOW	WIRING OPPORTUNITY	PERIOD OF GREATEST SUBSEQUENT ENHANCEMENT
Emotional development	Birth - 4 years	4 years - puberty
Trust	Birth - 14 months	4 years - puberty
Impulse control	16 months - 4 years	4 years - puberty
Social development	Birth - 4 years	4 years - puberty
Attachment	Birth - 12 months	4 years - puberty
Independence	18 months - 3 years	4 years - puberty
Cooperation	24 months - 4 years	4 years - puberty
Intellectual development	Birth - 4 years	4 years - puberty
Thinking Skills	Birth - 16 months	4 years - puberty
Cause and effect	16 months - 4 years	2 years - puberty
Problem-solving	Birth - 2 years	2 years - puberty
Language skills	4 months - 2 years	2 years - puberty
Early Sounds	Birth - 2 years	8 months - puberty
Vocabulary	4 months - 8 months	2 years - 5 years
Physical development	Birth - 2 years	2 years - puberty
Motor development	Birth - 2 years	2 years - puberty
Vision	Birth - 2 years	2 years - puberty

Adapted from Schiller, P. (January/February, 2009). Program practices that support intentionality in teaching. Exchange, 57-60. Reprinted with permission. All rights reserved.

Early childhood is a critical time in children's emotional and social development. During this period, typically developing children connect emotionally with the most important adults in their lives first, and then add connections to other family members, teachers, and peers. As development proceeds, children gradually come to know, understand, and adopt the expectations of their families, their neighborhood, and their community.

It is also during the early childhood period that we see indications that emotional development is or is not proceeding normally. When children have difficulty adapting to the expectations of the world around them, they may exhibit behavior that can affect relationships and delay or interrupt development and learning.

CHALLENGING BEHAVIORS ARE ON THE RISE

Signs point to an increase in challenging and difficult behaviors in young children, such as excessive tantrums, lack of impulse control, and aggression with peers. Experienced teachers report that working with children is more difficult now than in the past, and that they are faced with behaviors that don't seem responsive to teaching techniques which have worked before.

Signs all point to an increase in challenging and difficult behaviors in young children.

Psychologists, pediatricians, and early childhood intervention specialists confirm this reported increase in the number of children with developmental disorders. As diagnostic techniques improve, these disorders are being identified earlier. Autism is just one example of a developmental disorder that is on the rise. The rate of autism is as high as one in 68, up from one in 2,500 twenty years ago. This pervasive developmental disorder is characterized by a range of delays in the emotional, social, language, physical, and/or cognitive domains of development. It includes disturbances in one's ability to relate to others, and is often accompanied by language delays and sometimes by cognitive impairment.

The story of depression is similar. Historically almost unreported in children, depression is on the rise. One in 33 children are clinically depressed. Up to 2.5% of children and up to 8.3% of adolescents suffer from depression. Depression is reported earlier in life than in past decades and may persist into adulthood.

Advances in diagnosis and treatment of developmental delays and other disorders identify more children who need intervention. More children are on prescription medications, often without formal Food and Drug Administration approval for use in children, and with very few studies of their effects. Yet, families and teachers report that even medicated children struggle and continue to exhibit challenging behaviors at home and school.

Recent research suggests these developmental and emotional struggles are real and frequent. Children in pre-kindergarten classrooms are expelled from school at a rate more than three times that of their older peers in grades K–12. Expulsion rates are the highest in faith-based and for-profit programs. Boys are expelled at a rate over 4 ½ times that of girls. The author of this research, Yale University's Walter Gilliam, found that classroom teachers feel ill-prepared to handle the increasingly challenging behavior that comes to school with young children.

SOCIETY CONTINUES TO CHANGE

Families and communities have changed considerably in the last few decades. Mobility has forced the family unit to attempt to be nearly self-sufficient, depending on a limited range of neighbors or friends, because extended family members are not nearby. Suburban communities empty during the daytime as families go to work and drop off their children at child care, Head Start, or preschool programs. Commuting time is growing and can consume more than two hours a day of family time.

Children of working families often begin their out-of-home experiences during infancy.

Nearly two thirds of mothers with children under four are in the workforce full time. Children of working families often begin their out-of-home experiences during infancy, rather than during the preschool or early elementary years. While the impact of child care has been thoroughly researched and hotly debated, results indicate that any particular child's experience is closely tied to the family's characteristics and the child's unique temperament, rather than to the presence or absence of out-of-home care.

Another influencing factor is the quality of the care and education experience individual children receive. Requirements for early childhood programs vary widely. Few programs meet the recommendations of the National Association for the Education of Young Children's *Standards and Criteria for Accreditation*, particularly in relationship to teacher qualifications, group sizes and child/staff ratios, and curriculum. Low program quality has been shown to relate to a host of potential developmental consequences for young children, including behavior and academic problems that persist through adolescence.

CHILDREN SPEND, ON AVERAGE, SIX AND A HALF **HOURS WITH MEDIA EVERY DAY.** CHILDREN LIVING IN POVERTY AND IN URBAN AREAS WATCH AN AVERAGE OF 50% MORE TELEVISION THAN CHILDREN WHO LIVE IN SUBURBAN & RURAL AREAS. WHILE THEY ARE WATCHING MEDIA, CHILDREN WILL SEE OVER 8,000 MURDERS **AND** 100,000 ACTS OF VIOLENCE BY THE TIME THEY FINISH ELEMENTARY SCHOOL, INCLUDING 25 ACTS OF VIOLENCE PER HOUR **DURING** COMMERCIAL PROGRAMMING DESIGNATED FOR CHILDREN.

MEDIA EXPOSURE HAS INCREASED

We live in a consumer culture dominated by commercial advertisements, increasingly aimed at younger and younger audiences. Before they leave elementary school, children are exposed to 20,000 consumer-oriented messages. They spend an average of fifty hours per week exposed to television, radio, computers, electronic games, and print media. There are rising concerns about multiple media (TV, movies, Internet, video games, music, etc.) bombarding children with images and words that frighten, intrigue, and influence them in unknown and sometimes negative ways.

Horrific examples of failure to address emotional needs are regularly reported in the media. News coverage often focuses on murder and mayhem, and the shootings in Newtown, Connecticut and Aurora, Colorado brought the gravity of gun violence into almost every American home. The danger is not overstated. Although the rates of death due to gun violence have fallen in the last decade, nearly 20,000 children and adolescents are killed or injured by firearms annually.

> *"Repeated playing of violent computer games can function as horribly realistic rehearsals. With ready access to weapons and continued 'numbing to violence,' the long-term implications for the health and safety of American society is disturbing."*
>
> **James Styler**

The impact of societal change is not limited to young children. While detention rates in the juvenile justice system have declined since their peak in the late 1990s, the rates are still staggering, and minority teens are drastically overrepresented. Rates of mental illness among incarcerated teens are as high as 60% , and suicide rates in juvenile detention facilities are almost four times higher than they are for teens overall. The rate of teen deaths is higher in the US than in many other developed nations, based largely on higher rates of death from motor vehicles, homicide, and suicide.

As society has changed, the need to ensure early healthy emotional and social development for children has increased. **SET for Life** allows you to increase the positive impact you have on children in the classroom, while you enhance and expand your teaching skills at the same time. Read on to find out how.

THEORETICAL AND CLINICAL ROOTS OF SET FOR LIFE

SET for Life is grounded in widely accepted theoretical ideas from developmental and interactional theories. This theoretical foundation connects increasing emotional communication and symbolic thinking during the early childhood years with early interaction experiences. The way adults interact with children can impact emerging growth and development as much as biological characteristics. Experts believe that ideas about appropriate and desirable ways of interacting are culturally transmitted; that is, they are learned from the interactions that are observed, experienced, and modeled in the family, school, and surrounding culture.

The way you interact with children matters.

The clinical roots of **SET for Life** are found in play therapy. In therapeutic settings, trained play therapists address a child's developmental or behavioral difficulties over time. Play therapy meets children where they are, rather than requiring them to be where others expect them to be. Play therapists suspend their judgment and desire for children to be different. Instead, they allow children to *tell* them about their life experiences through play. As children are accepted and freed to be themselves, play therapists reflect their experiences and assist them in creating healthier attitudes and beliefs, which then influence and direct their behavior. Although **SET for Life** is founded on the principles of play therapy, it is not a therapeutic intervention. **SET for Life** is a way of "being" and "doing" in the classroom that offers benefits for children and teachers alike. In the classroom setting, adopting a positive attitude can help both children and teachers to be more successful in their classrooms.

SET for Life focuses your attention on the important work of building relationships that support the emotional and social development of all the children in your classroom, regardless of whether they are typically developing, have developmental delays, or pose behavior challenges. As you learn teaching strategies to help children master emotional and social skills, your ability to cope with challenges will improve.

"Forget mistakes. Forget failures. Forget everything except what you're going to do now, and do it. Today is your lucky day."

WILL DURANT, AUTHOR

CHAPTER 2
BUILD
POSITIVE
RELATIONSHIPS

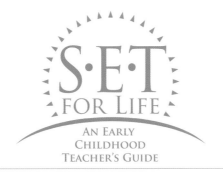

S·E·T
FOR LIFE
AN EARLY
CHILDHOOD
TEACHER'S GUIDE

> *"Nothing good that happens to children happens outside of warm, reciprocal relationships."*
>
> T. BERRY BRAZELTON,
> PEDIATRICIAN

Relationships matter because so much of how we experience the world occurs within them. The success of most of what teachers do depends on the relationships they develop with the children in their classroom. Positive relationships with teachers can shape how children view learning over the course of their entire school careers.

THE IMPORTANCE OF BUILDING POSITIVE RELATIONSHIPS

Investing in building positive relationships with children is the first principle of **SET for Life**. Your success in teaching young children will depend largely on the quality of the relationships you have with them. It really is an investment — relationships are formed through repeated interactions that take place over time. Developing relationships that foster emotional health requires an investment of both time and energy. This investment will pay off for young children as they grow up. And, it will pay off for you—their teacher—as you watch children's skills and abilities blossom in your classroom.

How do you know if you're building the right kind of relationship with children—one that forms a firm foundation for growth, development, and learning?

Positive teacher-child relationships are characterized by:

- A significant investment of time and energy in relationship building.
- Interacting with, rather than reacting to, children.
- Accurately reading and interpreting children's nonverbal and verbal cues.
- Anticipating children's needs and wants.
- Responding quickly and affectionately to any indication of distress.
- Considering personalities and temperaments in decision-making about what to do next.
- Including children in routines (particularly in caregiving routines).

- Being sensitive to over- or under-stimulation from the environment and the other people in it.
- Individualizing the schedule or pace of the day to match children's physical and developmental needs.

As you explore **SET for Life**, each of these important characteristics will be addressed. Let's begin by introducing interactional theory and its connection to healthy emotional development.

PREMISES OF INTERACTIONAL THEORY

The first principle of **SET for Life**—invest in building relationships—is based on one of the foundational theories of child development. This theory, called interactional theory, identifies five assumptions about the way children grow up.

Your success in teaching young children will depend largely on the quality of the relationships you have with them.

Theories are frameworks that organize and give meaning to ideas and actions, and guide decision-making. Theories help us organize the complexity of development into manageable ideas that describe, explain, and predict behavior in young children. Some theories try to explain how children grown and learn fairly comprehensively, looking across the entire developmental process. Others only describe specific portions of the developmental process.

The first premise of interactional theory is that healthy relationships, ones that are close, in tune, and mutual, form the foundation of healthy development. Noted pediatrician T. Berry Brazelton and psychiatrist Stanley Greenspan consider warm, nurturing interactions to be the first *irreducible* need of young children—one of the few things they cannot do without. Many others point to the profound effect that good relationships have on how children grow up and what they learn. When children and the adults who teach them like and enjoy each other, the benefits are enormous. They include increased cognitive and language learning, fewer conduct problems, greater social competence, and higher school achievement. This is particularly true for children whose families have the fewest resources and are under the greatest stress.

Irreducible: *Impossible to make less or smaller*

The first key to forming close, warm relationships is *reciprocity*— the give-and-take part of a good relationship. For example, when a baby coos and babbles, a teacher responds by mimicking the baby's sounds and then waits for the baby's reply, the interaction is reciprocal. The teacher's ongoing and adapted responses, which sustain the interaction, is reciprocity in action.

Reciprocity: Shared dependence, cooperation, or exchange between people; the "give-and-take" of a good relationship.

Synchrony: Occurring at the same time, with a similar level of intensity and responsiveness that seems to be meaningfully related.

The second key is *synchrony.* Synchrony is the part of a relationship that allows us to be in tune with each other, anticipating and meeting each other's needs just at the right times. When a teacher knows that a child has trouble saying goodbye to his mother every morning and makes sure to be close by to offer a hug and help him find something to do, she is demonstrating synchrony.

These concepts will ring true for many teachers, because you may be already doing them, without thinking much about it. **SET for Life** teachers are deliberate about anticipating potential problems. They recognize that changes and/or accommodations need to be made, and work with parents to prevent future difficulty. Finally they talk with the child about the plans put in place.

Note the synchrony between the adult and child in this photo. Both have similar types of emotions, levels of intensity, and an obvious connection exists between them!

The second premise of interactional theory is that interactions take place in, and are influenced by, a variety of different contexts, which shape our expectations about acceptable ways of communicating and behaving. These contexts are social (e.g., family, school, and neighborhood) and cultural (ethnicity, economic status, race, religion, etc.). Each family's expectations will shape the way their children respond to their teachers. That is one reason why it is so important that you are aware of a child and family's cultural context. This knowledge will help you find effective ways to address both accomplishments and concerns. (See Chapter 12 for more on partnering with families.)

The third premise of interactional theory is that there is interplay between the genes we were born with and the sum of our experiences. It is ongoing, and it influences development throughout our lifespan. Although genetics are unchanging, positive experiences during early childhood can unlock biological potential during sensitive periods of development. Such experiences can also compensate for early deprivation, missed opportunities, or mistreatment. For example, children who have experienced institutionalization (e.g., living in an orphanage), family upheaval such as divorce or death, or removal from their families by social services, may make up developmental delays when placed in environments where relationships are close, caring, and reciprocal.

This dynamic relationship offers hope for all children. It reminds teachers to stay focused on the present and on what we can do, rather than viewing either heredity or early experiences as growth-ending.

The fourth premise of interactional theory tells us that learning is directed by the interaction between children and the social, cultural, and physical world. This interaction allows children to continually construct, and reconstruct, their own knowledge and understanding. No matter how knowledgeable we are as teachers, we cannot **give** children knowledge. Instead, they **build** their own, using who they are, their experiences and relationships with others, their learning styles, and their interest level at the moment. For example, children who have been in the same school environment and have had very similar experiences may develop very different interests – one in exploring the outdoors, another in creative art. Each child's interests emerge from the combination of their life experiences, their genetic tendencies, and their unique construction of knowledge.

Premises of Interactional Theory

1. Intimate, reciprocal, synchronous relationships form the foundation of healthy development.
2. Interactions take place in, and are influenced by, a variety of contexts, including social and cultural contexts.
3. There is a flexible and ever-changing relationship between biological heredity and life experience.
4. Interactions between children and the social, cultural, and physical world direct learning.
5. Play is the interactive medium of development.

> *"The irreducible core of the environment of early development is people."*
>
> ROSS THOMPSON, PROFESSOR

The fifth premise of interactional theory is that play is the primary way children learn during the early childhood years. Emotional, social, physical, and intellectual growth takes place within the context of play — with objects and materials, in interactions with peers, and as facilitated by supportive adults. Play is the natural language of children. When children are playing, they are the most comfortable, expressive, and open.

Interactional theory helps explain why the way you relate to the children in your classroom is so important. **SET for Life** teaching strategies are embedded in classroom life—used when opportunities arise to build relationships, support children's interactions with others, and build on their previous experiences to help unlock their full potential.

ERIKSON'S PSYCHOSOCIAL THEORY

German-born Erik Erikson, who taught at Harvard Medical School in the 1930's, proposed a stage theory of psychosocial development that also adds insight into the importance of early relationships. He viewed each stage of development as a struggle, a crisis to be negotiated before continuing to the next stage. The resolution of each crisis influences the way the next stage unfolds.

Erikson's Stages of Psychosocial Development

Age	Crisis
0-1 year	Trust vs. Mistrust
2-3 years	Autonomy vs. Shame and Doubt
4-5 years	Initiative vs. Guilt
6-12 years	Industry vs. Inferiority
Adolescence	Identity vs. Role Confusion
Young Adulthood	Intimacy vs. Isolation
Middle Age	Generativity vs. Stagnation
Old Age	Ego Integration vs. Despair

The first stage of Erikson's theory is the struggle to develop a sense of trust. During the first year of life, babies discover that the world is a safe and responsive place to be, or, that it isn't. During this stage, it is important that children learn that caring adults will meet their needs, particularly when they are upset. Children also learn to use their own skills to impact what happens to them. The result is a sense of self-awareness and self-motivation. When children learn that their needs will be met and that they can make their needs known, they develop a connection and attachment to their caregivers that is crucial to future emotional development.

The second stage of Erikson's theory relates to feelings of autonomy, versus feelings of shame and doubt. Feelings of autonomy emerge as children successfully venture out from caregivers, and easily return when they need or want support from these important people. Success leads to feeling capable and being able to negotiate the social world, and is influenced by growth in language, physical ability, and cognitive skills.

Separation and reunion is a common example of the struggle of this stage. When children are comfortable in a new environment and can reconnect to a family member if needed, they experience an increasing awareness that they can safely venture out and explore. A successful resolution to this stage results in children who confidently participate in new and unfamiliar experiences.

Initiative versus guilt is the next stage in Erikson's theory—the one that predominates during the preschool years. As autonomy grows, preschool children seek to act on their newfound sense of independence. They take the initiative to dress themselves and help with routine tasks at home and at school. Children also become more receptive to adult input than they were during the previous stage.

When children learn that their needs will be met, they develop a connection and attachment to their caregivers that is crucial to future emotional development.

There is a risk during this stage that children will begin to feel appreciated and successful for what they **do** instead of who they **are**, particularly if they receive more attention for their failures than for their successes. Concern for this is warranted — high stakes testing and increasing academic pressures on preschoolers are two examples of current educational practices that can produce shame and doubt (Stage 2) and guilt (Stage 3) in children.

One of the encouraging aspects of Erikson's theory is that it offers hope for children whose early experiences are less than optimal. Failure to resolve an early dilemma is not irreversible. Renegotiation of any stage is possible at a later point in a child's life, although Erikson cautioned that it is not easy. For example, for children who do not develop a sense of trust in infancy, it is possible to help them renegotiate this struggle with consistent, responsive care. It may take a long period of intervention to reverse the mistrustful trend — longer than it would have taken to establish trust in the first place—but it can be done.

Erikson's theory is a good fit with ideas about development and learning occurring within the context of relationships. The identity crises of each stage are worked out in relationships with important people within the child's world, and as a teacher, you are one of those very important people. Children's experience of repeated interactions may create feelings of one kind (trust, autonomy) or the other (mistrust, shame, and doubt). Mindful attention to the kinds of interactions and relationships you have with children can influence their long term emotional health for the better.

GETTING STARTED WITH SET FOR LIFE IN THE CLASSROOM

Throughout the book we give easy strategies to use in your classroom. We begin with some ideas about how to build strong, reciprocal relationships with the children you teach. The most important of these strategies is SET Time – special time set aside, focused entirely on building relationships with the children in your classroom.

TEACHING STRATEGIES TO SUPPORT BUILDING POSITIVE RELATIONSHIPS

IMPLEMENT SET TIME

Every child in your classroom needs time to connect with you. SET Time helps you ensure that your relationship with each child receives attention. SET Time is a dedicated one-on-one time scheduled into the weekly routine, spent with a child or a small group of two or three children. It is "sacred" time, and never a punishment or reward. Inspired by Greenspan's idea called

Floortime, SET Time extends relationship-building experiences to small groups of children in the classroom setting as a routine part of the interactive curriculum. Adding SET Time to the planned activities supports building a warm relationship with each child in your classroom. Intentionally planning to interact with each child and facilitate children's play in small groups regularly supports their emotional and social development.

During SET Time, teachers spend more time talking *with* children, observing them, and listening, and less time talking *to* them. Use this time to help children express themselves when someone important is there to listen. It usually takes place on the floor in a defined play area (indoors or outdoors), with just a few interesting toys or materials. You, the teacher, are the only thing SET Time really requires. Your relationship with the child is the key.

SET Time in action.

To build healthy relationships in your classroom, plan for every child to spend some uninterrupted time with you on a regular basis. A reasonable goal is 20–30 minutes of SET Time, over the course of the week, and it can be scheduled or fit in when time allows. If there is time or your class is small, SET Time can be spent with each child individually. Otherwise, carefully selected groups of two to four children also work well.

During SET Time, the children are in charge. They make all of the decisions about what to do—you are the assistant and observer. If you are working with a small group, rotate the "in charge" position every 10 minutes, so that each child gets a turn.

SET Time is not teaching time. It is not a time to practice academic skills, or teach new lessons. It is a time to enjoy a safe place to play, for feelings to be experienced, and for thoughts to be expressed. It is a chance for children to practice decision-making skills, to make choices, and experience the consequences of those choices with the support of a caring adult. SET Time helps children practice being in control, an important lesson of the early childhood years. Being in charge gives children a chance to feel powerful and important.

SET Time Highlights
- Plan a regularly scheduled time for SET Time. Put it on the calendar and build it into your curriculum plans.
- Give SET Time a special name and use it with children.
- Suspend teaching agendas and expectations.
- Remember that children are in charge, not the teacher.
- All direction comes from the children. You are the assistant.
- Two ground rules: No breaking things and no hurting others.
- Classroom rules stay the same (such as, no sitting on tables).
- Avoid questions; make comments instead.
- Suspend judgment on particular types of play. Participate as a play partner —even if you would prefer a different type of play.
- Don't encourage pursuing one direction or another in play— follow the child's lead.
- Label, notice, and connect emotions with play—the idea is for the children to be able to feel whatever emotions arise.
- Be fully present—stay in the here and now. Attend to the children's actions, reactions, play, and language, and watch carefully to see what happens.

FOR EXAMPLE...

Mrs. Lopez is a pre-kindergarten teacher. She decides to implement SET Time in her classroom, starting with one child at a time, and planning to cover all of the children within a month. She tells the children during the morning meeting that, over the next month, each child will get to play with her one-on-one during center time. She posts a list, so she can keep track of who has had SET Time, and to assure children that they will each get a turn. She talks with the children about how the assistant teacher, Ms. Brown, will be available to children who need help while she is doing SET Time.

Mrs. Lopez is excited about getting started. She begins with Armand, who reluctantly joins her. He doesn't seem to want to choose an activity. After Mrs. Lopez provides several suggestions, Armand asks if he can go play with his friends. Mrs. Lopez feels disappointed, and she tells Armand that he can go.

She doesn't give up, though. She tries again with the next child on the list. Virginia is excited when Mrs. Lopez invites her to come to SET Time to play. Virginia chooses the doll house, and assigns Mrs. Lopez the "sister" doll and herself the "mommy" doll. Mrs. Lopez follows Virginia's lead and they play sister and mommy for the next 20 minutes. The following week, after seeing several of his friends enjoying SET Time with Mrs. Lopez, Armand joins her willingly, choosing play dough for his SET Time activity with her.

ADDRESSING POTENTIAL ISSUES WITH SET TIME

There are times when teachers do all the right things but children still don't respond. Let's discuss some of the potential pitfalls that teachers may encounter, and suggestions for dealing with them.

CHILDREN WILL GET WHAT THEY NEED – ONE WAY OR ANOTHER

Providing SET Time to all children is a big job in itself, but some children may need more than the 20 or 30 minutes normally set aside for them. Children tell us what they need through their behavior or misbehavior. They will get what they need—either through well-planned positive activities, such as SET Time, or negatively, through inappropriate behavior. Undesirable behaviors may appear in more and more contexts (at home, in the classroom, at the grocery store, etc.) if the child's needs continue to go unmet.

Managing inappropriate behavior is difficult, both for the teacher and the child. It is much more effective, not to mention more pleasant, to give children what they need in a supportive setting.

When children have their emotional needs met at the right time, they may be able to wait a little longer in the grocery line, take turns during group time, or tell a friend that they are angry instead of hitting. Even more importantly, children learn that they can get their needs met, receive empathy from others, and give and receive compassion from their friends.

Children who observe other children acting out or misbehaving can be given a simple, non-judgmental explanation, such as, "Harry is having a difficult time today. He is upset and it is hard for him to use words. Teachers will help him. You are not upset; you are a different boy, and you can play with blocks while I help Harry." This provides a framework for what is happening, and it tells children what will happen next and what is expected of them. It also reduces anxiety for children who are not having difficulty.

Effective teachers modify their interactions to match the needs of individual children and help children accept that they are similar to and different from others. Recognizing differences helps children begin to understand that the world is not necessarily a fair place, and that different children (and even adults) may need different, often unequal responses from others.

FOR EXAMPLE...

Jose is an older preschooler. At lunch, he spills his water right after Ms. Michelle pours it in his cup. She offers him napkins to clean it up. After watching Jose, Scott, a younger preschooler, pours his water on the table and begins to play in it. Ms. Michelle gently touches Scott's hands and says, "You are a different boy. Jose spilled his water; I think you decided to pour your water on the table. Water in cups is for drinking. Water in the water play table is for pouring." She then helps Scott clean up his water.

SET for Life Language

"You are a different girl (or boy)."

"Rosa needs extra time to get her body ready to sit. Jumping up and down in the block area helps her to be calm in the circle."

"Marcus needs to sit by me so he can really pay attention to the story. I know you want to sit by me and I will be able to sit by you later. Right now Marcus needs my help, and you are able to sit without my help."

FAIR IS NOT EQUAL

During the early childhood years, children feel very strongly about fairness. However, in children's minds, fairness means getting what they want at the moment. If they do not get what they want, it's not fair! Children may object if one child gets something they don't get, such as a longer SET Time. Teachers can help children understand that being fair does not mean that everything is equal.

Teachers themselves also struggle with concerns about fairness. You may feel it is not fair to give some children special attention, especially when that child's behavior is undesirable or problematic. You might worry that the other children will resent extra attention given to a child who acts out, or that usually cooperative children might imitate inappropriate behaviors to get extra attention themselves.

Just as children come in all shapes and sizes, they come with all kinds of needs. If you meet children's emotional needs in appropriate, positive ways (such as during SET Time), they have less need to demand negative attention. Children may try on inappropriate behaviors after seeing them in a classmate, but they rarely hold on to behaviors that don't work the same way for them.

WHEN TIME ISN'T ENOUGH

Teachers increasingly report that children with behavior problems seem immature, or stuck emotionally at a younger developmental stage. These children don't act like others their age — instead they act much younger. Sometimes, there are obvious reasons for these differences—temperament, individual differences, or developmental delays.

At other times, children exhibit this behavior as a result of stress or trauma. There can be many causes, including poverty, unskilled parenting, family changes (such as a traveling parent, moving, divorce, or death), trauma from abuse or neglect, institutionalization, physical injuries, or hospitalization. For young children, the age at which trauma(s) occurred can become the age at which the child seems stuck. Immature or developmentally delayed behavior may be the first indication that something is wrong and needs intervention.

It is important to not label a child as "hyperactive" or "anxious," for example, as you work to figure out what is going on. Instead, start with careful observation of the child in your classroom. Then, discuss your observations with an admistrator, mental health professional, or early intervention specialist, to determine how to approach family members about what you see in your classroom. Invite parents to share their perspective with you, as well. Then, encourage families to consult with their pediatrician, who can help them get a referral to a psychologist or other mental health professional.

Pediatricians, however, may not spend enough time with children during office visits, and some may not be able to recommend referral options for the child. If this happens, you can contact your local community mental health provider to explore other options. There may be resources or community-based services available to you as well as to the family. Persistence is often the key to helping families support their child's needs.

> **Immature or developmentally delayed behavior may be the first indication that something is wrong that might need intervention.**

Resources for Early Childhood Professionals to Consider

- Early childhood intervention programs, sponsored by state departments of education (program names vary by state)
- Zero to Three (www.zerotothree.org)
- Local child psychologists, social workers, play therapists, or other mental health providers who specialize in the early childhood period of development
- Local school districts
- Local community mental health centers
- Local children's hospitals
- Therapeutic preschool programs
- Early Head Start and Head Start programs

FOR EXAMPLE...

Carmen is an experienced teacher—she has taught toddlers for thirteen years. Jessie entered her classroom at 20 months of age. For three weeks, Jessie has cried every day for most of the day. He shows no interest in his teachers, or in the other children. He is inconsolable, except when he is playing with toy cars. Jessie lines them up repeatedly and becomes hysterical if another child comes near him or his cars. He throws the cars when asked to put them away. Jessie has a few words, but he often shrieks loudly. Carmen has only heard him say "Mama" in a teary frenzy, as his mother drops him off in the morning, yet he doesn't seem to notice when his mother returns. He begins to cry again when she picks him up to leave.

Carmen has tried everything she knows to help Jessie. She implements SET Time, but he seems uninterested in being with her. She partners him with other children, hoping that another child will interest him enough to help him play. She sets out his favorite activity—toy cars— each day. Nothing seems to work.

Carmen suspects that there may be a developmental issue. She consults with her director, who makes arrangements to observe Jessie in the classroom. After the observation, the director agrees that Jessie may need further intervention. The director and teacher meet with Jessie's parents and ask for more information about Jessie's development, and discuss their observations. They recommend that the family get a developmental evaluation for Jessie.

It is always best to first explore concerns about children's behavior or development with their families. However, if families don't agree to investigate your observations further, or if they reject your concerns, you don't have to give up. Continue to share information with the family, while you explore resources that can help you in the classroom.

Research has found that teachers who received classroom support from mental health/behavior consultants for dealing with children's challenges are more likely to find ways to respond to the child, and to address the behavior successfully. More importantly, the identified child was less likely to be expelled or asked to find another program, even if he or she had developmental issues.

So, don't give up. Talk to your colleagues, ask your director, principal, or administrator for help, and keep looking for resources. Successful intervention is more likely in early childhood than at any later stage of development. It is worth your time, effort, and persistence.

USING SET TIME TO SUPPORT SOCIAL AND EMOTIONAL GROWTH

Try to spend 15-20 minutes of SET Time with each child in your classroom, as often as you can. This may be more than enough for some children, and not enough for others. Be willing to invest extra time in children whose behavior tells you that they need it.

Introduce the idea of SET Time to children individually and during group meetings. Make sure they understand that it is special time spent together, when the child is in charge of what happens. Assure them that everyone will get a chance to have this special time with you.

Give this time a name. Call it Special Time, Kid Time, Teacher and Me Time, etc. If you'd like, let children come up with a name as a group.

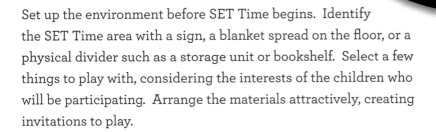

Focus on children's play. Show interest with nonverbal cues like smiles, head nods, and sitting close to the child. Give your full attention to the children involved. Don't take notes, watch the other children doing activities, or do teacher tasks during this time.

Set up the environment before SET Time begins. Identify the SET Time area with a sign, a blanket spread on the floor, or a physical divider such as a storage unit or bookshelf. Select a few things to play with, considering the interests of the children who will be participating. Arrange the materials attractively, creating invitations to play.

Meet children where they are during SET Time, putting teaching agendas and expectations on hold. During this time, focus instead on observing and gathering information. Resist the urge to point out concepts, comment on play choices, or set expectations.

Remind the children that they are in charge. They are the "director" or "boss," and you are the "assistant." When children have structured time to take charge, they may have less need to take control at other times, and may be more easily redirected.

Establish a few simple rules. "No breaking toys," and "No hurting others," are good places to start. General classroom rules stay in place. If children aren't allowed to sit on the tables or climb on the chairs in the classroom, those rules also apply during SET Time.

Avoid asking too many questions. Make comments like, "Looks like the goat is going up the mountain," instead of asking, "Where's the goat going?"

Remember, NO TEACHING. If child says a green truck is blue, then go with it. For now, call the green truck the blue truck! This isn't a time to test knowledge, learn vocabulary, or introduce new concepts.

Use the same time period, and the same location in the classroom, for SET Time. Create a sense of routine by having a consistent time and place to spend SET Time. For infants and toddlers, the SET Time area can be on a carpet near a shelf of manipulatives, in a rocking chair with the child in your lap, or lying on a blanket under a tree. For preschoolers and early elementary children, the SET Time area could be in the dramatic play area, the block area, or at a student work table. This designated area is not available to other children until SET Time is over. If children need help remembering that you and the children involved in SET Time are busy, make a sign to signal that SET Time isn't to be interrupted. Include children in making this sign, if at all possible.

SET FOR LIFE AND YOU

BE AWARE OF YOUR OWN EMOTIONAL HEALTH

As you work to support the emotional development of the children in your classroom, you must also be aware of your own emotional health. It is very difficult to give what you don't have. If you experienced appropriate and loving care as a child, it will be easier for you to provide the same for the children in your care. On the other hand, if you experienced harsh, neglectful, or abusive situations as a child, you may find yourself acting out some of those experiences with the children in your classroom — even if you're trying not to.

Attachment research shows that a majority of parents have the same attachment style with their children as they had with their own parents. For those who did not have a stable, loving environment with secure adult figures in their lives, it can be a monumental task to give to children what they have not experienced themselves.

If teachers are not aware of how they interact with others (including children in their classrooms) or how others interactions affect them, it may be hard to incorporate the strategies suggested in **SET for Life**.

If you are struggling to be effective, and you recognize that your own emotional history is part of your challenge, ask for help. If you are having a difficult time changing the way that you interact with children, despite your best efforts, you do not have to deal with it alone. Ask for support and feedback from a respected colleague or your supervisor, and make self-care a priority.

Helpful Points to Remember

- Relationships are the key.
- Fair is not equal.
- Every child needs SET Time, some more than others.
- Teacher emotional health is important.
- Ask for help from a supervisor if you feel you need it.

FOR EXAMPLE...

Mr. Neal is a new pre-kindergarten teacher. He has chosen the early childhood field against his family's advice, and he is determined to make his classroom the best. Neal is well prepared to teach academically, but by October, Neal is frustrated and angry. He has been unable to implement many of his plans because two children create daily disruptions. Neal is ready to quit and go back to get his MBA (his parents' preferred plan). He feels angry with himself and with his parents. On one hand, he feels his parents are pushing him to change his path, and on the other hand, he worries they might be right.

He tells the principal about his frustration. She is impressed with Neal's teaching skills, and she recognizes that he is struggling to meet the emotional needs of children. She asks how his own emotional needs were met during his childhood. Neal talks openly: his father was largely unavailable because he traveled often for work, and his mother was overwhelmed and sometimes depressed while his father was away.

The principal helps Neal see that it may be difficult to meet the emotional needs of sixteen preschoolers, when he may not have had his own needs met as a child. Neal admits that he feels unprepared to deal with the unruly behavior and neediness of the children in his classroom.

She suggests that Neal set aside his curriculum for a few weeks, and instead focus on the building better relationships with the children in his classroom, particularly the two who are so disruptive.

He starts by asking the families of the two disruptive children to extend their school day by 15 minutes—with one arriving early and the other one staying late while his assitant teacher is free to supervise any other children—so that each child gets some undivided positive attention. Then, he introduces SET Time, spending 10 minutes with a couple of children each day. He and the children spend this time in a cozy corner of the classroom doing puzzles, reading a story, drawing pictures, or just chatting.

During the course of the day, Neal creates more times with the two disruptive students when they are in learning centers. He decides to help children with their academic exercises in pairs and small groups, rather than trying to teach them all at once in a large group. After two weeks, Neal notices that the level of disruption in the classroom has begun to decrease, the two children with problematic behavior are managing themselves more successfully, and that he feels less frustrated.

Directors, principals, or other administrators should be available to discuss your emotional health when it affects your classroom, offering support and guidance when necessary, to create a healthy environment for everyone. If you don't find the support you need, ask for help to find ways to prevent your life experiences from impacting your effectiveness. Sometimes a referral to your employee assistance program or a local mental health provider will offer the needed support.

On the other hand, children should never be left to suffer because of a teacher's inability to create an emotionally healthy classroom environment. When situations like this arise, it is important to seek support and assistance to change things. Administrators who feel unable to support teachers in addressing emotional health issues can access community resources to find assistance.

FOR EXAMPLE...

Molly has been teaching for five years. She has a three-year-old son. Her husband recently told her that he wants a divorce. Molly is devastated. She arrives at school daily, feeling too upset to be present with the children in her class. Behavioral disruptions increase, and Molly's class becomes quite unruly. Many days, Molly is near tears by noon.

Molly's director, who observes in her classroom on a regular basis, notices the change. When she talks with Molly, Molly shares her personal struggles and concerns about her family's future. The director recognizes that Molly will need support. She refers Molly to a local mental health agency, and to a nearby law school that provides low cost legal consultations. Recognizing that all the teachers, not only Molly, could use stress reduction, the director begins on-site yoga classes. She provides child care and invites all teachers to participate. Molly comes to the yoga class and accepts the other referrals. As time passes, she gains the support she needs, and is able to continue teaching. As her confidence returns, so does the equilibrium of her classroom.

MORE TEACHING STRATEGIES TO SUPPORT BUILDING POSITIVE RELATIONSHIPS

GIVE CHILDREN YOUR TIME

In today's busy world, no one has enough time. Almost all of us report that there just aren't enough hours in the day to accomplish our long to-do lists. This is particularly true for teachers in this age of educational accountability. Many teachers find that, as more and more requirements are added to their curriculum, they regularly run out of time to get it all done. How, then, will you find the time you need to invest in building reciprocal relationships with children?

Think about the time you spend managing children. You guide, direct, redirect, and deal with problematic behavior. Many days, it may seem like there isn't time for anything else. **SET for Life** teaching strategies reshape how you interact with young children. As you begin to understand each child's particular temperament, stage of development, skills, and social and cultural context, your classroom's need for behavior management will diminish. The time you devote to relationship-building pays off, through increased understanding of what children need from you, and your ability to match your approach to specific children.

The amount of time that you share with each child makes a difference.

Both quantity and quality of time spent with children matters. Children know that where you spend your time is where your priorities are, and there is no doubt that building relationships requires time. In the classroom, you may feel pressured to move on to teaching content or skills instead and wonder how to find the time you need to focus on building relationships with children during your already busy day.

The amount of time that you share with each child makes a difference, although each child in your classroom will need a different amount of your time. For some children, a few minutes a day will do. These children fill up quickly, and will thrive with just a little extra attention. Other children will need much more of your time.

Whether you give it willingly or not, children will demand time from you. They find ways to get attention to meet their emotional needs, even if it is negative attention. The time invested in giving children negative attention rarely helps children build skills to use later in interactions with you and with other children. A focus on increasing positive interactions with children can reduce less appropriate demands for your time and attention.

To be effective, these interactions need to be deliberate and thoughtful — they require more than just physical proximity. Spending quality time with children means that you are truly **with** the child (not planning tonight's dinner, or mentally preparing for tomorrow's faculty meeting). It means that a child, or a small group of children, have your undivided attention.

But how exactly should you spend your time with the children in your classroom? SET Time is one of the most important and meaningful ways to invest your time wisely with children.   In the sections to follow, we will suggest several other kinds of time investments, each with different purposes, and all supporting healthy relationships with children.

BUILD IN DOWN TIME

Children need down time. Modern lives are so busy that children often miss out on simple relationship-building activities like taking walks, watching others play, looking at books, or showing off new skills. Down time offers children and teachers the opportunity to spend time together in conversations about experiences without any external pressures.

Down time is a time just to be.

Down time is integration time—time to integrate experiences into thinking and practice. It helps children blend new skills with previously acquired ones. To become integrated, or automatic, skills need to be practiced again and again. Repetition helps children focus on what matters in their interactions with others, and to learn from the various outcomes. For example, when a child builds the same structure over and over again, he is integrating both motor and cognitive skills.

But integration is also a process; it takes time. Ten minutes of down time may be more than enough for one child, while another child may need hours of down time, over several days, weeks, or months before integration is complete.

Down time can be any activity children choose on their own. The key is that nothing is required of the child. This is a time to just be. A baby on a blanket in the grass, a toddler building with blocks, a preschooler reading in the book corner on a bean bag chair, or an early elementary-aged child doodling in her notebook are all good examples.

INCORPORATE OBSERVATION TIME INTO YOUR TEACHING ROUTINE

In order to truly know a child, you must spend time observing them in uninterrupted, self-directed play. Observation allows you to understand children. It can transform teaching by offering insights that are only available from careful watching.

Comment on what you see children doing. This lets them know you are interested in them and their activities.

Children know you need to spend time watching and observing them in action. Infants and toddlers turn repeatedly to see if you are watching them as they play. During the preschool years, every child demands, "Watch me!" Children ask you to watch for a reason. They need you to know what they are doing, and how they are succeeding and faltering. This way, you can adjust your interactions, curriculum, and classroom to their emerging skills and individual challenges. Observation is so important that we are devoting an entire chapter to it. You will learn much more about observation in Chapter 3.

FOR EXAMPLE...

Four-year-old Louise is playing with the blocks. She repeatedly asks her teacher, Mr. Collins, "Do you see what I'm doing?" "Isn't this neat?" "Am I doing a good job?" "Is this cool?" She continues to ask, even after he reassures her that she is indeed doing a good job. Mr. Collins finally stops putting away the paint jars, comes to where Louise is building, and kneels on the floor next to her. For a couple of minutes, he just watches, repeating his admiration for Louise's structure. Louise beams. After a few more minutes of observing, he goes back to cleaning paint jars and Louise continues to build in the block area, occasionally looking over at him, without verbally demanding his attention any further.

SET for Life Language

"I am watching you."

"I see your important work."

"You worked hard to get that built."

"I think you want me to watch you."

CREATE TIME TO FOCUS ON THE SAME THINGS

Children also need time to focus. Learning colors and shapes, having a classroom meeting, or learning a new math or reading skill are all good examples of focused time.

In order for children to be able to focus, the size of the group needs to be small enough for them to be able to concentrate. Ideally, focus time should be done in groups of two to five children.

These small groups allow teachers to help children focus their attention on the important parts of their interactions. Young children are not very good at screening out all of the non-essential information available in busy classrooms. Paying attention to the right things, and ignoring unimportant details, takes focus and practice.

FOR EXAMPLE...

Seven-month-old Hailey and her teacher, Ms. Munro, are rocking while Hailey drinks a warm bottle. As she drinks, Hailey swats the bottle, arches her back, and turns her head to see what is going on in the rest of the classroom. Ms. Munro takes Hailey's hand and holds it gently over the bottle. She says, "Hailey, it is time for you to drink your bottle. When you are finished, you will be able to play with the children on the floor. Right now, it is time to eat." Then, she turns the chair slightly, so that Hailey can't see the other children in the room, and can focus on drinking her bottle while she gazes at her teacher.

Teachers can also help children screen out non-essential information. Adults are usually able to ignore background noise and focus on important details around them, particularly details related to the task at hand. Children are often distracted by less relevant details, such as air-conditioning noise or voices in the hallway, and they need your help to focus on what is important for them to notice.

FOR EXAMPLE...

Ms. Josie is distributing snack to the children in her group. Zoe, a younger preschooler, is looking at the construction workers outside the window, listening to the, "beep, beep, beep," of a truck backing up. She has a hard time paying attention what is happening at the snack table.

Ms. Josie says to Zoe, "I think you find what they are doing outside very interesting. They are building a new gym for us. It will be ready next spring. Right now we are having snack and I need your eyes and ears to be here at the snack table with us. If it is too hard, then I can close the blinds."

SET for Life Language

"Take a look."

"Look, you might be interested."

"Right now, we are talking about the book. I need you to look over here. You can look out the window later."

HELP CHILDREN DIFFERENTIATE BETWEEN THINGS THEY CAN CONTROL AND THINGS THEY CANNOT

Children, in general, want to be in control. Yet, when they are allowed to take charge of tasks beyond their developmental ability, they may instead feel anxious and insecure. They may also feel responsible for controlling their behavior, yet they know they are not able to do it. Children need help from adults to understand and accept when they are in control and when they aren't.

You can help children to feel safe by taking charge. When toddlers are practicing independence, preschoolers enter a bossy phase, or anxious children try to use control to make themselves feel better, they need reminders of who is in charge at the moment.

When children can be in charge varies by age, developmental stage, and circumstance. Younger children are in charge of fewer things, but even toddlers can decide where to play, whether to put on their tops or bottoms first after a diaper change, and what they want for a snack from a limited number of choices. Preschoolers can take control over more responsibilities, such as brushing their teeth, choosing to eat their green beans or their chicken first, or deciding who they want to play with. Early elementary age children can choose which friends they would like to play a board game with, what table they want to sit at for lunch, and so forth. Over time, children will learn to feel proud of the tasks they are in charge of, and they will learn that they don't have to be responsible for things that are beyond their ability.

FOR EXAMPLE...

Alison, a 4 ½ year old, tries to leave her classroom to go check on her baby brother in the toddler classroom. Her teacher knows that Alison is often left in charge of her brother at home when their mother works late. She says, "Alison, at school you do not have to worry about your brother. His teacher will take good care of him and keep him safe, just like I will keep you safe in our classroom. You do not have to worry about him while you are at school."

SET for Life Language

"You are safe here. I will take care of you."

"You want to be in charge and you are too little to be in charge."

"That is not your worry. I will take are of it."

FOR EXAMPLE...

Ms. Steinberg assigns jobs in her classroom. One job is to turn off the light switch at naptime. Every day, five-year-old Jerad runs to the light switch and flips it off, even though he knows that he is not the light helper.

JOBS	CHILD'S NAME
Pass out napkins for snack	Julio
Turn classroom lights off on the way to the playground	Sandra
Turn classroom lights on after playground time	Chloe
Help set table for lunch	Liling
Help Ms. Santa Anna put out naptime cots	Leila
Turn off lights at naptime; turn them back on after naptime	John

Ms. Steinberg thinks that Jerad is worried about naptime because he often has difficulty staying on his mat and not disturbing others. She talks to Jerad about this, and together they arrive at a plan for him to have some control over his transition to naptime. He puts his special blanket on the nap mat prior to lunch, so he knows it is waiting for him there. He selects a book, or other quiet activity, and puts it on the mat, too. After a while, he stops running to the light switch every day, and becomes more able to rest comfortably or play quietly on his mat.

SET for Life Language

"You want it to be your turn to be the light helper and it is not."

"I think you are worried about naptime and how hard it is to stay on your mat."

"You are a boy who can figure out what you need to stay quiet at naptime."

SET APPROPRIATE LIMITS AND APPLY THEM CONSISTENTLY

In order for children to be able to learn new skills, teachers must set appropriate limits and apply them consistently.

Children's emotional development is supported when limits are:

- **humane and not punitive.**
- **clear and enforceable.**
- **accompanied by reasons.**
- **consistently applied.**

When limits are too subtle, change frequently, or are inappropriate for the child's developmental stage, children will often test boundaries repeatedly, checking to see what is really off limits. When limits are clear, children are able to relax and interact positively with the learning environment and the other children in it.

Classroom Rules

- Touch friends softly.
- No grabbing toys from friends.
- Ask a teacher if you need help.
- Quiet voices inside.

Post your classroom rules, and make up reminders in the form of finger plays or chants, so children are clear about your expectations. Repeat them often, as you deal with situations that require your intervention. Also, share your expectations with families, so everyone is on the same page.

HELP CHILDREN "FEEL FELT"

When children "feel felt," they know that another person understands the way they are feeling. Teachers can help children to accept what they are feeling and move on by reading nonverbal, verbal, and behavioral cues, sharing their observations with the child, and reflecting out loud about having felt the same way at one time or another. When children "feel felt" by important adults in their lives, they understand that their emotions are natural and normal, rather than something scary or threatening.

FOR EXAMPLE...

Five-year-old Brody sits at table where children are playing a board game. He won't participate or take his turn. His teacher says, "It is hard to be the new child at school. Desiree, do you remember how hard it was when you started school?" "Yes, it was so hard, I didn't want to play when I was new," says Desiree. Brody continues to sit for a couple more rounds. Then, he picks up his piece and joins in the play.

SET for Life Language

"Desiree remembers that being new is hard."

"When I was a little girl, I liked painting and coloring, too."

"I think you are feeling sad about leaving your mother at home with the new baby. Marco felt that way when he had a new baby at home."

"I can tell it feels hard. I know that feeling."

"Your face tells me you don't want to talk to me right now."

"I remember feeling sad when I had to stop running and I didn't want to."

ALLOW SECURITY ITEMS

Access to security items helps children cope with and adjust to new situations and to manage stress. Young children experience entirely too much anxiety because adults remove the very support they need to be successful when they are away from their families. Transitional objects are **good** for young children. In new situations, they serve as a much-needed connection to the people who love and care for them.

Children often use objects to help them cope with their anxiety. As any experienced teacher will tell you, security items from home can ease the pain of separation from family members and make a boo-boo better far quicker than a Band-Aid™.

As a child develops a sense of self, these security items literally remind them of who they are, and where and to whom they belong. They are a bridge from the known and comfortable to the unknown and uncomfortable, and help children move forward more confidently in new or unfamiliar settings.

Taking these security items away before children feel comfortable giving them up on their own may prolong the time it will take to adjust. It is important to trust children to make the right decision for themselves about when it is time to leave their security item in their cubby or inside during outdoor play. When they are rushed by an external timetable, such as their age or program level, they may be pushed to do things they are not ready to do, interrupting ongoing development and creating problems that would have otherwise resolved on their own without intervention.

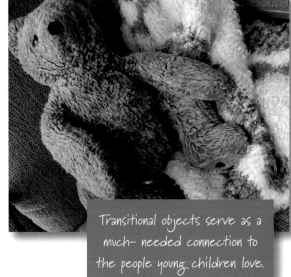

Transitional objects serve as a much-needed connection to the people young children love.

This situation is complicated by the public's view of security items. Unsolicited comments from well-meaning adults, such as, "You are too old for that pacifier," don't help. You can support children by allowing the use of security items during stressful times and reminding families that this is an appropriate, useful coping strategy.

FOR EXAMPLE...
Eighteen-month-old Laura is going to school for the first time. She carries her blankie with her. Her fear and anxiety are obvious.

During the first month of school, she gets to know her teacher, learns the routines of her class, and most importantly, figures out that her mommy comes back for her. Her teacher allows her to carry her blankie wherever she goes, seeing that it helps ease her anxiety. Her blankie keeps her from playing with certain toys, but it provides Laura with the comfort she needs to be able to stay at school without being so upset that she can't participate at all.

Slowly, as Laura becomes comfortable and builds a trusting relationship with her teacher, she begins to leave her blankie lying around. Her teacher sees it is time to make a plan about where to keep her blankie so it stays safe and can be found when she does need it. The teacher and Laura agree to keep it in her cubby, where it is readily accessible should she feel distress. She no longer needs it to be with her every moment.

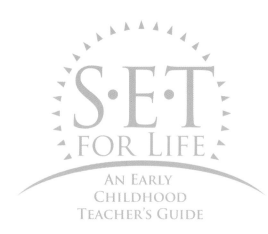

SET for Life is not about using all of these teaching strategies perfectly every time. It is about practicing them to improve your ability to support children's development and learning. Few teachers will be able to use **SET for Life** strategies (or any other teaching skill) 100% of the time. But, you can begin to incorporate these techniques into your teaching style, and with practice, make them routine.

SUMMARY: TEACHING STRATEGIES TO SUPPORT BUILDING POSITIVE RELATIONSHIPS

Your success in teaching young children will depend largely on the quality of the relationships you have with them.

IMPLEMENT SET TIME
Every child needs time to connect with you. SET Time is time designated specifically for building relationships with children. It is a key strategy for **SET for Life**.

- Relationships are the key.
- Every child needs SET Time, some more than others.
- Sometimes time is not enough. Developmentally delayed behavior may be a sign that further intervention is needed.
- Teacher emotional health is important. Ask for help from a supervisor if you feel you need it.

GIVE CHILDREN YOUR TIME

- Children will get your time and attention, one way or another.
- Positive and well-planned time supports relationship-building, as well as children's development and learning.
- Look for additional resources if time is not enough.

BUILD IN DOWN TIME

- Down time is integration time.
- Down time requires nothing from the child.

INCORPORATE OBSERVATION TIME INTO YOUR ROUTINE

- In order to truly know a child, you must spend time observing him or her in self-directed play.
- Observation allows you to understand the meaning behind a child's behavior.
  > *"I am watching you play."*
  > *"I see your important work."*

CREATE TIME TO FOCUS ON THE SAME THINGS

- Focus time is goal-oriented.
- Focus time typically occurs in small groups or with individual children.
- Children need your help to screen out distractions and focus on the important parts of what is happening.
  > *"Look, you might be interested."*
  > *"Right now we are talking about weather. What is the weather like outside today?"*

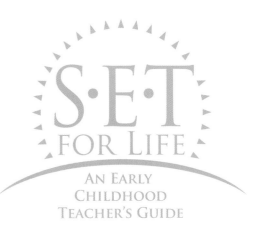

HELP CHILDREN DIFFERENTIATE BETWEEN THINGS THEY CAN CONTROL AND THINGS THEY CANNOT

- You can help children feel safe by being clear about who is in charge.
- What children can be in charge of varies by age and circumstances.
  > *"You want it to be your turn to be a light helper and it is not."*
  > *"I will be in charge of snack. It is not your worry."*
  > *"You are a boy who can figure out how to rest quietly on your mat during naptime."*

SET APPROPRIATE LIMITS AND APPLY THEM CONSISTENTLY

- Rules and limits should be:
    - Humane and not punitive.
    - Clear and enforceable.
    - Accompanied by reasons.
    - Consistently applied.

HELP CHILDREN FEEL FELT

- Let children know you understand how they feel.
- Reflect out loud about times you and others have felt the same way in the past.

    "When I was a little girl, I loved painting and coloring, too."

    "I think you are feeling sad about leaving your mother at home with the new baby. Marco felt that way when he had a new baby at home, too."

    "I can tell it feels hard. I know that feeling."

    "Your face tells me you don't want to talk to me right now."

ALLOW CHILDREN TO USE SECURITY ITEMS

- Security items help children to bridge the gap between the familiar and comfortable to the unknown and uncomfortable.
    - Security items remind children of where and to whom they belong, and support their ability to participate in new experiences.

        "You can hold your blankie during circle time."

        "Your pacifier is in your cubby. You can get it at naptime."

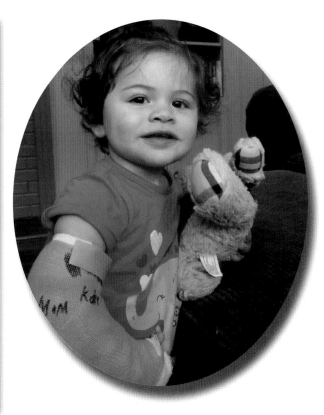

BECOME A GOOD OBSERVER

Careful, frequent, and focused observation is one of the most important strategies an early childhood educator will ever use. When you pay attention to the way children interact with each other and with key adults in their lives, you gain important knowledge about their personalities, temperaments, developmental patterns, and abilities.

In this chapter, we will look at the important role of observation in the classroom. Before you begin observing children, you must first reflect on how your perceptions are influenced by your own background and experiences. We will explore how your previous experiences may shape your choices in the classroom. Then, we will discuss different ways of observing children and how these observations can help you to be more effective at building relationships with children and their families.

"It is necessary; therefore, it is possible."

G. A. BORGHESE, WRITER

Finally, we will then look at the ways that temperament— personality traits that are genetically determined—can vary between children and talk about why understanding temperament is so important. We will provide you with tools for determining a child's temperament, and then with ideas for working with children with different temperamental types.

Taking time to observe children gives you valuable information.

In addition to providing strategies for better classroom management, observation serves another important purpose. It helps us be more deliberate in the way we respond to children, to choose the best response over our initial instincts and reactions. Sometimes, our first response is not the one to act on. Let's talk about the reason why.

WHY YOUR CHILDHOOD EXPERIENCES MATTER

When you walk into your classroom, you don't come in alone. You bring with you the influences of all the important relationships in your life. Some of these influences are positive, and others are not. When children and families come into your classroom, they also bring their own histories. This can make for a crowded room! Being aware of how our own backgrounds affect us can make us more effective and sensitive as teachers.

My Family Diamond

Take a look at the family diamond. To fill it in start with your parents (birth, adoptive, foster, etc.) and anyone else who took on a parenting role while you were growing up. Now add others from your neighborhood and then your community who greatly influenced your life. You can find a blank copy for you to complete and an example in Appendix A.

Me

If you think back on important moments in your life and the role that the people on your diamond played in them, you'll realize that we all carry a part of these important people with us. Those relationships inevitably come into play in our interactions with children. Sometimes, we embrace the models and experiences, seeking to imitate them in our own lives. Sometimes we reject them, trying to create new experiences that are as different from our prior experiences as possible. Regardless of whether we embrace or reject the models we had as we were growing up, our experiences in these families, neighborhoods, and communities are right there with us in the classroom.

All of the people you added to the diamond influence how you respond to children. Many of these influences can help you support children's emotional development. For example, if your aunt made a gravestone and planted flowers with you when your dog died and helped you to deal with your grief, her positive response may allow you to support children who are experiencing sadness by showing them the same compassion and understanding that you received.

Some of these influences, however, can make it harder for you to support the emotional development of children. If your bike was stolen from your garage and someone important to you yelled at you for not locking it up, that response might have made you feel ashamed about neglecting your responsibilities and fearful of making additional mistakes. Lingering feelings of shame and worries about making mistakes might lead you to be less understanding of other's mistakes or cause anxiety about your ability to make the "right" choices in the future.

> **Observation can prevent reacting in a way you may later regret. When you take a moment to observe, it is easier to think about, access, and use the teaching skills you know are most appropriate.**

This exercise illustrates why teaching is such a dynamic process. The relationships you have with the children in your classroom are constantly influenced by your previous experiences within your own family, and with the other important people in your life. These influences shape important teaching decisions, such as to yell or not to yell, whether or not to offer a pacifier to a crying infant, or how to work with a family who makes parenting choices you don't approve of. A deeper understanding of the influences that guide you in your day-to-day actions can help you make more deliberate choices and allow the positive influences to come into play as you teach.

THE POWER OF OBSERVATION

Observation and reflection before action lead to informed decisions. They create the opportunity to respond to a situation thoughtfully and purposefully, instead of just reacting. Magda Gerber, an infant development specialist and educator, was a vocal advocate for respecting infants and children as equal participants with adults in interactions. She was also a pioneer in describing how observation can influence interactions with children. Gerber was particularly uncomfortable with adults who underestimate or dismiss children's ability to recognize their own needs, regardless of the age of the child. Her view of children as competent in interacting and responding when they experience the respect of an adult who recognizes and believes in their abilities, altered the way we look at initiating interactions.

Gerber felt that teaching requires observation prior to responding. While teaching medical students about child development at the University of California at Los Angeles, she advocated observation as the way to begin any interaction with a young patient.

A situation she often describes is picking up a baby she didn't know. Gerber recommends first gazing at the baby and looking for cues about whether the baby is interested in being picked up. She would wonder out loud if the child wanted to be held and respond only after some indication—maybe a coo or a smile—communicated the child was also interested. Most adults rarely consider this point of view. We typically direct almost all of young children's routine experiences, without pausing to consider the child's perspective. Observation helps us to understand better how a child experiences these everyday interactions.

Observation creates the opportunity for teachers to think before acting. It gives you time to survey the situation in front of you, ask important questions about what is really happening, and then to think about what you want to do before you make a decision about how to respond. Acting without thinking often causes guilty feelings—wishing a different action had been chosen. Observation can prevent reacting in a way you may later regret. When you take a moment to observe, it is easier to think about, access, and use the teaching skills you know are most appropriate. Further, observation leads to a better understanding of each individual child. This knowledge can help you judge actions more accurately, and respond most appropriately to that child's specific needs or behaviors.

Another important purpose of observation is to help you identify the emotional meaning behind behavior. Behavior often has emotional meaning. Sometimes we jump to conclusions based on our own personal experiences, instead of noticing the particular emotional meaning for a child. This is another reason why regular observation of the children in your classroom is so important. When you know a child well, it is easier to accurately identify the emotional meaning behind his or her behavior.

When children get their emotional needs met in positive ways, inappropriate behavior may decline and emotional meltdowns are less likely. Children whose needs are met also tend to be more cooperative and flexible. These things combine to help your classroom run smoother on a day-to-day basis. But you should be aware that this change will not happen overnight—it requires extended effort to discover and address the emotional meaning of children's behaviors.

OBSERVATION TECHNIQUES

Thorough, accurate, systematic observation and analysis of children's interactions with you and other children in your classroom can shape and improve all aspects of your teaching. Such observation will give you plenty of examples to share with families when you talk with them about their child's development and learning. Sharing these observations can help you build positive relationships with families, which benefits both you and the children in your care.

To become a good observer, you will need to know a variety of observation techniques. Several are described here, to get you started. As you become more skilled, you may want to explore even more ways to observe in your classroom.

Some Observation Strategies

- Anecdotal Notes
- Checklists
- Rating Scales
- Frequency Charts

ANECDOTAL NOTES

Start observing with the simplest strategy—writing anecdotal records. These are brief narrative accounts that describe events and situations that happen with a child or a small group of children. In these notes, answer the basic questions—what is happening, when and where is it happening, and with whom. Describe what you are seeing in as much detail as you can. Write things down as they happen, while you are working with children.

The idea is to note things that will help you to recall events later. You can fill in details when you are not supervising children. For example, you might write, "Joey and Minh disagreed in block center before snack today," and include the date. Later, you could add in details about what the argument was about, how it was resolved, or other circumstances might have come into play that day (e.g., *Minh was not feeling well, and Joey's parent was on a business trip.*)

Anecdotal records can be cumulative, used to collect bits of information in a written format over a period of time. When you review and analyze your notes, notice patterns *(Joey and Minh always argue when they are at centers together right before snack.)* and try to discover why *(Right before snack and lunch when they are hungry, they have a hard time getting along.)*

Look for trends and think about what an interaction might have meant to a child. Consider the classroom context or environment for clues (for instance, more meltdowns on Tuesdays, right after music), and think about ways to adjust future situations (such as including more reminders about transition time for once-a-week activities).

Avoid jumping to conclusions beyond the information you have. Instead, use what you discover to focus future observations so they continue to add to your knowledge of the children you teach. What you learn can help you make modifications for the children, the classroom, and in your teaching. A blank note is included in Appendix B for your use.

CHECKLISTS

Checklists are usually used to analyze and document specific skills or behaviors. They are useful for teachers because they focus your observations. They often contain milestones that measure developmental progress (such as the number of words in a child's vocabulary or the ability to perform certain motor skills), and they can be used to assess whether children's development

Anecdotal Note

Child's Name: Jordan
Date: May 3, 2012; 10:20 am

Jordan and two of his friends, Carlos and Brent, are playing at the sensory table. Jordan has started a game of "spin the sand wheel" where he drops the sand onto the wheel and watches it spin. Carlos asks for a turn. Jordan says, "No!" Brent says, "Aw, come on. We want to play." Jordan looks at his friends, takes one more turn pouring sand on the sand wheel, then hands the measuring cup to Carlos. He says, "Just one time. Then it is Brent's turn." Carlos nods, and pours sand on the wheel. Brent holds out his hand for the cup. Carlos looks at Jordan, saying, "One more turn, please, please!" Jordan says, "OK." Brent says, "No fair. You said I could have a turn." Carlos pours the sand on the wheel and hands the cup to Brent. "You can," Carlos says as he hands it to Brent.

Recorded by: Ms. Pamela

is progressing normally. When you use a checklist, your observation focuses on determining whether a particular item on the list is present or absent. For example, you might note whether or not a two-year-old can combine two or three words to make a sentence, if a six-month-old is able to roll over unassisted, or if a preschooler is making letter-like marks.

A number of developmental checklists are readily available from pediatricians and child development specialists. And, you can make your own using objective, easy to see traits, behaviors, or skills. Use checklists to confirm that a child's social and emotional development is proceeding normally, figure out what skills a child may be having difficulty with, or if he or she may need additional support from you or referral for further assessment.

RATING SCALES

Rating scales are similar to checklists. The difference is that you must identify the degree to which the child demonstrates the trait, behavior, or skill. They usually use numbers or points on a continuum. For this kind of observation to be effective, you must be aware of how children vary. For example, you might rate a child's activity level on a scale of 1 to 10, with a very active child receiving a 10, and marking a more sedentary child at a 3. Rating scales are a good tool to use when the skills in question are more complex, such as a child's ability to play independently. Scales are often used to share information with pediatricians, psychologists, or child development specialists to help identify children with developmental or learning difficulties.

Social Problem-solving Skills Rating Scale

Uses indiscriminate aggression directed at everyone and everything	Always	Often	Sometimes	Seldom	Never
Uses physical aggression with peers and adults	Always	Often	Sometimes	Seldom	Never
Uses physical aggression with peers, adults, toys, and the environment	Always	Often	Sometimes	Seldom	Never

You may want to develop your own rating scales to make your observations easier. For example, if you want to know how many of the children in your classroom are using social problem-solving skills, you might create a rating scale like the one on the previous page that allows you to identify which children in the classroom have the identified skills and rate their level of accomplishment in using the skill. You could modify it to observe other skills, such as internalization of self-control.

FREQUENCY CHARTS

Frequency charts are designed to help you record how often specific behaviors, such as hitting, are occurring. Behaviors you might want to track with frequency charts are ones that are problematic for the child and require your intervention. These charts can also be valuable for sharing information with parents or other concerned parties.

Biting Frequency Chart

Biter	Victim(s)	Location in the classroom	While playing with what toys/ materials	Time of incident	Who else was near?	What was the teacher doing?	Where was the teacher in the class-room?	Intention or goal of biting?	Extenuating circumstances?
Sara	Emma	Art	Watercolors and brushes	9:45 am	Sam, Julia	Reading to Kylie	Library	?	?
Sara	Emma	Construction	Waffle blocks and star builders	10:12 am	No one	Helping Sam	Art	To play with waffle blocks	?
Sara	Emma	Construction	Waffle blocks and star builders	3:30 pm	No one	Helping children get up from nap time	At the changing table	To play with Emma?	The blocks and the star builders were mixed up on the floor between Emma and Sara
Sara	Emma	Construction	Waffle blocks and wooden animals	5:50 pm	No one	Talking to a parent	Near the door	Needs teacher's attention late in the day?	Emma's mother was later than usual

Frequency charts are easy to make and modify to fit particular situations. They also allow additional observers (e.g., family members, other teachers) to collect similar information at different times during the day, broadening the picture of what is happening. The chart on the previous page is an example of a frequency chart related to biting. You can design similar ones related to many other behaviors.

TEACHING STRATEGIES TO HELP YOU BECOME A GOOD OBSERVER

INVEST IN REGULAR OBSERVATION OF CHILDREN WHILE THEY PLAY

Observing, without interrupting or intervening, is a valuable use of your time as a teacher. It helps you get to know individual children and notice how they are similar to and different from their peers. We know that your teaching day is already busy. Many teachers report that there just isn't enough time to observe. You don't need to devote hours of every day to observation. Instead, you might choose just one child, or a small group of children, to observe over the course of a week. Then move on to a different child or group the next week.

Taking time for observation can save time in the long run by reducing the time spent managing disruptive behaviors on a day-to-day basis. With a deeper understanding of the children that you teach, you may be able to respond more appropriately to their emotional needs, which can reduce disruptions overall. Consider what other activities you could put on hold temporarily, so you can work regular observation into your routine.

When children exhibit challenging behavior, observation should be your first intervention. Take time to watch. Try to see what is really happening. Don't assume that you know why the child is behaving as she is. Before you draw any conclusion about what the problem might be or how you should address it, take the time to observe.

Remember, behavior often has meaning, and it is driven by emotion. Looking for the underlying cause of the behavior is the first step. Taking the time to look for the emotional meaning that is behind a behavior will make it more likely that the intervention you decide to try will be successful.

FOR EXAMPLE...

During the last week, three-year-old Jada, who is rarely aggressive, has had three instances of losing control and hurting a friend. To find out what is going on, her teacher, Mrs. Alexander, begins observing her for short periods of time throughout the school day. She notes with whom Jada plays the most, and when and where she is playing when she loses control.

Behavior generally has emotional meaning.

During her first day of observation, she notices that Jada doesn't seem to have a favorite playmate. She also notes that she has trouble when it is time to transition to the playground. She gets silly and pushes her friends, although no one gets hurt. On the second day, she observes that Jada continues to select several different children to play with. She hits Sara when they line up to wash their hands at lunch time. On the third day, she observes Jada continuing to select a variety of playmates without incident, until right before the music teacher arrives. During this special time of the week, the children wait for the teacher to arrive, seated in a circle. Right as she walks in the door, Jada hits Juan, the friend sitting next to her.

After reviewing her anecdotal notes and frequency chart, Mrs. Alexander notices three things. First, Jada doesn't seem to have a special friend in the classroom. Second, she seems to have problems right before or during transitions and when waiting. Third, when Jada hurts other children, it is often directed at whoever is near, not towards a particular child.

After considering this information, she begins her interventions by reminding Jada before each daily transition about what is happening next and what she will have to do.

Next, she pairs Jada up with Nicholas, a child she selected as a playmate every day she observed her. She seems to enjoy playing with Nicholas, who has never used aggression in the classroom. She tells Jada that she and Nicholas will be partners during transitions. Her goal is for Nicholas to help model appropriate behavior and scaffold Jada's behavior during transitions, so she can stay under control. Finally, she decides to let Jada and Nicholas be first in line during most of the transitions for the next few days to see if pairing Nicholas with Jada is working, and to limit the length of time Jada has to wait.

This intervention works wonders for Jada. Subsequent observations indicate that Jada is tolerating the transitions better with Nicholas's help and the reduced waiting time. There are no more incidents during the following two-week period. Although she is pleased with the progress, Mrs. Alexander still plans to do several more short observations in the next month, so she can further support Jada's emerging social skills and self-regulation.

OBSERVE TO DOCUMENT STRENGTHS

We often begin observations when we notice a problem. It is also important to document children's strengths. Children have a wide variety of temperaments, learning styles, and all sorts of developmental variations. When one of your observation goals is to find out about how children are unique, different, and special, your observations can lead to insights into each child's particular strengths. When you know what children's strengths are, you will be more likely to find ways to use them to help you address their other needs.

One other benefit of paying attention to children's strengths as you observe is that you will have a host of wonderful examples to share with their families. All families like to hear good news about their children. Hearing about strengths from you helps families to know that you feel connected to their child. This, in turn, may encourage them to collaborate with you to support their child's learning and development, and to address together any challenges that arise.

A good rule of thumb is to use observation to document five positive experiences or interactions about a child for every one observation you record that identifies a concern or documents a challenging behavior.

DISCUSS YOUR OBSERVATIONS WITH OTHERS

Once you start observing children, it helps to discuss your observations, interpretations, and action plans with others. Start with your coworkers in the classroom. Find out whether they have seen the same things you are observing. Ask them to share their observations—including those that are similar and those that are different—and to talk with you about what those might mean. Then, plan to observe again to see what else you might uncover.

One benefit of paying attention to children's strengths as you observe is that you will have a host of wonderful examples to share with their families.

The knowledge and experience of your colleagues is a valuable resource. Sometimes, talking with colleagues will help you untangle puzzling observations and figure out what they might mean. More experienced teachers may have had similar experiences and have ideas for handling things in ways you might not have thought of before. Sharing your written records, taken over a period of time, may be especially helpful, since they can show patterns over the course of several days or weeks.

Staff meetings can include a time for teachers to talk about problems and work together to find solutions. Ask your administrator to allow you to share your observations, ask for input from others, and get suggestions for things to try.

TALK TO CHILDREN ABOUT WHAT YOU OBSERVE

Normally, discussing your observations of children is not something that happens in front of them. However, externalizing your observations—saying out loud your objective observations so that children are aware of what you see—can be an effective teaching strategy.

Talking about what you see happening with the children can change the way children interact with you and with each other. When you comment objectively on what is happening between and among children to bring it to their attention, interesting things might happen. Children may be able to use your observations then or later on, to solve problems or make plans.

FOR EXAMPLE...

Three children are in the puzzle center. They have almost completed the puzzle and are beginning to argue over who will be the one to put the last pieces in. Mrs. Williams, who is standing next to the puzzle center, and says aloud to her co-teacher, "Mrs. Parker, it looks like that puzzle is almost complete. I wonder if the children will figure out how to get the last pieces in." The children, noting the teacher's attention to their problem, refocus and soon figure out how to work cooperatively on finishing the puzzle.

One caution here, though. It is never appropriate to discuss your concerns about children when they are present, or to use a conversation about the child with another adult to embarrass the child or impose discipline. Such attempts almost never work and may damage your relationship with the child.

As you learn to fine tune your observation skills and begin to develop detailed written records of the children in your classroom, you will undoubtedly discover patterns of behavior in particular children. When you analyze this information, one factor you will need to take into consideration is the temperament of each child. In the next section, we will explore temperament, how it affects your classroom, and how understanding temperament can help you as a teacher.

THE IMPACT OF TEMPERAMENT

Every child is born with a personality—a temperament that guides and influences her approach to the world. Genetically determined, a child's temperament shows up in a variety of character traits, which are present regardless of environment, parenting, and culture. These differences in personality can often predict how children may cope with challenges and obstacles later in life. There are many different ways of looking at temperaments and each can give us insight into things we see happening in the classroom.

An understanding of temperament helps teachers avoid blaming all challenges in the classroom on behavior. When you take temperament into account when choosing teaching strategies, your likelihood of success increases. In addition, considering your own temperament may help you respond appropriately, instead of just reacting, especially when working with children whose temperaments differ from your own. Further, awareness of temperamental types helps in grouping children, assigning play experiences, and making the most of individual strengths.

Every child is born with a temperament that guides and influences her approach to the world.

TEMPERAMENT TRAITS

Nine character traits shape a child's temperament. As you observe, avoid focusing on one area of a child's temperament and neglecting the others. While one area may strike you as particularly challenging, it is the combination of traits that will guide you in understanding a particular child.

TEMPERAMENT TRAITS

Temperament Traits	Continuum
Activity level	(varies from low activity to high activity)
Regularity of biological rhythms, such as sleeping, eating, eliminating	(varies from very regular to highly irregular)
Approach/withdrawal tendencies	(varies from easy to approach/rarely withdraws to has difficulty approaching/often withdraws)
Mood	(varies from positive to negative)
Intensity of reaction	(varies from low intensity to high intensity)
Adaptability	(slow to adapt to quick to adapt)
Sensitivity to light, touch, taste, sounds, and sights	(varies from low sensitivity to high sensitivity)
Distractibility	(varies from low distractibility to high distractibility)
Persistence	(varies from low persistence to high persistence)

From Albrecht, K., & Miller, L.G. (2001). Innovations: Infant and toddler development. Lewisville, NC: Gryphon House. Reprinted with permission. All rights reserved.

Where children fall on each of these scales gives you more information about individual children's temperaments. It makes sense to collaborate with families in identifying temperament. Asking them to help you understand their child's temperament is a good place to begin to build a relationship, because families are typically keenly aware of the temperamental characteristics of their children.

Awareness of children's temperaments informs the way you teach.

Teachers can observe and identify where children are and use what they discover to better address each child's individual needs. For example, if you realize that a student falls on the high end of the intensity scale and is also slow to adapt, you might take his temperament into consideration when making classroom changes, and take extra measures to prepare him for the transition. Having enough preparation may help your student get through the changes without struggling to adapt.

TEMPERAMENT TYPES

Some experts group these traits together, combining them to describe more general temperament types. Psychologist Alicia Liebermann combined the traits of temperament into three temperament groups: *flexible*, *fearful*, or *feisty*.

THE FLEXIBLE CHILD

The traits of flexible children include regular biological rhythms, easy adaptability to new situations, low intensity, low sensitivity, and positive mood. In school, flexible children are easy to spot; they are often described as laid back, and easy-going. They are sometimes overlooked in a busy classroom, because they demand so little attention. You will want to find ways to devote attention to these easy-going children, even though they don't always demand it.

FOR EXAMPLE...

Jamilla is a capable 3-year-old girl who shows up to school each day with a smile. She rarely takes much of her teacher's time or demands her attention. She does her work and generally gets along well with peers. Occasionally, she will ask the teacher for assistance or express distress due to a dispute with a friend, but usually Jamilla goes with the flow. She is willing to listen to the ideas of friends and is easily redirected when she gets off task. She raises her hand when she knows an answer in circle time, but generally doesn't seem to mind if the teacher calls on her or not. Jamilla is friendly with most everyone in the class, though she has a best friend with whom she spends most of her playground time. She has many friends and well liked by her teachers. They all say she is a pleasure to be around.

THE FEARFUL (OR CAUTIOUS) CHILD

Fearful children often avoid new situations. They may be slow to warm to new people and experiences. Their cautious ways mean that teachers must go slowly with them, allowing them to observe a new activity or situation before approaching it. Teachers may also need to directly introduce fearful children to new activities, gradually withdrawing their support as children become more comfortable, and as caution gives way to interest and enjoyment.

Some educators prefer to call this temperament "cautious" or "slow to warm," because of worries that this style will be perceived as negative, instead of just a normal variation in the way a child approaches the world. The intent of temperamental styles isn't to label children's temperaments as positive or negative. Its purpose is to help understand the impact of temperament on behavior, development, and interactions. It is important to help children learn to capitalize on their natural strengths and develop skills to cope with the parts of their personalities that may create extra challenges or distress.

FOR EXAMPLE...
Two-year-old Lori is loud and sassy at home, but in new environments she looks like a completely different child. She hides behind her mother, refuses to speak, and generally looks terrified. When Lori visits her classroom before the start of school, her teacher, Ms. Lopez, notices her anxiety and fear.

Hoping to help Lori settle in as easily as possible, Ms. Lopez tries to find out more about her during the pre-enrollment visit with her mother. She learns that Lori loves animals, has a cousin who attends the school in a different classroom, and that her favorite song is "Twinkle, Twinkle Little Star." On the first day of school, Ms. Lopez places a chair slightly behind the rug where the children will be for circle time. She puts several stuffed animals next to the chair. She also speaks with Lori's cousin's teacher, and they plan to have her cousin join them at the start of the first day of school.

When Lori arrives, Ms. Lopez invites her in. Lori is carrying her blankie from home, and Ms. Lopez lets her know she can hold on to it for as long as she needs to. She tells Lori that her cousin is visiting to help her feel comfortable, and that he will stay for awhile before he goes to his classroom. Lori enters hesitantly, but after a while begins to talk quietly with her cousin. When it is time for circle, Ms. Lopez shows Lori the chair with the animals. She tells Lori that she is welcome to sit on the carpet with the others or in the chair if that feels better to her. Lori chooses the chair. She holds tightly to her blankie, and picks up a doggie and a bear. Ms. Lopez ends the circle time with songs, starting with "Twinkle Twinkle Little Star." Lori doesn't participate on her first day, but she does almost smile when Ms. Lopez makes eye contact with her.

THE FEISTY CHILD

Feisty children have irregular rhythms and are very active, intense, easily distracted, sensitive, and moody. They run rather than walk, push the limits, and respond impulsively with intense emotions. Well-planned transitions are important to feisty children who resist being rushed. Feisty children need opportunities for active play, as well as a chance to experience quiet play when the mood strikes.

For Example...

Four-year-old Roman is a spunky boy whose energy is obvious from the moment he enters a room. He is loud and rambunctious. He rarely walks, preferring to run. He climbs on everything, and often knocks things over. He seems to be unaware of where his body is in space or the impact he has on his environment. In his former classroom, his teacher struggled with Roman's behavior, and complained often to his family. His new preschool teacher, Mrs. Jones, loves energetic, spirited children. She prefers to allow them to manage their own behavior within a set of classroom limits that are carefully introduced, explained to children, and consistently enforced. She steps in only if there is a physical altercation. The rest of the time, she encourages children to work out their own disagreements and conflicts with her nearby as a resource if needed.

Roman's parents are glad that there are fewer complaints about Roman's behavior from Mrs. Jones, but they worry that he doesn't seem to be making friends in his new classroom. When they ask Mrs. Jones about it, she notes that Roman does play alone quite a bit. Mrs. Jones decides spend some time observing Roman, watching more carefully how he plays with his classmates. She notices that other children shy away from Roman. They often won't let him play because they worry he will destroy what they are playing with. She sees that Roman's rambunctiousness is causing him some difficulties with getting to play with friends. She also gets a good view of his need for physical activity, and that he needs help to slow his body down so that he can interact with his peers appropriately.

Mrs. Jones decides to shadow Roman for a week and help him play more successfully with his classmates. When other children complain that Roman will "tear it up" or "knock it down" if he joins them in the block area, she asks Roman if he thinks he can play carefully, without causing damage to his friends' projects. At first Roman says, "No." Mrs. Jones asks if he might be able to get his wiggles out first by jumping on the mini-trampoline, and then come back and play without knocking anything down. Roman agrees to try it, and after he jumps for a while, Mrs. Jones helps him join the other children. This time, Roman is able to control his body and play without being destructive.

A widely used temperament assessment is included in Appendix C. You might want to complete one for each child in your classroom, ask each child's parents to complete one, and use the combined information to better understand and respond to the children in your classroom.

TEMPERAMENT STABILITY

Temperament is relatively stable, but not unchanging. Our experiences play a large role in the way we express our natural tendencies. Under ideal circumstances, these experiences can help children make the most of their innate temperaments. For example, with support from caring adults, a cautious child can learn to approach new situations less fearfully and to manage their anxiety as they try out new experiences. Feisty children can learn to manage intense feelings and express them appropriately, when teachers meet their emotional outburst with gentle guidance and understanding. Flexible children can learn how to ask for attention when they want it, even though the adults around them are busy.

A cautious child can learn to approach new situations less fearfully.

On the other hand, when there are mismatches between a child's temperament and the temperament of his teacher, what he experiences can make innate differences in temperament even more difficult for him. For example, when feisty children who need help to manage their impulsivity, are in a classroom with flexible teachers who are less likely to set firm limits, problems with behavior, interactions, and learning may arise. This is another reason why careful observations of the temperament of children, as well as understanding of your own temperament, is so important.

By around the age of two, what you see of a child's personality is a combination of their inborn temperament and how the important people in her life respond to it. The result for the child is a worldview that is accompanied by particular expectations for responses from all adults, including teachers, based on their experiences.

Fiesty children can learn to express intense feelings appropriately.

In Roman's case, his temperament didn't change. He still has traits of a feisty child. He will continue to need Mrs. Jones competent, sensitive, individualized response to his need for physical activity before he can calm down enough to control his fidgeting and play successfully with others. Over the course of the school year, Mrs. Jones' continued support may be enough for him to integrate new coping strategies into his behavior. He is still active, physical, and impulsive, but now has some ideas about how to manage that activity and impulsivity so he can play successfully with his peers. He also knows his teacher can be depended on to help him cope. Repeated experiences with teachers like Mrs. Jones are likely to result in a child who has many ideas about what to do when his physicality and impulsivity are problematic for him, his peers, or his teachers.

It is worthwhile to note that teachers' temperaments also affect the classroom atmosphere. It is easy to see where a feisty adult might not have much in common with a cautious child, or how a cautious teacher might have difficulty with a feisty child. You might consider filling out the temperamental chart for yourself, and having your partner, a close friend, or family member fill one out for you, as well. The better you understand your own temperament, the more perceptive and flexible you can be when working with children.

When the fit between a teacher's temperament and a child's temperament are at odds, it is even more important for the adult to be aware of temperament, and individualize interactions to minimize these differences. When you realize that a child rubs you the wrong way, it is important to pay close attention to how you react and respond to him or her and make specific plans for how to ensure that each child in your classroom gets responses from you that support his or her individual temperamental differences.

TEACHING STRATEGIES TO ADDRESS CHILDREN'S INDIVIDUAL TEMPERAMENTS

ASSESS CHILDREN'S TEMPERAMENT

In order to best address the needs of children in your care, it is important to be aware of their temperaments. The overall temperament (e.g. flexible, feisty, or cautious) is a good place to start, and children's ratings on particular aspects of temperament (intensity, perseverance, adaptability, etc.) are important. It is also good to know that many people will have some aspects of more than one temperamental style—their own unique version of temperament. These children require even greater insight, and perhaps more observation, since they don't fall into easily identified temperamental patterns.

FOR EXAMPLE...

Alicia is a first grader. She is a cooperative child, and her teacher, Mr. Morris, considers her to have a flexible temperament. However, he notices that Alicia has difficulty transitioning to music class on Tuesdays. The music teacher reports that Alicia doesn't participate in class and often seems scared. Mr. Morris talks with Alicia about music class. Alicia says that music class is too loud, especially when they use cymbals and drums.

Mr. Morris consults with the music teacher and they discuss the situation and possible solutions. The teachers meet with Alicia and talk about their ideas. They also ask her for her own ideas about how to make music class work for her. Alicia likes the music teacher's idea of wearing earmuffs and sitting near the door. The next week, the music teacher brings a basket of earmuffs for children to use if they'd like to, and Alicia and several of her friends put a pair on, giggling at each other. She enjoys wearing the earmuffs and is able to participate in music class that day.

PLAN FOR TEMPERAMENTAL DIFFERENCES

Once you have a more complete understanding of the temperaments at work in your classroom, you can begin to plan for these differences in ways that support children's emotional development and help your classroom run more smoothly. Here are some ideas about how you might plan for and address temperamental differences.

For feisty children who need to move, include active play and opportunities for children to move their bodies regularly throughout the day in the classroom and extended time in outdoor play. Mini trampolines, exercise balls, jump ropes, and songs, rhymes, and finger plays that require movements can be used indoors to help children get their wiggles out and stay in control emotionally.

Active and outdoor play needs to be an integral part of early childhood and elementary programs and is critical to all children's emotional and social development, although it is particularly critical for feisty children. Schools have been eliminating or limiting outdoor play and/or recess for a number of reasons (testing, punishment for disruptive behavior, etc.) This practice probably makes the problem worse. For children with fiesty temperaments whose bodies NEED to move, restricting their movement works against this basic need.

Before transitioning to quiet activities that require focus or attention, all young children will benefit from 3–5 minutes of stretching, calisthenics (jumping jacks, squats, arm circles, etc.), or moving to music (conga lines, Hokey Pokey, If You're Happy and You Know It, for example.) Also, it is crucial that teachers don't forget, shorten, or eliminate outdoor play.

For more cautious children, don't push too hard. Allow time for them to get ready before you encourage them to participate. Let them watch other children try things out first, and answer their questions about what might happen. Give extra reminders about what will happen next and make the sequence of upcoming events clear for them, with words and pictures if necessary. Support them by staying close. For children who seem easily overwhelmed, a cozy corner with plush animals, pillows, or rocking chairs can give them a way to watch from the sidelines as they decide whether to participate in a particular activity.

While flexible children need less help from you to participate successfully in classroom activities, it is always good to check in with them and see if they need or want any extra support or guidance from you. Be sure to give them the opportunity to be close to you during the day, during SET Time, reading a book, or as helpers in the classroom. These children need your attention, too, and you may need to keep track of the time you spend with them to be sure they are not overlooked.

Accommodating Temperamental Differences

For Children with FEISTY Temperaments

- Implement SET Time regularly, adding more time if children's behavior tells you they need it.
- Make sure the environment is predictable.
- Make changes incrementally rather than all at once.
- Assign one special adult to spend time with in the classroom.
- Use redirection.
- Remind children in advance of transitions.
- Provide active opportunities followed by calming activity choices.

For Children with CAUTIOUS Temperaments

- Implement SET Time regularly.
- Build relationships over time.
- Allow children access to security items and control over when they use them.
- Support emerging independence.
- Hold children's hands as you take them over them to activities.
- Stay close as they become comfortable, before moving on to your next teaching task or responsibility.

> **For Children with FLEXIBLE Temperaments**
> • Implement SET Time regularly.
> • Check in often.
> • Provide opportunities to be close to the teacher periodically during the day.
> • Keep track of interaction times (on a class roster or on your curriculum plans) so they don't get overlooked.

Observation is vital to good teaching. Observing before we intervene helps to build relationships with the children in our classroom and improves the odds that the interventions we choose will be successful. Understanding the factors that influence our own perceptions and experience can help us understand children better. With that understanding, we can meet their emotional needs and help them to develop in healthy ways. Familiarity with various temperaments that children may present and knowledge of strategies to meet these children's needs helps to ensure that our role as important adults in their lives is one that helps them to grow and thrive.

SUMMARY: TEACHING STRATEGIES TO BECOME A GOOD OBSERVER

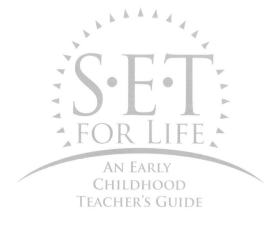

Careful, frequent, and focused observation is one of the most important strategies an early childhood educator can use.

INVEST IN REGULAR OBSERVATION OF CHILDREN WHILE THEY PLAY
• Observing, without intervening or interrupting, is a valuable use of your time.
• When children exhibit challenging behavior, observation should be your first intervention.
• Taking time to observe will save you time in the long run because your interventions will be more effective.

• Some techniques to document what you observe include:
- Anecdotal notes.
- Checklists.
- Rating scales.
- Frequency charts.

OBSERVE TO DOCUMENT STRENGTHS
• When you know what children's strengths are, you will be more likely to find ways to meet their needs.
• A good rule of thumb is to document five positive experiences for each documentation of a concern or challenge.

DISCUSS YOUR OBSERVATIONS WITH OTHERS
• Talking with colleagues may help you untangle puzzling observations.
• Sharing written records, taken over a period of time, can be especially helpful.

TALK TO CHILDREN ABOUT WHAT YOU OBSERVE
• Talking with children about what you see happening can sometimes change the way they interact with you and with each other.
> *"You are almost finished with your puzzle! I wonder what you will do next."*
> *"You and Jacob seem to be having a hard time playing together today. I wonder what might help."*
• This strategy should never be used as discipline.

TEACHING STRATEGIES TO ADDRESS CHILDREN'S INDIVIDUAL TEMPERAMENTS

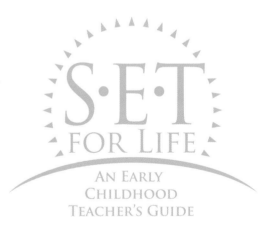

Temperament is genetically determined, and shows up in a variety of character traits, which are present regardless of environment, parenting, or culture. You can support children by recognizing and accommodating their individual temperaments.

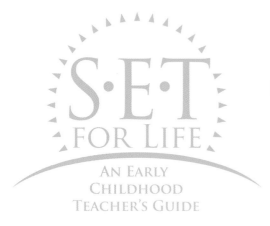

ASSESS CHILDREN'S TEMPERAMENTS

- In order to best address the needs of individual children, it is important to be aware of their temperaments.
- There are a variety of ways to assess temperaments. Getting input from families and other teachers may provide more understanding.

PLAN FOR TEMPERAMENTAL DIFFERENCES

- Awareness of temperamental types helps in grouping children, developing play experiences, and making the most of individual strengths.
- When all temperamental types are accommodated, you will spend less time redirecting, and more time teaching and interacting with children in more positive ways.

CHAPTER 4
MAKE HEALTHY EMOTIONAL CONNECTIONS

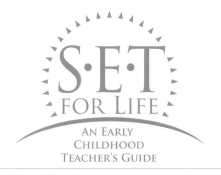

S·E·T
FOR LIFE

AN EARLY
CHILDHOOD
TEACHER'S GUIDE

I n the last chapter, we talked about the benefits of observing young children as they work and play in your classroom. Here, we will give you more tools for understanding emotional development, so you can use that information to build relationships with children.

> *"I hope that while so many people are out smelling the flowers, someone is taking the time to plant some."*
>
> HERBERT RAPPAPORT, SCREEN WRITER

WHAT IS ATTACHMENT?

Attachment is the developing capacity to form and maintain healthy emotional relationships that begins at birth and continues through early childhood.

Unique Features of Attachment Relationships

1. An enduring form of connection with a special person.
2. Involves soothing and comfort by this special person and frequent pleasurable experiences with him or her.
3. Distress is evoked by loss or threat of loss of attachment figure's presence that intensifies as the relationship grows.
4. Serves as a secure emotional base.
5. Presence of attachment figures supports venturing out and exploring the wider world beyond the immediate vicinity.
6. Results in feelings of safety and security when the attachment figure/secure base is nearby.

ATTACHMENT NETWORKS

When relationships are brand new, strong feelings of love and caring draw parents and primary caregivers to their child. The development of these warm feelings is what we call **bonding**. Experiences during this time build a lifelong connection between caregivers and children.

Attachment is a little different. It has more to do with how the child feels towards a caregiver, instead of the other way around. Positive emotional ties between children and adults allow children to be comforted when they are upset or experiencing stress. They also allow caregivers to serve as a secure base

Most often, children's primary attachment figure is their mother or other most frequent caregiver.

for exploration of the wider world. Secure attachments enable children to trust that their needs will be met by caring adults, and to feel that they can make things happen in their world. How the *child* feels is the important dynamic of attachment.

UNDERSTANDING PRIMARY ATTACHMENT

The way primary caregivers respond during a child's first two or three years determines how this relationship forms and how it will impact future emotional development. When children have close, positive, and reciprocal relationships, they develop a sense of trust and security that lasts their whole lives. Relationships with family members and primary caregivers can flourish when these important adults respond quickly and warmly to children's needs, talk to and play with them, and are sensitive with daily routines such as diapering and feeding.

Primary Attachments: *The relationships children form with their most important caregivers, usually their parents.*

Most often, the first attachment relationship that children form is with their mother (or other most frequent primary caregiver.) However, in most children's lives, there are also networks of additional attachment relationships. They usually have one or two primary attachments at home and then a circle of secondary attachment relationships with other caring adults, including extended family members, neighbors, and teachers. All of these relationships have the ability to positively influence children's emotional development.

FOR EXAMPLE...

Marisa was six months old when she was adopted from foster care. Before she was adopted, she lived with a foster family and had a warm, caring relationship, and a strong attachment to her foster mother. When she went home with her adoptive family, they were equally responsive and caring. Over time, Marisa developed a secure attachment to her adoptive mother and father, as well as a special bond with her grandmother, who cares for her while her parents are at work. When she starts preschool, Marisa quickly forms a positive relationship with her teacher. Repeated positive experiences with caring adults allow Marisa to build successful relationships at home, in her extended family, and at school.

THE STAGES OF ATTACHMENT

Attachment is a process that happens in stages, over time, with each stage building on the previous one. These stages are characterized by behaviors that give clues about where children are in their attachment development.

Stages of Attachment

Stage 1: Indiscriminant Attachment
→ Child is responsive to most caring adults. (birth – 5 months)

Stage 2: Discriminant Attachment
→ Child begins to show preference for primary caregivers. (6 months- 1 year)

Stage 3: Separation Anxiety
→ Child show strong preference for familiar adults, becomes cautious with unfamiliar faces. (1 year – 18 months)

Stage 4: Stranger Anxiety
→ Child shows fear and distress with unfamiliar adults. (18 months – 2 years)

The first stage is called **indiscriminant attachment**. During this stage, babies generally respond the same way to most caring adults. Although even newborns show a special preference for their biological mothers, who are familiar to them even before they are born, most infants will allow any responsive adult to meet their needs, as long as these caregivers provide sensitive care. Feeding babies when they are hungry and holding them when they are uncomfortable or upset are examples of responsive care. Warm, caring, and prompt attention allows children to begin forming early attachment relationships, and a preference for familiar over unfamiliar grows stronger as babies head into the second stage.

The second stage is called **discriminate attachment**. During this stage, babies begin to smile, babble, and coo at familiar adults and show definite preferences for the people they know best. It is during this stage that most babies learn that familiar, caring adults will meet their needs, and that they can trust the world to be a safe and responsive place. Babies become less tolerant of care given by unfamiliar adults, and may not be as easily comforted by people they don't know well.

The third stage is called **separation anxiety**. During this stage, children's preference for the people they know becomes much stronger. Friendliness toward unfamiliar adults goes away. Children move closer to a trusted adult when new people enter the room, and they may cry when familiar caregivers leave.

Don't underestimate their anxiety: when children first enter this stage, they believe that loved ones who are out of sight have simply disappeared. Because of their developmental stage, they don't yet know that these special people will come back. It takes many experiences with separation and reunion, and additional time for cognitive development to proceed, for children to learn that family members exist even when they can't be seen, and that they will always come back.

The fourth stage, **stranger anxiety**, is one that almost every teacher has seen. During this stage, children develop a fear of unfamiliar adults. The cautious behavior, seen during the separation anxiety phase, is replaced with clinging, crying, and other anxious responses to strangers and to separation. A child will resist almost any approach by unfamiliar adults, no matter how friendly, and show great distress when family members or a teacher leaves. This stage can be especially trying for parents and teachers alike.

FOR EXAMPLE...

Mrs. Rogers is walking her toddler class to the playground when the custodian, Mr. Frank, walks by and greets them cheerfully. Twenty-month-old Moses shrieks, dashes over to Mrs. Rogers, and buries his face in her legs. Mrs. Rogers gently peels him off her body, and kneels down, putting her arms around him. She says, "Mr. Frank is here to sweep the floors. He comes every day. I will keep you safe." She holds Moses' hand and helps him continue walking towards the playground. Mrs. Rogers later invites Mr. Frank to come by her classroom and show the toddlers his broom and mop so his presence in the hall can be better understood by all of the children (particularly Moses).

At the end of this stage of attachment, children are typically ready to venture out into the social world and form new relationships on their own. And remember, because development is unique to each child, some children experience these stages at different times and with varying levels of intensity. Your ability and willingness to make accommodations for individual differences will help children through these stages.

However, progress through attachment stages isn't guaranteed. Children's experience at each stage of attachment affects the next stage and the way the child will develop emotionally in the coming months and years.

TYPES OF PRIMARY ATTACHMENT

There are two types of primary attachment of children to their significant caregivers: **secure** and **insecure**. It's important to remember that in either case, we are talking about how connected the child feels to her caregiver, not necessarily the way the caregiver feels about the child.

When children are securely attached, they use members of their attachment networks as a secure base. From there, they can explore the environment and the people and things in it. When they are with these important people, children want to stay near them, particularly in new or unfamiliar situations. When they are in situations where they feel more comfortable, they explore the environment, and then return to touch base with the adults they know and trust. By doing this, children recharge their interest and emotional readiness for further exploration. Children who demonstrate these kinds of behaviors are said to have secure attachment.

In contrast, insecure attachment can show up in several different ways. It usually falls into three categories: *ambivalent*, *avoidant*, and *disorganized*. When children have ambivalent attachment, they tend to react inconsistently to their primary caregivers. One minute they might cling to a family member or teacher, and the next moment, they may refuse contact altogether. For example, a child with an ambivalent attachment may run to his mother after a fall or disagreement with a sibling or friend, but when his mother stoops down to offer a hug, he may push her away, or even run in the opposite direction.

Secure and Insecure Attachment

Secure Attachment:
These children feel safe and secure with their primary caregivers and seek them out in unfamiliar situations. They can be soothed and comforted, and feel safe enough to explore the world around them with support from the important people in their lives.

Insecure Attachment:
These children do not look to the important adults in their lives for comfort, reassurance, and emotional connection. Insecure attachment can have many causes, including trauma, separation, or health issues, and may show up in a variety of ways in children, depending on their circumstances and temperaments.

When children have avoidant attachment, they appear disinterested when their parent or other caregiver leaves or returns, when in reality, they are quite upset and just don't show it in the same ways securely attached children do. They may be more affectionate with strangers than with their primary caregivers or other familiar adults. Children with avoidant attachment may also react inconsistently to separations and reunions, sometimes showing great distress when their caregiver leaves, but appearing angry or unresponsive when this person returns and tries to approach them.

Children who have disorganized attachment may appear unable to manage or control their behavior or their emotions. They may move about in a frenzy, or seem completely apathetic and uninterested in what is happening around them. These children do not seek help from their caregivers when they are upset, and tend to be all over the place emotionally and behaviorally. They often have a hard time accepting adult assistance.

The behaviors associated with insecure attachment can be a real challenge for both families and teachers. The way that a child demonstrates insecure attachment can vary depending on both their experiences and temperament, but all children who struggle with developing secure attachments will need extra support and guidance from caring adults around them.

The good news is that most children display secure attachment. Of children demonstrating signs of insecure attachment, avoidant is the most common, followed by disorganized, and then ambivalent. It is important to realize that attachment disorders can occur in all kinds of families. In the media, attachment disorders are most often linked to adoption and abuse, but they also can occur in children in other situations including children with chronic medical problems, those who have depressed or mentally ill primary caregivers, and children experiencing family upheaval.

Insecure Attachment

Ambivalent:
Child reacts inconsistently one minute running to an attachment figure for comfort, but then pushing them away when comfort is offered.

Avoidant:
Child seems disinterested in parent or caregivers, and may even be more affectionate with strangers than with their primary caregiver.

Disorganized:
Child seems to display confused or contradictory behaviors. They may not seek comfort from adults when they are upset, and may resist adult assistance.

If you observe some of the behaviors described above, or suspect an attachment problem with a child, resist the temptation to label any child's behavior (e.g. unattached, or attachment disordered). Instead, make a referral to a mental health specialist for further exploration and guidance. While many people falsely believe that there is no treatment or cure for attachment disorders, therapy and other interventions offer hope for children and families. Further, the best time to address issues related to attachment is as early as possible, as soon as signs appear. At this point, children may be more responsive to intervention than they would be if intervention is postponed until the problem gets worse.

UNDERSTANDING SECONDARY ATTACHMENT

Young children have a different kind of relationship with their teachers than they do with their families. The attachments children develop with their families and most frequent caregivers are called *primary attachments*. Children also develop many *secondary attachments* with their teachers, extended family members, friends, neighbors, and other less frequent caregivers. While still very important, secondary attachments are often more temporary and somewhat less intense. Secondary attachments can often serve as substitutes when primary attachment figures must be away, providing children with comfort and reassurance in the meantime. Secondary attachments can also be shared – one adult can serve as a secondary attachment figure for several children at one time, as in the case of a classroom teacher or caregiver.

> **Secondary Attachments:** *The relationships children form with other caregivers and friends in their lives, including extended family, neighbors, and teachers. These attachments are usually less intense, and not always as long lasting as primary attachments.*

Children need both kinds of attachment relationships. When their primary *and* secondary attachments are strong and reciprocal, children can engage fully with the world around them, and their emotional development can continue uninterrupted. Secondary attachments introduce children to the variety of relationships in the social world. They broaden children's social exposure and help them learn about and accept differences between people. The more children are comfortable with secondary attachments, the more secondary attachments they are willing to build.

Education about attachment is important, both for parents and teachers. Understanding the differences between primary and secondary attachment, and the special role that attachment plays in helping children grow up emotionally healthy, can help smooth common points of conflict between families and teachers. This understanding can also help ensure that children are supported in building strong primary attachments to their primary caregivers and vibrant secondary attachments to teachers and other caring adults in their lives.

The secondary attachments children develop with their teachers can positivley influence the quality of their attachments to others.

WHY THE QUALITY OF ATTACHMENT MATTERS

Why does attachment quality matter? Secure attachments set children up for success in all aspects of their lives, and those advantages last a lifetime. When children sense that the world is a responsive place, they feel free to explore, they manage their feelings more easily, and are more emotionally stable throughout their lives. Securely attached children handle stress better, and approach new situations with confidence and persistence. They are more likely to become self-reliant, have a positive sense of self, and develop healthy friendships. They even show advanced memory skills. In adolescence, children who were securely attached to their primary caregivers during their early years are more independent, have lower rates of mental illness, and generally do well in school, and in life.

TEACHING STRATEGIES TO SUPPORT ATTACHMENT

As a teacher, the time and effort you put into building strong attachments can pay off in a calmer classroom environment, better relationships with families, and higher achievement in children. Here are some strategies to add to your repertoire of teaching skills.

SPEND ENERGY, EFFORT, AND TIME BUILDING POSITIVE RELATIONSHIPS WITH CHILDREN

In Chapter 2, we discussed the importance of reciprocity and synchrony, and how they relate to our ability to build healthy relationships with children. The ability to respond appropriately, at the right time, helps strengthen the bond between you and the children you care for and teach. When you know when to agree, when to distract, when to confront, and when to wait, children come to trust that most of their attempts to communicate will work. They can relax and benefit from the experiences you plan for them in the classroom. When children feel this synchrony, they can take the interactive risks that lead to learning. They also are more likely to hang in there with you, when communication goes awry or you misinterpret their cues.

Because routine caregiving is almost impossible to implement without a child's cooperation, these moments are a great time to develop reciprocity and synchrony with the children in your classroom. You can't feed a baby until she opens her mouth. And, it's difficult to redirect a toddler or a preschooler until you have his full attention. By "ping-ponging"— responding and waiting for a response—during these moments, you can take advantage of this important one-on-one time. So, rather than rushing through routine times, such as diapering or toileting, snack or lunch time, and clean up time, embrace these opportunities to sustain interactions and strengthen relationships.

FOR EXAMPLE...

Baby Elizabeth is in Mrs. Amhed's arms, gazing at her. Mrs. Amhed looks at her, and smiles. Elizabeth smiles back, obviously pleased at having gotten her caregiver's attention. Her smile causes Mrs. Amhed to giggle, which in turn, elicits a belly laugh from Elizabeth. This turn-taking continues until Elizabeth hears another child banging two toys together on the floor, causing her to turn her head to look at him. When Elizabeth looks away, Mrs. Ahmed notices and comments, "You hear Jacob making a big noise!"

Four-year-old Sanjay brings a doll to Ms. Herzbon. He tells his teacher that the baby has a terrible rash and has to go to the doctor. Ms. Herzbon looks concerned and wonders what could have caused such a bad rash. Sanjay replies that it wasn't his fault since he changes his baby every time she needs a clean diaper. Ms. Herzbon empathically nods. She agrees that he takes good care of his baby, and that sometimes babies just get diaper rashes. Sanjay nods in agreement and heads to the doctor kit. On the way, he asks Vonda to come play doctor so he can bring his baby to see her.

RESPOND PROMPTLY TO DISTRESS

When you respond to children right away when they are upset, regardless of the cause, they learn to trust that you are a resource to help them get their needs met. When children *don't* get the attention they need, particularly when they are upset, or responses are inconsistent or insensitive, they are less likely to develop the trust they need to build healthy relationships now, and later in life.

Developing this important sense of trust begins in infancy and continues through the early childhood years. (See p. 16 in Chapter 2, to review the important ideas in Erikson's stages of psychosocial development.) When a child in your classroom is upset, go to her right away. Prompt response is one of the building blocks of trust.

Some children will arrive in your classroom without having experienced prompt, appropriate responses to their distress. Children who have lived in orphanages, those traumatized by abuse or neglect, or children who live in homes where their caregivers are unable to meet their needs because of addiction, poverty, or mental health issues, for example, may need even more responsive attention from you to develop a sense of trust. Sensitive responses from you can help children overcome their previous experiences, begin to build trust, and subsequently, build good relationships with you and others.

Forming a trusting relationship with a child who has a traumatic or chaotic history may not be easy. When children have not gotten the responses they needed from other caregivers, they may worry that the world won't or can't meet their needs. It takes many positive and sensitive experiences with caring adults, over long periods of time, to begin to impact those feelings of distrust. Learning to trust is the foundation of children's emotional well-being, and deserves as much attention as you can devote to it.

FOR EXAMPLE...

Clara was eighteen months old when she was adopted from Russia. She is now a quiet three-year-old, pleasant and sweet in the classroom. After a week in her new early childhood program, her teacher, Ms. Powell, sees Clara taking food from other children at snack and hiding it in her pockets. Later, she notices Clara looking in her pockets repeatedly, to see if the food is still there.

Ms. Powell decides that the issue of food hoarding is something she needs to discuss with Clara's parents, and she asks them to come in for a conference. During the conference, the parents report that they feel that Clara is attached to them, but share that her anxiety regarding food is a problem at home, too. They remind her often that she no longer lives in the orphanage and that in her home there will always be enough to eat, but it has not stopped her need to hoard. They are open to new strategies to help their daughter feel safe and learn to trust that she will have enough food when she needs it.

Ms. Powell and Clara's parents decide to offer Clara small bags of food to carry with her at all times. At home, her parents put bags of crackers and raisins by the bed and keep fruit in a bowl where she can reach it. They tell her often that she can have food whenever she is hungry and always let her have it when she asks. Ms. Powell also tells Clara that she may carry snacks with her in her pocket, keep snacks in her cubby, and leave a snack bag next to her nap mat. She gives her complete access to food whenever she wants or needs it. Ms. Powell places a basket of snacks out in the classroom where Clara can see it at all times, and reminds her daily that she will always have enough food at school. When the issue comes up with other children in Clara's class, Ms. Powell gives them their own basket of snacks. She also talks with them about being different children, and not needing to carry snack bags around.

After a couple of months, Clara's need to hoard begins to decrease. Although she still wants to know where her snack bags are, it's now rare for her to actually eat the food. Her classmates, who already trust that there will be enough food, and were initially very interested in their snack basket, now rarely seek it out. By recognizing the source of Clara's worries and meeting her emotional needs, Ms. Powell and Clara's parents have helped her begin to trust that her basic needs — in this case, for enough food — will be met.

LET FAMILIES TEACH YOU ABOUT THEIR CHILDREN

Parents and other primary caregivers know their children well. Ask them to share their knowledge with you. They are usually happy to tell you about a child's temperament, history, eating and sleeping habits, likes and dislikes, typical schedule, and other useful information. It's a good idea to get this information in writing so you can keep track of all of the details you learn about children in your classroom.

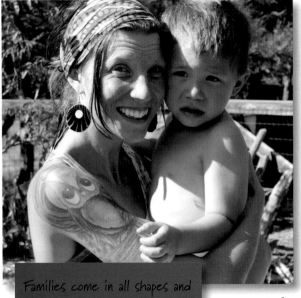

Families come in all shapes and sizes. Your classroom should make all families feel welcome.

Another good way to get to know families is to invite them to attend a "Get to Know the Teacher" session before they start in your program. During this first visit, encourage families to come without their child, if possible, or provide an activity area for children who come along and can tolerate separation from their family members. This is a good time for you to focus your attention on the family, learn about their hopes and concerns for their child(ren), and explore what their expectations are for you and your program. The more you know about the children in your classroom, the better prepared you will be to support them and help them learn. If a face-to-face meeting isn't possible, you can improvise with other strategies such as email, or a phone or Skype call.

Getting to know the families of the children in your classroom is very important for many reasons. It is vital that you have information that will help you to support all of the children (and their unique family compositions) because the messages children receive about themselves, family formation, and diversity at school play a large role in how children see themselves. You need to ask, for example, what names children use to refer to their caregivers, how the family talks about possible visible differences (such as transracial or gay/lesbian families), and gather any other relevant data that will help you to make the child feel comfortable in your environment.

Provide an inclusive environment that welcomes all families. Practice and use inclusive language, and be sure to consider adoptive families, multicultural families, gay/lesbian families, military families, and grandparents who are parenting grandchildren.

Lessons and assignments can be modified when they prove difficult for children who have been adopted or live in foster care (for example, ask children who may not have baby pictures to bring pictures of themselves at different ages or on various holidays). Paying attention to these kinds of details will provide an environment in which all children feel valued, while minimizing possible triggers of grief and loss for children in less traditional families or who have experienced trauma (such as divorce, displacement, deployment, etc.).

Examples of Inclusive Language
- Caregiver instead of parent
- Birth parent instead of real parent
- Parent instead of mom or dad

GIVE CHILDREN AND FAMILIES TIME TO SETTLE IN

Gradual enrollment is another important part of helping children settle in while supporting the relationship building process. Invite the family members to spend time in your classroom with their child. Start slowly, with a one or two hour visit. Gradually increase the time the child stays in the classroom with a familiar adult, until they have spent a full day there. This gives children time to get used to you and to their new surroundings with the support of a familiar and trusted person. It also gives children, teachers, and family members time to get to know each other before they need to rely on each other completely.

The way families identify themselves is highly personal and sometimes sensitive. You can use a family questionnaire to find out the way families refer to each other and their extended family.

Neuroscience supports this process. In the brain, there are dedicated cells called mirror neurons that help children read other people's nonverbal cues and adopt their state of being as their own. Children can pick up negative as well as positive emotions and translate them into their own experiences. We can use this neurological process to help children cope with transitioning to the new environment of child care or school.

FOR EXAMPLE...

Mrs. Harper arrives with her three-year-old son Jonathan for his first day at preschool. Johnathan is Mr. and Mrs. Harper's only son, and he has been cared for at home until now. He was born prematurely and suffers from asthma. Despite a visit to the classroom prior to starting school and a home visit by the new teacher, Ms. Peterson, Mrs. Harper is highly anxious as she approaches the classroom door. Jonathan looks terrified, clinging to his mother and hiding behind her skirt as she talks nonstop.

Ms. Peterson approaches them, greets Mrs. Harper and bends down to say hello to Jonathan. He covers his face with his mother's skirt. Mrs. Harper continues to talk: "Jonathan is so scared; he's never been away from me. I am worried he may have an asthma attack. Do all the teachers know that he has medication? What if he needs me? How will I know that he is alright?" Ms. Peterson sees that Jonathan is becoming more upset as his mother continues to talk. She invites Mrs. Harper to come into the classroom and reminds her that she may stay as long as she would like. She brings a chair over and tells Jonathan that his mommy will stay until he has time to get used to the classroom, since this is all very new for him.

Ms. Peterson calmly talks with Mrs. Harper, reassuring her that she understands this is a big transition for the family, and that parents are welcome in her classroom any time. She shows Mrs. Harper the medicine cabinet and the labels, pointing out that the cabinet has a laminated card showing Jonathan's medication and describing how is it to be administered. She offers Mrs. Harper some tea and invites her to sit and read a book with Jonathan while she welcomes the other children and parents into the classroom. As his mother relaxes, Jonathan also calms. They settle into the room and begin reading a book. After a few minutes Ms. Peterson notices Jonathan start to look at toys, and then slowly leave his mother's side to get one.

The gradual enrollment process could take from one to four weeks or even longer for children under three. Although there is no single way to do gradual enrollment, it often looks like this:

- Children come to school with parent(s) or other primary caregiver.
- The family member(s) stays with the child as he or she moves around the classroom, allowing the child to play and to watch the teachers and other children.
- The child's teacher stays nearby during this time, but does not rush to interact. Teachers can take advantage of this time to observe the child and the family members in action, while continuing with the day's routine and tending to other responsibilities.
- In the beginning, the family member provides routine care (feeding, aiding in going to sleep, diapering or toileting, etc.). The teacher observes, learning the child's usual routines.
- Gradually, over several days, the family member and the teacher begin to trade places — the family member becomes the observer, and the teacher takes over care of the child.

Giving children time to settle in can ease the transition from home to school.

In full-day, full-year programs, gradual enrollment can take place over a couple of weeks. However, it is also important to support families who can't fully participate in gradual enrollment, due to work schedules or other responsibilities. Encourage all families to do gradual enrollment for at least a few days. If this is not possible, family members can spend 20-30 minutes in the classroom before leaving, helping their child make the transition and then return at lunchtime for a visit.

At the end of the day, encourage families to spend another 20-30 minutes in the classroom to reconnect with their child before heading home. This transition time can be slowly reduced over several days or weeks, as the child settles in.

For programs with traditional academic schedules that begin in the fall, gradual enrollment will look different. Here are some ideas for gradual enrollment for a traditional academic schedule:

- Begin the children in small groups, rather than starting everyone at once.
- Stagger start times; children arrive in two or three small groups, for the first few days or weeks.
- Shorten the length of the school day during the first few days or weeks, to allow time for adjustment.
- Schedule one or two play days before school starts to let children explore their new classroom and get to know their teachers.

Gradual enrollment is extremely valuable. Providing the time for good relationships to get started the right way helps everyone — families, teachers, and children — know what to expect from their school experience and get off to a good start.

When families do not participate in a gradual enrollment process, both parents and children may have a harder time settling in. Misunderstandings between families and teachers or administrators are more common without gradual enrollment. It takes more time at the beginning, but the benefits will last through the child's entire time in your program or school.

MATCH EACH CHILD TO ONE CAREGIVER/TEACHER

Primary caregiving is another important strategy for supporting children's emotional development. Primary caregiving focuses on developing a warm, sensitive, and reciprocal relationship between children and you, their most frequent secondary teacher. It also provides you with the opportunity to develop close ties with families and children, building relationships that are successful and rewarding for everyone involved.

Your first task as a primary caregiver is to invest in relationship building with a smaller group of children in your classroom. In a class with two or more teachers,

Primary caregiving has many benefits.

children are simply divided among the adults. As a primary teacher, you will spend time observing each of the children assigned to you, gathering information about their families, individual schedules, personalities, and cultures. This valuable information will help you match your responses to individual children.

A second task is developing a good relationship with each child's family. Because family members are the most important people in a child's life, the quality of this relationship can make or break a child's school experience. You will likely be the person that families first contact when they have a concern about their child. How much families feel they can trust you will strongly influence the relationship you are able to build with their child.

Primary caregivers/teachers:

- interact with rather than react to children.
- anticipate what children might need and want.
- respond quickly and affectionately when children are hurt or upset.
- wait for signs of readiness from children before requiring action.
- consider children's individuality and temperament when interpreting their cues.
- interact warmly with children during routine caregiving, such as diapering or toileting, snack and mealtimes, or napping.
- are sensitive to over- or under-stimulation from the environment, and the adults and children in it.
- individualize the schedule or pace of the day to meet children's individual needs.

Your third task is building a special relationship with each child in your primary teaching group. The time you spend observing them will help you get to know their unique personalities and circumstances. This kind of fine tuned attention will help build a strong bond between you and each child, as well as a sense of connection between the children within the group.

It is important to know that primary teaching is not exclusive teaching. Teachers who share responsibilities in a classroom must be willing to help each other to ensure that the needs of all children are met. For example, if the other teacher in the classroom is busy helping his group with painting, and one of his assigned children is upset in the block area, you should respond to that child, even if you are not her primary teacher.

FOR EXAMPLE...

Ms. Nguyen and Mrs. Roberts are taking their preschool class on a nature walk. Ms. Nguyen walks at the front of the group, pointing out the changing autumn leaves to the children. Most of the children in her primary teaching group stay near her as they walk, with Mrs. Robert's group following close behind. Mrs. Roberts walks at the back of the group, making sure the whole class stays together. She notices that Charlotte, one of the children assigned to Ms. Nguyen, is falling further and further behind the group, and looking more and more upset. When Mrs. Roberts sees that Charlotte is about to cry, she kneels down next to her and asks what is wrong. Charlotte tells her that her shoe is unbuckled, and she doesn't want to get left behind if she stops to fix it. Mrs. Roberts quickly buckles Charlotte's shoe, and encourages her to run to catch up with her best friend, who is walking next to Ms. Nguyen.

BE AVAILABLE OVER TIME

When teachers are dependable, children learn that caring adults will provide what they need. But this awareness takes time to develop. Being available over time is something you can do to support emotional growth in the classroom.

Called continuity of care, looping, or sustained instruction, leaving children in the same learning groups for longer periods benefits children's emotional growth. Ideally, children would have one teacher during infancy and toddlerhood, another one for the preschool years, and the same teacher for two or three of the early elementary years (K-3). Teacher changes can make it hard for children to develop strong secondary attachments, and it is especially problematic for children whose primary attachments are not secure.

If it is not possible for children to remain with the same teacher for the ideal amount of time, you can help them compensate and adjust to change by providing long, well-planned transitions before they have to leave familiar teachers behind. How these plans are implemented depends on the children who will experience the transition.

When a new teacher comes into a classroom, and a familiar one is leaving, plan an overlap when both teachers are available. Similar to gradual enrollment (when children transition from their families to the classroom), the familiar teacher follows the day's usual routine at the beginning, while the new teacher observes. The teachers then work together, allowing the children to see both of you in action. Eventually, the new teacher begins to interact more with children, reading stories, passing out snacks, and helping with diapering or toileting, until she has gradually taken over most of the classroom responsibilities. Plan at least two weeks of this kind of overlap with new teachers in a preschool classroom, and a month or longer for younger children.

When both the classroom and the teacher change, allow even more time. Schedule regular visits to the new classroom and have the new teacher(s) spend time in the current classroom in the weeks leading up to the transition. Encourage new teachers to observe, so they can learn how familiar teachers work with particular children in the group.

Then, plan for children to spend short periods of time in their new classroom, with both their new and current teachers. Begin with familiar events, like storytime, or lunch. Soon, familiar teachers can begin to leave the new classroom for a little while, so children can practice depending on and trusting their new teachers.

Slowly increase the amount of time familiar teachers are out of the new classroom, making adjustments if children seem anxious or stressed, until the transition is complete. Familiar teachers should return for high stress times, such as arrival and departure time, and at other routine times, such as mealtime and naptime. An example of a transition schedule for toddlers moving to a preschool classroom is in Appendix D.

FOR EXAMPLE...
Two-year-old Andrew is transitioning from the younger toddler classroom to the older toddler classroom. He has a very strong attachment with Greta, the younger toddler teacher. Greta and Priscilla, the older toddler teacher, have made a plan to assist Andrew in the transition. Andrew has visited Priscilla's classroom for fifteen minutes for two days with Greta, who stays the entire time with him. She helps him explore the room and find the trains, his favorite toys. Priscilla comes over to engage with Andrew and Greta, lingering a bit longer each day. On the third day, Greta tells Andrew she needs to get her notebook from the other classroom. She tells him that Priscilla will stay in this room with him and that she will be right back. Priscilla kneels down to offer Andrew another train. Andrew immediately looks to Greta, who reassures him that he is safe, that Priscilla will take good care of him for a couple of minutes, and she will be right back. Greta's calm voice and reassuring words help Andrew to remain in his future classroom, while she gets her notebook. Just as she said, Greta comes right back. Although Andrew notices her return, he continues playing with Pricilla and the trains.

Understanding and supporting attachment relationships will help you build positive relationships with children and families, and to provide support during times of stress. When children sense that the world is a responsive place, they may feel more free to explore, manage their feelings more easily, and be more emotionally stable throughout their lives.

SUMMARY: TEACHING STRATEGIES TO SUPPORT ATTACHMENT

The way teachers respond determines how their relationships will impact children's future emotional development.

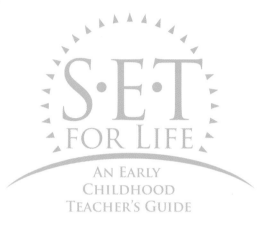

SPEND ENERGY, EFFORT, AND TIME BUILDING POSITIVE RELATIONSHIPS WITH CHILDREN

- The ability to respond at the right time, in the right ways, helps strengthen the bond between you and the children in your care.
- Embrace routine caregiving moments (feeding, toileting, clean-up time, etc.) as opportunities to practice synchrony and build relationships with children.

RESPOND PROMPTLY TO DISTRESS

- When a child is upset, respond right away, regardless of the cause of his or her distress.
- Prompt response to distress is a building block of trust.
- Building trusting relationships with children who have a history of trauma can be challenging, but it can make a difference in their emotional health over their entire lifetime.

    "Ouch! That really hurt! You can sit on my lap until it feels better."

    "You didn't want Mommy to leave today. She will be back after naptime, and I am right here if you need me."

    "You didn't want it to be Landon's turn on the swing. You can hold my hand until you are ready to play again."

LET FAMILIES TEACH YOU ABOUT THEIR CHILDREN

- Parents and other primary caregivers know their children well — ask them to share their knowledge with you.
- Accommodating and validating all kinds of families helps children and families feel welcome and safe.

GIVE CHILDREN AND FAMILIES TIME TO SETTLE IN

- Gradual enrollment is an important part of helping children settle in, while supporting the relationship-building process. Invite family members to spend time in your classroom with their child.
- Providing time for good relationships to get started helps everyone — families, teachers, and children.

MATCH EACH CHILD TO ONE CAREGIVER/TEACHER

- Matching small groups of children to individual teachers helps support children's emotional growth. Work to build a positive and reciprocal relationship with each child in your group.
- Primary caregivers also work to build strong relationships with the families of the children in their group.
- Primary caregiving is not exclusive caregiving. Teachers who share a classroom must be ready to meet the needs of all of the children, not just the ones in their small group.

BE AVAILABLE OVER TIME

- When teachers are dependable, children learn that caring adults will meet their needs.
- Children benefit from long-term relationships with their teachers, built over several years.
- Gradual and sensitive transitions to new classrooms or caregivers are important to supporting children's emotional health.

CHAPTER 5

UNDERSTAND EMOTIONAL DEVELOPMENT

S·E·T
FOR LIFE

AN EARLY
CHILDHOOD
TEACHER'S GUIDE

Emotional development involves learning about two related processes during the early childhood years—**emotional expression** and **emotional regulation**. By the age of three, children experience and express a wide range of emotions, even if they are only able to name some of them. The challenge during these years is to learn to manage — or regulate — these intense emotions in order to be successful at home, in school, and in the wider community.

UNDERSTANDING EMOTIONAL DEVELOPMENT

GREENSPAN'S THEORY OF EMOTIONAL DEVELOPMENT

Stanley Greenspan, a child psychiatrist, describes play as a gateway to emotional learning and proposes that emotional development proceeds in a series of overlapping stages. Understanding them can help you address children's needs at each stage and give you clues about how to modify your teaching strategies to support progress through the stages. The ages given for these stages are not set in stone, but are useful in understanding where children might be emotionally and why they experience their emotions in particular ways.

During **Stage One** (*birth- 3 months*), children learn to calm themselves, start to focus on things happening around them, and begin to develop a sense of security about getting their needs met by caring adults. **Stage Two** (*2 months-7 months*) is sometimes called a time of falling in love. During this stage, children develop a joyful interest in the human world and are more engaged with the people who care for them. This is the age when babies begin to light up at the sight of familiar faces. **Stage Three** (*3 months-10 months*) sees babies developing intentional communication and seeking cause and effect interaction with familiar adults. For example, they will reach their arms up to be held or clamp their mouths shut tightly when an unwanted bite of food is offered. When caregivers do a good job of interpreting and responding to these cues, children begin to learn how to communicate their needs and interact successfully with their caregivers.

> "It is not the strongest of the species that survive, nor the most intelligent, but the one most responsive to change."
>
> CHARLES DARWIN, NATURALIST

Emotional Expression: *The way emotions are demonstrated to the outside world.*

Emotional Regulation: *The way emotions are managed internally.*

Stage Four (*9 months-18 months*) finds children forming a sense of themselves as separate from their caregivers. They begin to link one experience to another and can solve some problems on their own, such as remembering where to find a favorite toy when they want to play with it. Their communication skills become more sophisticated. Instead of crying for a bottle, they take their caregiver's hand and pull her over to the refrigerator, point, and say "ba."

During **Stage Five** (*18 months-30 months*), children begin to use language successfully to get their needs met and interact with others. Children connect behaviors with emotions, (e.g., understanding that Mom's hands on her hips means she isn't pleased), and they can use words, rather than actions, to express emotions (such as saying, "I'm angry!" instead of throwing a toy in anger). It is during this stage that pretend play also emerges.

As children get older, they enter **Stage Six** (*2 ½ years-4 years*), when they begin to create an internal world and connect feelings to actions. This ability helps them to anticipate consequences and change behaviors to avoid them (for example, they notice that they are feeling angry, but decide not to throw a toy, because they want to continue playing with it). In **Stage Seven**, children are able to understand multiple causes for emotions, and deal with gradations in feelings.

Greenspan's Stages of Emotional Development

Stage 1: Being Calm and Interested in the World (*birth – 3 months*)

Stage 2: Falling in Love (*2 months – 7 months*)

Stage 3: Becoming an Intentional Communicator (*3 months – 10 months*)

Stage 4: Learning to Interact to Solve Problems (*9 months – 18 Months*)

Stage 5: Creating Emotional Ideas (*18 months – 30 months*)

Stage 6: Building Bridges between Ideas (*2 ½ years – 4 years*)

Stage 7: Multiple-Cause and Triangular Thinking (*4 years – 7 years and up*)

Stage 8: Gray-Area, Emotionally Differentiated Thinking (*6 years – 10 years and up*)

For Example...

Three-and-a-half year old George sat on the pillows in the cozy areas, screaming. If anyone came near him, he growled and screamed louder. Children covered their ears and moved away. When teachers tried to redirect, distract, or set limits with him, he grew louder or lashed out by hitting or pinching. Mrs. Harris walks over and kneels down near him saying, "You are really upset. You are screaming, yelling, pinching, and growling. You must be really, really mad." He growls at her as she moves away.

Later on, while playing at the sensory table, George says to Mrs. Harris, "I'm ready to talk." She sits by him and says, "I'm glad you are ready to talk. You were really mad before and didn't want to talk to anyone! Maybe I can help now that you aren't so mad." She waits, making a few comments about what he is doing at the sensory table.

After a few minutes of her nearby presence, George begins to tell her what had made him so mad. He had been playing at the sink and someone wanted to wash her hands. He didn't want to move, so instead, he hit that child. As a result, Mrs. Harris helped him leave the sink area and asked him to take a minute to get under control in the cozy area. Mrs. Harris and George talk about what else he might have done instead of hitting. She lists several things and asks him which one might have worked. They make a plan to keep him from getting so mad the next time someone needs to wash their hands while he is at the sink.

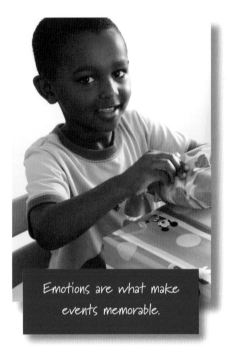

Emotions are what make events memorable.

INTELLIGENCE AND EMOTIONS ARE CONNECTED

In addition to a stage theory of emotional development, Greenspan offers another important idea: intelligence and emotions are connected. Each intellectual skill is first tagged and organized in the brain by the emotional response that accompanies it. Emotions increase the ability to recall the experience and access the related skills that were learned at the time. Without an emotional connection, the skills acquired during that experience may not have much meaning over the long term.

The importance of emotional connection applies to memories as well as skills. It is easier for us to remember events that were more emotionally intense than it is for us to recall things that didn't cause an emotional reaction. That may be why, as adults, we don't remember the toys we received at a specific birthday party unless the toy had emotional meaning beyond that occasion. On the other hand, you might have vivid memories of a certain doll that provided comfort during a difficult time in your childhood — the emotional meaning attached to the toy makes the doll memorable.

Skills and emotions are closely linked in children's development. As children gain increasing control over their emotions, they become more able to focus their attention and behavior—crucial skills for learning. The reverse of this is also true: if children can't manage their emotions, they may struggle to access the skills they have learned or benefit from planned classroom experiences. Supporting emotional development in the classroom is tremendously helpful for children in many other aspects of their learning, and especially beneficial for learners who are at risk for language difficulties or other learning differences.

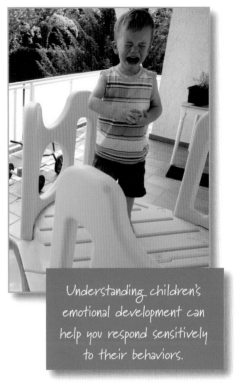

Understanding children's emotional development can help you respond sensitively to their behaviors.

Behaviors, and the underlying emotions that accompany them, tell us a lot about a child's stage of emotional development. They can also show when a child is in need of specific kinds of teacher interaction. Since young children aren't always able to explain the meaning behind their actions, it often falls to the teacher to figure it out. The challenge is for teachers to suspend judgment and action (or reaction) until the underlying meaning of behavior can be discovered and addressed.

It's important to consider what emotional meaning is attached to the experiences a child has in your classroom. Here are some things you can do to help children attach positive emotional meaning to classroom experiences:

- Focus your interactions with children on building relationships.
- Watch for children's verbal and nonverbal responses to classroom experiences.
- Record observations for further review.
- Individualize and modify interactions to support emotional connections between children and yourself.
- Build Down Time into the routine to help children recharge and get ready for new experiences.
- Plan activities to match children's age and stage development.
- Make sure learning activities are concrete, hands-on, and enjoyable.

· Include age-appropriate humor and even some silliness in transition activities.
· Work in small groups, so children get enough of your attention and encouragement to feel successful.
· Assure that learning is fun by using engaging and developmentally appropriate teaching strategies.

EMOTIONAL EXPRESSION

HOW CHILDREN LEARN ABOUT EMOTIONS

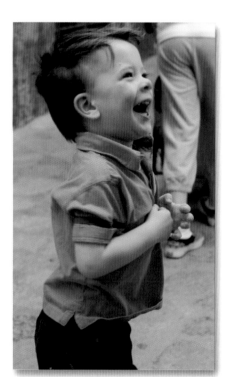

During infancy, children express themselves primarily by crying. They send nonverbal signals as well, such as averting their eyes or turning their heads away. As they learn to differentiate their cries, matching different situations with different intensity, tone, and persistence, their caregivers get better at recognizing the purpose of particular cries, and then at anticipating what the baby might need, before crying starts.

Toddlers grab, bite, hit, and wail, using their bodies to express themselves as they learn the give-and-take of nonverbal and verbal communication. As language develops, children have more options for self-expression. However, their early emotional vocabulary is not extensive, and often the gestures or words don't come fast enough to help others interpret their needs. As a result, they physically act out their feelings, instead of accessing the words to describe how they are feeling.

As children grow, their understanding about emotions also expands. Preschoolers have more experience with expressing their emotions in play. They can use these prior experiences to influence what others do by trying what worked in previous situations. For example, we have all heard a preschooler say, "I won't invite you to my birthday party if you don't let me play," hoping to influence the outcome of a situation. Preschoolers can also show great compassion and generosity when they feel inspired to help others feel better.

TEACHING STRATEGIES TO SUPPORT EMOTIONAL DEVELOPMENT AND EXPRESSION

MAKE YOUR FEELINGS OBVIOUS FOR CHILDREN TO SEE

It can be hard for children (and adults!) to tell the difference between emotions. For a toddler, there is a very fine line between frustration and rage. Noticing the difference between anger and irritation, for example, requires attention to very subtle cues, such as changes in the way a mouth looks or what the eyes are doing. Children sometimes miss these important details. You can help them learn to read these cues by exaggerating facial expressions and combining them with other physical cues, such as putting your hands on your hips or making big gestures with your hands.

This advice may seem contrary to some cultural and societal norms about expressing feelings. Families have all kinds of views about emotions. Some encourage children and adults to hold on to their feelings and not display them, or suggest that expressing emotions in various contexts is inappropriate. For children in the early childhood period, this hinders learning about emotional expression. In the classroom setting, clear identification of how you are feeling helps children learn from you about emotional expression.

Your expression and gestures help children notice differences in emotions.

Ms. Thomas is trying to put a puppet on a high shelf, but it keeps falling off. She tries three times, and every time it topples down. After each fall, she sighs loudly and rolls her eyes. Eventually, she throws her hands us and puts the puppet on a low shelf. Then she says, "That was so frustrating! The puppet just wouldn't stay on the puppet shelf. I guess it is too crowded."

Mrs. Henderson's class is building birdhouses. As she is demonstrating hammering a nail, she misses and hits her finger. "Ouch!" she yells, dropping the hammer. She shows the children her red finger and says, "That really hurt. I didn't mean to hit my finger. That was a big mistake! Make sure your finger is out of the way before you hit the nail."

SET for Life Language

"Ouch!! I dropped a book on my toe! It really hurt!"

"I am disappointed it is a rainy day and we can't play outside."

"I am so excited about our special visitor!"

"I don't like that you hit me."

"I am mad about the broken toy. And, we will find a way to fix it or replace it together."

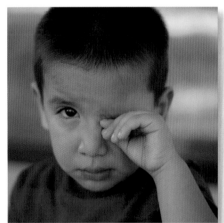

DON'T TRY TO "FIX" CHILDREN'S FEELINGS - ACKNOWLEDGE THEM INSTEAD

When children are upset, it's natural to want to comfort them by making their big feelings go away. Emotions don't need fixing. We don't want to remove emotions from a child's experience. We have all said, "You're okay," to a crying child who is obviously not okay, or "Stop crying," to a child who is upset. In the **SET for Life** approach, we suggest teachers resist the urge to tell children they should feel differently than they do.

Instead, focus on helping children name the way they are feeling and manage their intense emotions. Recognize and validate that the emotions are present and real to the child. Then, connect intense emotions to appropriate behaviors (such as taking deep breaths, or sitting in the cozy corner), and teach children to use problem-solving skills, like calling for help from an adult or making a plan to get what they want. This helps children manage how they feel without dismissing their feelings.

When you use typical guidance strategies like redirection and logical consequences, it's easy to incorporate language that acknowledges children's feelings. Doing this helps them figure out how to make different, more appropriate choices the next time they have similar feelings.

Using **SET for Life** teaching strategies helps you focus on how the child feels rather than on what he or she should do about it. Although learning what to do when you feel mad is crucial, you must first know what that emotion looks and feels like, and how it is similar to and different from other emotions, such as joy or irritation.

FOR EXAMPLE...

Four-year-old Rachel is crying in the dramatic play area. The teacher approaches and asks what is wrong. At first, Rachel just shrugs her shoulders and keeps crying. After a few minutes, Rachel tells the teacher that her daddy and mommy yelled at each other that morning. Her teacher says, "I wonder if that made you sad and maybe a little scared, too. The teacher continues, "I think it can be pretty scary when mommies and daddies don't get along. Maybe you are worried about what will happen when you go home after school. You are safe here. Your tears are helping you show your worry. I will stay right here with you until you feel better."

SET for Life Language

"You are really mad!"

"Your face says you are sad that you lost the game."

"I hear you. You are really angry."

"She said 'No!' I think that was hard to hear. You really wanted her to say yes."

"When Daddy is gone, I think you miss him."

LABEL FEELINGS FOR CHILDREN

Recognizing and labeling feelings supports emotional development. For teachers and families, this means being able to put word labels on feelings as they are experienced.

When children feel understood and are given words to name their feelings, they are supported in all areas of development, not just in the emotional domain. This understanding is what we mean when we talk about "feeling felt." It allows children to receive support from adults as they experience emotions by letting them know that someone understands how they feel. The more children feel understood and respected, the easier it is for them accomplish the important developmental task of understanding and managing their emotions.

You play an important role in showing children how to label their feelings. Start by naming happiness, joy, anger, fear, and sadness. Later, you can move on to more subtle emotions, like irritation, generosity, worry, relief, frustration, confusion, embarrassment, pride, jealousy, disgust, etc.

FOR EXAMPLE...

After reading the book Sometimes I Feel Like a Mouse, *by Jeanne Modessitt, to a group of children, Ms. Garcia asks children to point to the picture that shows how they feel. Travis, who is four, points to the illustration of "happy" and says, "I'm happy." Next Mrs. Garcia asks six-year-old Gabriella how she feels. Gabriella says, "Actually, I feel four, no, five things!" Ms. Garcia says to Gabriella, "I wonder if you might be worried about giving the right answer. You may have many different feelings. Which one is the biggest feeling right now?"*

SET for Life Language

"I think you might be angry." (or mad, sad, happy, irritated, content, calm, lonely, etc.)

"You sound mad." (or sad, happy, frustrated, disgusted, exasperated, suspicious, etc.)

"You have your hands on your hips. Are you mad? Exasperated?"

"I'm wondering if that face means you're frustrated or irritated."

"Your eyes look surprised."

TEACH CHILDREN TO NAME THEIR FEELINGS

Naming feelings lets children know that their experiences are normal, and gives them a way to think about what is happening. Emotional vocabulary allows both children and adults to talk about emotions, giving children a chance to identify how they feel, and to think about how to respond at that moment, as well as later when they have the same feeling again. This kind of reflection leads to talking about feelings, instead of acting on them immediately.

Naming feelings, and talking about the way they are expressed, is a good ongoing emotional curriculum project. Collect photographs of children in your classroom as they express various feelings. Older children, who might feel singled out or embarrassed by being photographed, can look at selected magazine pictures that illustrate children and adults expressing various emotions. When you lead a small group discussion of what the people in the pictures might be feeling, children can learn from you about naming emotions.

The easiest emotions for teachers to label are usually happiness, anger, and sadness. However, there are many feelings worth naming — jealousy, frustration, loneliness, fear, and fury, to name a few. But, there are many more! A feelings chart can help you and the children name the wide variety of emotions we all experience. For example, you might comment on a child's disappointment when she isn't selected to be her best friend's bathroom buddy, saying, "Shucks, you wanted her to choose you. She didn't. I think you are disappointed."

SET for Life Language

"Check your body. What is it telling you? How are you feeling?"

"You have tears in your eyes. I wonder how come."

"That is a very big smile. I wonder how you are feeling."

"What did you feel to make you stomp your feet?"

"You're sitting with your arms crossed. I wonder how come."

"How come you want to play by yourself?"

USE EMOTIONAL LANGUAGE IN THE CLASSROOM

The early childhood years are a great time to introduce language related to emotions because children are adding vocabulary at a remarkable rate. There are many ways to incorporate this important vocabulary into your classroom. Label feelings the same way you label numbers and colors. Read books about emotions, play charades and act out feelings, play classical music for children to move to the feeling of the music, and play emotions games where children match the faces of their friends by acting out similar emotions.

You can include emotional language toys and materials in your classroom as well. Here are some ways to do so:

- Provide mirrors (locker mirrors, full length mirrors, and pocket mirrors) to check out how emotions look.
- Post an emotions chart where children can see it and use it to help children figure out what they are feeling.
- Provide photo cards of emotions for children to look at, label, and match.
- Read children's books that show various emotions.
- Talk about how emotions are handled.

It is also important for children to see you own and label your feelings. Talk to children about things that happen to you and how you feel about them. When you do, children can learn from your example as you show them how you look when you experience various emotions.

FOR EXAMPLE...

Mr. Collins is late for school one morning. During his morning meeting with his class, he tells them why he was late: "My car had a flat tire on the way to school this morning. I was worried about getting here on time. It took the tow truck twenty minutes to get to me! Then it started to rain, and I left my umbrella and my lunch in my car at the car repair shop. I was very frustrated this morning because so many things were hard. I am glad to be at school now and I am feeling calmer. Mrs. Jones is coming in to read a story to you while I go pick up my car at the shop and get my lunch and my umbrella."

MODEL APPROPRIATE RESPONSES

The next step, after validating feelings and teaching children to name them, is to connect appropriate responses to their emotions. We can't fix or take away feelings, but we can teach acceptable ways to express them.

Hitting and grabbing are common examples of how anger or upset feelings are demonstrated in an early childhood classroom. When these things happen, it is important to focus your attention on the child who has been hit or grabbed from first, instead of immediately addressing the offending child. Then, you can model language and ways of behaving that are acceptable and show children an appropriate level of upset to match what has happened.

For Example...

Joseph is building a tall tower with unit blocks and all of a sudden the tower falls down. Furious that it fell, he sweeps all the blocks across the floor and then kicks them around. Ms. Ochello says, "Joseph, you are really angry that your tower fell down. You are a boy who can rebuild your tower. You can be disappointed about your tower falling and you may not kick blocks. I can help you find a way to keep your tower standing when you are ready."

HELP CHILDREN CONNECT EMOTIONS WITH APPROPRIATE BEHAVIOR

Children connect emotions to behaviors quite naturally as they grow up. They begin by copying the behaviors they see in important people in their lives — we've all seen toddlers do perfect imitations of their scolding family members! When children are very young, these connections can be charming.

When emotions are attached to hurtful behaviors or physical action, you must respond. Intervention often means keeping children from hurting themselves or others further, giving children time to recover from emotions so they can work on a solution, and comforting them until they can calm down. Once everyone is calm again, you can help children talk about other things they could have done, instead of acting on their emotions. Talk about what happened, and offer other problem-solving strategies that might work next time.

After toddlerhood, the connection between the intervention and the discussion of alternatives can wait until both you and the child are ready to talk and have time to process the experience. When emotions aren't so intense, you will often find children know what they were supposed to do, and were just too upset to do it. This is perfect opportunity to shift the conversation to talk about how to manage intense emotions. Suggest calming ideas such as taking deep breaths, taking a break in the cozy corner, rubbing your hands with hand cream, taking a walk around the room, or looking out a window at the natural world.

FOR EXAMPLE...

Two-year-old Xavier is playing in the sandbox. His classmate Melissa walks up to him, and whacks him on the head. He begins to cry. Mrs. Alvarez, the teacher on playground duty, quickly walks over to Xavier and says, "Xavier, Melissa hit you. You can tell her, 'Don't hit me!'" Mrs. Alvarez kneels next to him and puts her arm around his shoulder to comfort him. She says again, "Tell her, 'Don't hit me!'"

Before Xavier repeats her words, Melissa darts away. Mrs. Alvarez calls to Ms. Alonzo, the other teacher on the playground, asking her to bring Melissa back to the sandbox. When they return, Mrs. Alvarez prompts Xavier to tell Melissa again not to hit him. Xavier tells her again in a stronger voice and Ms. Alonzo helps Melissa to stay and hear Xavier's words.

Staying with the two children, the teachers begin to talk with each other. Mrs. Alvarez explains to Ms. Alonzo what happened, wondering out loud why Melissa hit Xavier. Melissa blurts out, "He took my bucket!" "I see," says Mrs. Alvarez, and then asks Melissa how she might get the bucket without hitting. Melissa shrugs, and doesn't reply. So, Mrs. Alvarez helps her make a plan to have a turn with the bucket she wants. When it is time for Melissa's turn, Mrs. Alvarez models telling Xavier that it is her turn with the bucket and helps Xavier give it to her.

> ## SET for Life Language
>
> *"You can tell him/her: 'Don't hit me!' 'I don't like that!' 'It's my turn!' 'Stop!'"*
>
> *"I can help you get a turn."*
>
> *"What could you do the next time your body feels out of control?"*

UNDERSTAND EMOTIONAL SELF-REGULATION

WHAT IS SELF-REGULATION?

Self-regulation refers to our ability to adapt or control behavior, emotion, or thinking. It means we are able to stop doing one thing and start doing something else, even when we don't want to. It determines how much we are able to control our impulses. It begins as babies learn to successfully communicate their needs, then moves on to developing the ability to manage emotions, and learning to calm down after being upset. Next, children learn to focus their attention on a particular task, and finally, they learn to control their behavior. Adults can see the progress in self-regulation as children become more independent, needing less and less direct adult support to make good choices, stay safe, and play successfully.

WHY YOUNG CHILDREN NEED ADULT SUPPORT TO LEARN SELF-REGULATION

Young children can't self-regulate on their own. The pathways in the brain that direct communication are not fast enough to get messages where they need to go reliably and in time to regulate emotions or the actions that follow. Children need caregivers' support in managing their emotions and behaviors.

Self-Regulation: *The ability to adapt or control behavior, emotions, and thinking.*

Further, children are trial-and-error learners and have a hard time predicting what might happen next, especially in unfamiliar situations. They have low impulse control, and that makes it hard for them to wait and delay gratification. They often have a hard time screening out irrelevant features in their environment and can be completely distracted by what seems like background noise to adults (voices in the neighboring classroom, or the hum of a refrigerator, for example), missing important details of interactions, and sometimes learning opportunities. Just the quantity of information provided by the environment is enough to make self-regulation hard for young children, as they can be overwhelmed by the constant stream of stimulation they experience.

Internalization of Self-Control

Infancy
Completely supported by adults or the environment

Toddlerhood
Support from adults or the environment

Preschool
Adult-supported self-control

School Age
Mostly internal self-control

EMOTIONS

Intense and physical responses

A few positive emotions regulated

Almost no negative emotions regulated

Intense & physical emotional responses

Some positive emotions regulated

Most negative emotions unregulated without assistance

Regulates some emotions

Regulates attention when emotions are under control

Controls most behaviors when assisted by adults

Regulates most emotions

Regulates attention most of the time

Controls most behaviors

Still needs adult assistance to regulate intense emotions

A final reason children need your help to self-regulate is because of language. Language is still developing during the early childhood years. When emotions are intense, children can't always access words and use them as problem-solving tools. As a result, they end up communicating through actions. Children need teachers to support them with vocabulary to use to address their feelings when they happen, so that they are able to make appropriate choices about how to behave.

Self-regulation is also a developmental process. It proceeds from completely external to the child, to external with support and reminders, to internal self-control across the early childhood period of development. As children age, they are increasingly able to self-regulate. Adults can see this progress as children become more able to function independently without direct adult support.

FOR EXAMPLE...
Three-year-old Jackson loves to be first in line to go outside. His teacher, Mrs. Raj, keeps a rotating list, so that each child gets a turn. Today, it is not Jackson's turn, but he rushes to the front of the line anyway. When Mrs. Raj begins to walk towards him to redirect him, she can see that his eyes are already welling up with tears, and his face is getting red. She kneels down in front of him, puts her arms around him and says, "You really want to be first in line. You may be first in line another day. Today it is Sasha's turn. Would you like to sit on my lap for a minute, while Ms. Kim helps the other children line up?" Jackson nods and curls up in her lap. He is still sad, but is able to stay in control, and join the other children outside after a few minutes of cuddling.

Five-year-old Shien is at the writing center, but is having a hard time getting started. She shuffles through the stacks of paper and looks through the bins of markers, but then gets distracted by looking outside at the playground.

Ms. Johnson notices that Shien is not writing and asks her to get her notebook. By the time Shien gets the notebook, Ms. Johnson is across the room helping another child. Shien takes out a variety of markers and decides to get some pink paper, which is at the bottom of the stack.

She discovers this is too difficult and tries to get a green sheet instead. In the process she knocks over a bin of pencils. When she bends over to pick up the spilled pencils, she finds some stickers on the floor and picks them up and puts them on her notebook.

When Ms. Johnson sees that Shien has still not started writing, she comes back to help. She moves Shien and her notebook to a table in a quiet corner of the room, bringing just one marker. She tells Shien that it is time to write in her notebook. She asks Shien what she would like to write about — Shien decides to write about her trip to the beach. Mrs. Johnson tells her she will come back in five minutes to check on her work. Shien picks up the marker to get started as Ms. Johnson walks away to help other students.

WHY SELF-REGULATION MATTERS

Self-regulation is critical to success in almost every aspect of children's lives, and without it, they may struggle both at home and at school. It is related to success in school and to self-control during the teenage years. When children have the ability to regulate their emotions and behavior, they can better manage the stress caused by life's inevitable challenges.

Self-regulation is important for physical health, as well as emotional development. When we experience stress, the brain releases a hormone called cortisol that inhibits neural network connections. Emotional conflict, stressful transitions, and crises in family life may increase levels of cortisol. When children have help to regulate their powerful emotions, cortisol levels usually drop back down, minimizing any long-term effects. When children are left to cope on their own, cortisol levels can remain at high enough levels to affect brain development by damaging cells and interrupting communication between neurons.

In the first chapter of this book, there is a chart that illustrates the windows of opportunities for optimal brain development (see p. 5). These windows are relatively long during the early childhood years, and addressing self-regulation during this period of development is critical. Teaching self-regulatory skills is a prerequisite for other important learning during this time and later on. The ability to self-regulate has further implications for academic and life success. Children with good self-regulation skills get along better with others, including their parents, teachers, and friends. They are more likely to follow directions and comply with cultural and societal expectations. They are able to generate solutions to conflict and they persist when they are faced with challenging tasks. You can help the children in your classroom to succeed by implementing the teaching strategies that follow.

FOR EXAMPLE...

Two-year-old Sierra has been in Mrs. Hunter's class for six months, when she suddenly starts having trouble in the morning when her father drops her off. Her mother has recently had a new baby, and the transition has been hard on Sierra. When her father brings her in, Sierra clings to his leg, screams, and has to be physically held to keep her from following him out the door.

Mrs. Hunter understands that Sierra is probably reacting to all the changes in her life. When it is time for Sierra's father to leave, Mrs. Hunter wraps the screaming toddler in her arms, holding her close and speaking softly in her ear, saying, "You are very upset now, and you want to go with your daddy. Right now, it is school time, and I will hold you close until you feel ready to go play." She sits down with Sierra in a rocking chair, and begins to rock. Sierra's screaming turns to quiet crying, and then tapers off altogether. After a few more minutes, Sierra is ready to choose an activity and play.

TEACHING STRATEGIES TO SUPPORT SELF-REGULATION

OFFER CHOICES AMONG ACCEPTABLE ALTERNATIVES

Children feel empowered when they are given the opportunity to choose. When you see a child gearing up for a fight, give her choices about what will happen next, offering *only acceptable alternatives*. Here are some examples:

- "Do you want to climb into your car seat or do you want me to put you in?"
- "Do you want to start putting blocks away now, or in one minute?"
- "Do you want to walk by yourself or shall I carry you?"
- "Do you want saltines or graham crackers for snack?"

In these examples, either choice is acceptable. Children are more likely to comply when they feel they have a say in the matter.

On the other hand, when there isn't an option, don't offer one. When it is time for a particular activity, such as group time or outdoor play, use a statement instead of a question to let children know. For example, announce playground time by saying "It is time to go outside. Meet me at the back door."

Statements let children know what is expected. If teachers instead said, "Would you like to go outside now?", some children may answer, "No." One special education teacher thought this point was important enough to write on her chalkboard: *Don't ask a question unless "no" is an acceptable answer.*

SET for Life Language

"Do you want goldfish or vanilla wafers? A lot of goldfish or a little?

"Do you want to play with him or ask him to play with you? With the cars or the blocks?"

"Do you want to sit by Alexia or Carmen?"

"Do you want to put that in your pocket, in your cubby, or under your chair?"

"You can stop your body or I will help you stop."

"You can choose or I will choose for you."

When giving instructions, be especially careful not to add, "Okay?" to the end of your sentence. Saying, "Let's get ready for lunch now, okay?", turns an instruction into a request, leaving room for disagreement. "Time for lunch" is a better way to let children know what is happening next, and what they will need to do.

Following through is also important. Some children will resist making choices when they don't like either option. You may have to help some children act on their choices (e.g., choose a graham cracker for them) or help them comply when choice is not an option (e.g., help them walk to their cots).

EXPECT AND ACCEPT PROTEST, RESISTANCE, AND MELTDOWNS

Children often need to protest or resist before they are able to comply. You can validate the feeling, while at the same time clearly stating the expectation.

Allow extra time for protest as you prepare children for what will happen next, especially if it is something that is likely to be unpopular. For example, a few minutes before it is time to finish center time, you might say, "In five more minutes, it will be time to stop playing in centers, clean up the classroom, and wash our hands for lunch." When children protest, say, "It is hard to stop playing; it makes you sad (or mad, or furious, etc.) **AND** we will clean up in five more minutes."

Notice the **AND**. Children often interpret *but* the same way they interpret *no*. Using **AND** clarifies the next steps and may keep children from tuning you out.

> ## SET for Life Language
>
> *"You would like to play longer AND it is time to stop."*
>
> *"Going outside sounds fun AND right now we are having snack. We will go outside later."*
>
> *"I hear that you are very angry AND you may not scream at her."*

USE BOOKS TO HELP CHILDREN DEAL WITH LIFE EVENTS AND STRESSORS

Children's books are valuable teaching tools in addressing emotions, life events, and stress. They can help children see familiar situations and explore outcomes they may not have considered. When a storybook character tackles the topic, children are often able to recognize the ideas presented and use the solutions suggested. Reading about characters who have similar experiences helps children realize that their varied emotions are normal. It can also help them process feelings with some distance between themselves and the characters in the story.

Books can be used to help children cope with many challenging events: adoption, birth of siblings, death, divorce, peer conflict, nighttime fears, etc. They can also give children ideas for how to handle common experiences related to new developmental experiences, such as giving up a pacifier, having an imaginary friend, losing a tooth, or learning to ride a tricycle. You can find some suggestions of where to find helpful book lists in Appendix E.

FOR EXAMPLE...

Three-year-old Sally is worried about monsters, and having trouble going to sleep. After a conversation with Sally's mother, her teacher, Ms. Trujillo, decides to read There's a Nightmare in My Closet, *by Mercer Mayer, at story time. Over the next week, she incorporates other books about children's fears. She makes a list of children's fears on an experience chart, and talks with individual children about how they handle fears. In small groups, Ms. Trujillo shares what she has learned and asks children more about their ideas. Sally is able to identify with the books and talk about her own fears. After a few weeks, Sally is less afraid at bedtime and is able to go sleep without much difficulty.*

You can also create teacher-made books for children for specific incidents in their lives to help them understand feelings, identify concerns or fears, or learn a new skill. When the book about the new baby getting all of the attention has a child's own name and photograph in it, it can be easier for him to work through feelings about the new sibling. Stories about a specific incident can help children understand and remember what is required of them, and they are a wonderful tool for children who have developmental delays or need to hear, see, and experience things in many ways before internalizing them.

FOR EXAMPLE...

Michael is having trouble staying in his seat on the bus. His teacher helps him make a five page book about riding the bus to school. Michael draws pictures and his teacher adds the words: "I get on the bus." "I sit down and buckle my seat belt." "I can talk to friends or look out the window." "When the bus stops, I can unbuckle and get off." "I can sit on the bus." Every day, she reads the book to Michael. After a few weeks, Michael can sit on the bus and keep his seat belt buckled until he gets to school.

SUMMARY: TEACHING STRATEGIES TO SUPPORT EMOTIONAL DEVELOPMENT, EXPRESSION, AND SELF-REGULATION

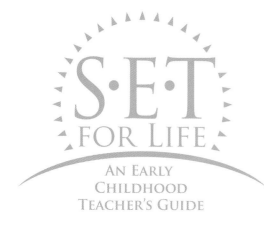

Emotional expression and emotional regulation are two important developmental tasks of the early childhood years. Children must learn to manage intense emotions in order to be successful at home, in school, and in the wider world.

TEACHING STRATEGIES TO SUPPORT EMOTIONAL DEVELOPMENT AND EXPRESSION

MAKE YOUR FEELINGS OBVIOUS FOR CHILDREN TO SEE

- Children sometimes miss cues indicating the emotions of others.
- Talk about your own feelings and exaggerate your facial expressions and body language to help them pick up on this important information.

  "I am so excited about our special visitor!"

  "Shucks! I am so disappointed it's raining. I really wanted to go outside."

  "Ouch! I dropped a book on my toe! That really hurt!"

Don't Try to "Fix" Children's Feelings – Acknowledge Them Instead

- Resist the urge to tell children that they should feel differently than they do. Instead, help them name the way they are feeling, and manage their intense emotions and the behavior that may accompany them.
- Help children connect feelings with appropriate ways to express them (such as hitting a pillow when they are angry, instead of a friend).

    "I see that your knee really hurts."

    "I hear you. You are really angry." (Or sad/disappointed/upset)

    "She said 'no.' I can see that was hard to hear. You wanted her to say 'yes.'"

    "It is okay to be angry. It is not okay to hit your friends. You can hit this pillow instead."

Label Feelings for Children

- When you give children words to name their emotions, they "feel felt," and all areas of development are supported.

    "You look happy." (Or sad/angry/disappointed, etc.)

    "You have your hands on your hips. Are you mad? Exasperated?"

    "I wonder if you feel angry?" (Or mad/happy/irritated/calm/ lonely, etc.)

    "Your eyes look surprised about what happened."

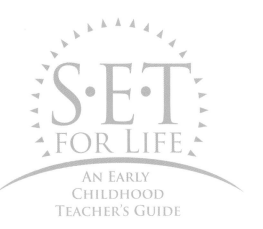

Teach Children to Name Their Feelings

- Labeling feelings lets children know that their experiences are normal and gives them a way to think and talk about what is happening.
- Vocabulary related to emotions can be an ongoing curriculum project.

    "Check your body. What is it telling you? How are you feeling?"

    "You have tears in your eyes. I wonder how come?"

    "What did you feel that made you want to stomp your feet?"

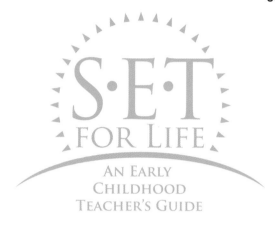

Use Emotional Language in the Classroom

- Early childhood is a great time to introduce vocabulary related to emotions.
- Provide emotional language toys and materials in your classroom, so children can explore how feelings look, sound, and feel.
- Talk about your own emotions, so children can learn from your example.

    "Let's look at the Feelings Chart. Which one looks like how you feel?"

    "That was hard to do! Whew!"

    "I was so surprised to see Ms. Sultana!"

Model Appropriate Responses

- When children react to their emotions in inappropriate ways (hitting or biting, for example), model language and behavior that is acceptable in a classroom setting.

    "You can say, 'I want a turn.' Grabbing the truck from Gabby's hands is not okay."

    "Joseph, you are disappointed that your tower fell down. You are a boy who can rebuild your tower, and you may not kick blocks."

Help Children Connect Emotions with Appropriate Behavior

- When emotions are connected to hurtful behaviors, you must respond.
- When children are calm, discuss what they might do differently next time.

    "You really want to hold that toy. I can help you get a turn."

    "What could you do next time your body feels out of control?"

TEACHING STRATEGIES TO SUPPORT SELF-REGULATION

OFFER CHOICES AMONG ACCEPTABLE ALTERNATIVES

- Children feel empowered when they are able to make choices. Support them by offering only acceptable alternatives.
- If there are no options, use statements instead of questions to let children know what is expected of them.

    "Do you want to climb into your seat, or do you want me to put you in?"

    "Do you want to put blocks away now, or in one minute?"

    "Time to go inside for lunch."

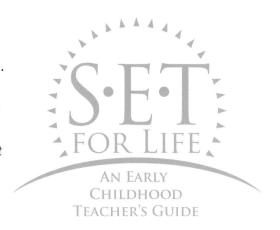

EXPECT AND ACCEPT PROTEST, RESISTANCE, AND MELTDOWNS

- Allow extra time for protest as you prepare children for what will happen next, especially if it is something that is likely to be unpopular.
- Use AND instead of *but* to help children comply.

    *"You are having a good time in the sand, **AND** in five minutes, it will be time to go inside."*

    *"Going outside sounds fun, **AND** right now we are having snack. We will go outside later."*

USE BOOKS TO HELP CHILDREN DEAL WITH LIFE EVENTS AND STRESSORS

- Books can help children see familiar situations and explore outcomes they may not have considered. They also can help children process feelings with some distance between themselves and the characters in the story.
- Teacher-made books for specific needs can help children remember what is expected of them and process events in their own lives. These books are especially helpful for children with developmental delays or other learning differences.

    "Remember the girl in The Chocolate-Covered-Cookie Tantrum? *I wonder if you could try what she did to calm down."*

    "Before you get on the bus, let's read your book about staying in your seat until the bus stops."

UNDERSTAND SOCIAL DEVELOPMENT

S·E·T
FOR LIFE

AN EARLY
CHILDHOOD
TEACHER'S GUIDE

Social development during the early childhood years is a fascinating developmental process. Because human beings do not live in isolation, we have to learn to live, play, and work together. Social development starts as increasing self-awareness during infancy. Before you know it, children seem socially competent, confident, and have a growing awareness of their own abilities, as well as their limitations. They learn to make friends and be a friend, and to compare their choices with the ones others make. At the end of early childhood, children are typically prepared to become successful citizens in the broader social world.

There is little doubt that the foundation for social success has its roots in the caring relationships between children and their primary caregivers. Upon that foundation, teachers help build the more advanced social skills that lead to productive participation in the wider social world. In this chapter, we will explore how social development unfolds during the early childhood period, and then discuss ways you can support and facilitate children's optimal social development.

VYGOTSKY'S SOCIO-CULTURAL THEORY

Lev Vygotsky, a psychologist working in Russia at the turn of the 20th century, introduced three ideas that have had tremendous impact on early childhood educational theory. First, he believed that the child's social development and intellectual development are dependent on each other—connected in a way that causes experiences in either developmental domain to influence the other one. He also believed that learning couldn't be separated from socio-cultural experiences children have at home and at school. He believed that young children learn by doing, talking about what they are doing, bouncing ideas off of each other before trying them out, and working together until they are successful. Further, Vygotsky thought that these kinds of social interactions contributed significantly to children's learning.

"People who need people are the luckiest people in the world."

BOB MERRIL, SONGWRITER, & JULES STYNE, COMPOSER

Vygotsky's second idea was what he called the **zone of proximal development**—the range of tasks children cannot handle on their own but can manage with the help of more competent peers or a supportive teacher. Because children seem to learn best when working in this zone, social interactions between children, and with supportive adults and more competent peers, play a significant role in the learning process.

> **Zone of Proximal Development:**
> *The range of tasks children cannot handle on their own, but can manage with the help of more competent peers or a supportive adult.*

The teacher's role in supporting learning in the zone of proximal development is a dynamic one because this is when children are most receptive to learning, and teachers can be most effective. Vygotsky believed that teachers can best help children learn by encouraging conversations and participating in children's interactions and play in small groups. Knowing when to ask a question, what new information to add, which suggestion to make, and when to let children move forward independently, are delicate considerations. The right teaching strategy can scaffold learning to an even higher level, while the wrong one can disrupt the flow and derail it.

Addressing each child as an individual makes the role of an early childhood teacher very different from the traditional elementary classroom instructor. Vygotsky felt teachers had to be keen observers, and use their observations to discover each child's zone of proximal development. Armed with intimate knowledge of each child in the classroom, teachers are then poised to offer the right kinds of experiences and information at the ideal moment.

> ## Vygotsky's Socio-Cultural Theory
> 1. Social and intellectual development are dependent on each other.
> 2. Children learn best when working within their **Zone of Proximal Development.**
> 3. Children learn primarily through play.

The idea that play fills a central role in children's learning during the early childhood years was Vygotsky's third idea. As children play, their conversations, discussions, conflicts, and negotiations extend and enhance all of their skills and abilities. When children are playing, their communication with each other is a primary mechanism for advancing what children know and can do. (We will discuss more about play and its importance in Chapter 7.)

Vygotsky's theory is a part of the theoretical foundation of the **SET for Life** approach. **SET for Life** advocates learning social skills through interactions in the classroom, with the help of intentional, supportive adults. As a teacher, your job is to help children work and play together successfully. Your teaching scaffolds their social development, which in turn facilitates children's readiness to learn. Scaffolding entails helping children practice social skills that may be just beyond their current skill level but not outside of what they can do with help (in other words, within the child's zone of proximal development).

> **Scaffolding:**
> *The support provided by a more capable peer or supportive teacher that helps a child accomplish tasks he or she can't do on his or her own, but can manage with help.*

IMITATION AND MODELING

Imitation is copying the behavior of another person or thing. It begins early and is one of the chief ways that young children learn. Very young babies mimic the facial expressions of the important adults in their lives. Young children imitate the ways they see others interacting around them.

To benefit from imitation, children must first learn to pay attention to what is going on around them. Observing, watching, listening to conversations, and picking up on subtle emotional messages are all important parts of social learning.

Teachers often use demonstration to help children figure out appropriate behaviors for particular social situations. When children observe you saying, "Thank you," for example, they are more likely to thank others at a later time. Teachers also recognize that children learn all kinds of things from observing others, some teachers like (blowing kisses) and some teachers do not like (biting or name-calling). The way you respond to both positive and negative modeling will help determine which behaviors become a permanent part of children's skill repertoire. Many situations in the classroom create opportunities to support children's imitation and modeling of *appropriate* social behaviors.

THE ROLE OF FACILITATIVE TEACHER

Good teachers intentionally scaffold children's social development in the classroom, jump starting children who need a little help to be successful in peer relationships, and providing ongoing support to children who need more help (particularly those with developmental delays, speech and language delays, attention deficit/hyperactivity disorder, autism, or social anxiety). These children have an even greater need for supportive scaffolding by the teacher to interact successfully with their classmates. Whether children struggle due to lack of confidence or experience, or due to other individual or learning differences, you can help each child interact more easily with their peers by teaching them the skills they need to find success in the social world.

You can help children learn the social skills they need to succeed with their friends.

Seeing ourselves as an important resource to help children succeed in their peer relationships is a big shift. It means that we change our perspective: helping children succeed socially becomes our first priority, instead of just responding or reacting when their struggles turn into conflicts and get our attention. This role requires you to be proactive and flexible, attending to interactions before problems arise, and matching your response to the needs of individual children.

After observing children to discover where they are succeeding and where they are struggling, join in children's play at the moments when you are needed. This doesn't mean that you take charge of the interaction between children. You are there to support children by lending a hand, so that they can use the skills they have, as well as practice new ones with your help. As children become more capable, be ready to take a less involved role, sitting back and observing on the edge of play until the children can manage completely on their own.

. . . .

FOR EXAMPLE...

Four-year-old Brandon and five-year-old Freddie are playing with the castle and knights. Both boys are playing happily alone, but next to each other. Brandon is playing with the horses, while Freddie raises and lowers the drawbridge. Ms. Wright watches for a few minutes, then picks up a dragon and enters the play. In a surprised voice, she says "Brandon, I think a dragon is trying to get in the castle. Quick, ask Freddie to bring over the knights to help us fight the dragon!"

Brandon (a bit confused, but pleased to have his teacher's attention), says to Freddie "We need the knights! A dragon is coming!" Freddie scoots two knights across to where Ms. Wright has set the dragon down. Ms. Wright then comments to both boys "Yikes! It looks like a scary dragon, guys! What are you going to do?" Brandon says "We can kill him! We're super strong!" Freddie adds, "Yeah, we have super powers!", as he knocks the dragon over with a knight.

Ms. Wright comments again to both boys, "Hmm, looks like the draw bridge is up. How are you going to get back in the castle?" Brandon says, "I know how it works," and opens the bridge. Freddie brings the rest of his knights and horses in the castle. Ms. Wright lines up a few more "intruders" for the boys to fight, and then sits back to watch a few minutes as the boys continue their play.

Facilitating interactions and play is like a dance; sometimes you lead until the children can take over, and then you follow (until the children need you again). Notice in the previous vignette that the teacher's role is proactive, facilitating skill building when there is no conflict. In this case, one small intervention helps Brandon feel noticed by his teacher, and he and Freddie play together instead of side by side. Then, although she isn't needed in the end, she stays nearby to make sure their play is successful.

TEACHING STRATEGIES TO SUPPORT SOCIAL DEVELOPMENT

ENCOURAGE POSITIVE MODELING

When children use the positive social behaviors you model, such as helping a friend or working out a problem without help from teachers, point out the behavior and encourage the child to use it again. Encouragement makes it more likely that the new behavior will become a part of the child's social repertoire.

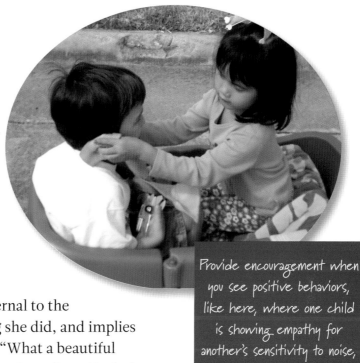

Provide encouragement when you see positive behaviors, like here, where one child is showing empathy for another's sensitivity to noise, by covering his ears.

Encouragement is crucial to helping children internalize positive behaviors. But it is different from praise. Praise is external to the child. It tells her someone likes something she did, and implies an evaluation or judgment by the teacher. "What a beautiful painting!" can be confusing to a child, if she doesn't particularly like how her painting turned out.

On the other hand, encouragement offers no judgment ("You are working hard on your building project!"). It lets children place their own evaluation on the experience. Encouragement supports effort, and conveys the message that you noticed it. When the skill and effort feel important to the child, they are more likely to become a regular part of his or her skill set.

Comment often on the positive behaviors you notice in the classroom. Doing this helps all children to understand what behaviors you are looking for and which ones are appropriate in the classroom. It is also offers a more effective way to help children remember classroom rules and expectations. They will remember better when they are encouraged for following rules (and attach positive emotional connections to rule-following) than they will if they are lectured for forgetting them (and reject your input because they have negative feelings about following the rule).

When children are working to solve problems on their own, be sure to provide encouragement for the effort, even if the solution isn't the one that seems best to you. If both children accept the solution, allow them to follow through on it and discuss the outcome later, if necessary.

FOR EXAMPLE...
Josie, who is a third grader, sees Bryan raise his hand to get their teacher's attention. Mr. Mendes goes over to Bryan, thanks him for raising his hand and waiting patiently, and then helps him with his question. When Josie sees how well Bryan's strategy works, she raises her hand as well. Soon, Mr. Mendes comes to her desk.

Ms. Sears notices that seven-year-old Emma is helping her friends, Libby and Corey, to negotiate how they will play a board game. Libby and Corey are arguing over who will go first. Emma suggests that they could play the game two times and each girl could have a turn to go first. The children like her idea and agree to try it. Ms. Sears says aloud, "Emma, you found a way to help your friends work out this problem. That was very helpful."

Nero is twenty-two months old and has mastered the hammering ball set. He puts the ball on top and with one good whack can send it whirling through the maze, while twenty-six-month-old Jonas watches. Later, Mr. Roberts sees Jonas pick up the hammer, and then drop it. Mr. Roberts asks Jonas if he'd like some help with the hammering balls. When Jonas nods, Mr. Roberts gets the hammering balls and models for Jonas how to hit them. Jonas tries to imitate Mr. Roberts, but misses. Mr. Roberts says, "I'll help you." He takes Jonas' hand and hits the ball a few times. After a few more tries on his own, Jonas hits it. Mr. Roberts cheers for him. Watching Nero, followed by Mr. Roberts' supportive model, Jonas has learned a new skill.

SET for Life Language

"You did it!"

"You used your very good brain to figure that out!"

"You really worked hard to make that happen."

"You have figured out that I will come if you raise your hand, even if you have to wait a few minutes."

HELP CHILDREN LEARN SOCIAL PROBLEM-SOLVING SKILLS

You can help children learn to solve the problems that they will inevitably encounter as they negotiate the social world. **SET for Life** suggests that you teach children how to resolve conflicts. Introduce these steps as individual children are able to negotiate them, first with your help, and then on their own.

STEP 1: CALLING FOR HELP

Responding quickly to a baby's cries lets her know she has been heard, and helps her to feel safe and valued. The same applies for toddlers and preschoolers. When young children call for your help, go to them as soon as you are able.

Remind children to call for help if the strategies they are using do not seem to be working. For example, when two children want the same toy, they both may grab it and begin to scream for help. Respond and validate the call for help. Then, help them to find a way to play together. Reassure them that you will help if their own attempts aren't working.

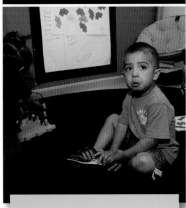

Be available to help when children have conflicts over toys.

SET for Life Language

"I can help you figure it out."

"Hold on – I'm coming!"

STEP 2: TRADING

Most of what happens in early childhood classrooms is not really sharing; it is teacher enforced relinquishment. Children don't really understand what sharing really means until they are almost five. But even very young children can learn to trade when we teach them how to exchange something they have for something they want.

When a child wants a toy that a friend is playing with, help her find a different, equally interesting toy to offer as a trade, prompting her with, "Ask him to trade with you." Regular practice with trading (exchanging one thing for something of equal perceived value), rather than sharing (which requires you to give something up), helps children solve problems with resources. True sharing can only occur when children feel they have enough of what they need and want, and are confident enough to willingly give it to others. Until children reach this point, support learning to trade.

Social Problem-solving Skills

Step 1: Calling for Help
Step 2: Trading
Step 3: Taking Turns
Step 4: Sharing Resources
Step 5: Plan-making

FOR EXAMPLE...
Toula and Gabrielle, both three, are at the dramatic play center. Gabrielle has the only phone with working push buttons. Toula, who wants the phone, has a grocery cart full of things. Mrs. Jones watches Toula's attempt to persuade Gabrielle to give her the phone. After a couple of unsuccessful attempts, Mrs. Jones prompts Toula to offer Gabrielle a trade from her grocery basket. Gabrielle chooses a purse from the basket and they trade toys.

SET for Life Language

"Ask him to trade toys with you."

"She doesn't want to give you the phone. Maybe she would trade you for the teapot."

STEP 3: TAKING TURNS

After children learn to trade, help them learn to take turns. Taking turns is hard because it requires children to wait and watch until the other child is ready to give him a turn. But learning to say, "First you, then me," helps children see that waiting a little while can help them get what they want in the end. Children will need your help to be patient while they wait for a turn. Explain what is happening and provide the physical support and supervision children need while they practice taking turns.

FOR EXAMPLE...

Three-and-a-half year old Ying and four-and-a-half year old Harmony are at the water table pouring with cups and bowls when Harmony picks up a boat from a nearby basket. Ying screeches with delight and reaches for it. Harmony pulls it to her chest quickly. Mrs. Thibodeaux, having heard Ying's screech, moves close to see what is happening. She remarks, "Wow, you found a boat, Harmony. It looks like fun. You girls are really enjoying the water table together. Ying, are you wanting a turn with the boat Harmony found?" Ying replies, "Yes!"

"Ah, I see," remarks Mrs. Thibodeaux, turning her attention to Harmony. "You both want the boat. You can take turns with it." Mrs. Thibodeaux asks, "How long will you need for your turn, Harmony—three minutes or five minutes?" Harmony quickly chooses five minutes, and Mrs. Thibodeaux turns on the timer, letting both girls know when they hear the 'ding' of the timer, it will be Ying's turn with the boat.

SET for Life Language

"You both want the boat. You can take turns with it."

"First Jose, then Raul."

"I wonder how you can each play with it?"

"Is there a way for everyone to have a turn?"

"You have a dilemma. What would you like to do about it?"

STEP 4: SHARING RESOURCES

Once children can trade and take turns, they can learn to share resources – dividing up toys or materials so that everyone has some to use. Sharing resources is different than trading or taking turns. For this to work, there must be enough of something so that it can be divided between the children who want to use it. In the beginning, children will need you to show them how to do this. For example, when two children both want to build with Legos®, show them how to divide the blocks into two separate and relatively equal piles, so that both of them are able to play. Most children can do this by the age of three or four, but they may sometimes still need your help and reminders to be successful. Sharing resources can enable children to continue to play with each other.

SET for Life Language

"You can both play with the blocks – here are some for you, and here are some for Jonathan."

"We have enough dolls for each of you to hold a baby."

STEP 5: MAKING PLANS

The most sophisticated social problem-solving skill during the early childhood years is plan-making. Plan-making helps both children get what they want, regardless of what it is. It's a complex skill to learn, though, and children will need support from you until they become good at developing and accepting plans on their own.

When two children are arguing over a toy, it's a good time for you to step in and introduce plan-making. Tell the children that you have an idea about how to solve the problem, and both children will get what they want. The child who was playing with the toy already will get to keep it for three (or five) minutes. You will help the other child to make a plan to get the toy afterwards for three (or five) minutes. While the second child is waiting, help him choose another activity even if that activity, is sitting and waiting with your support! If the child who originally had the toy wants another turn, this process can be repeated.

Plan-making is a step up from turn-taking. Taking turns is an 'in the moment' decisive action. Plan-making requires thinking ahead and mentally holding on to what you want, trusting you will get it while waiting for it. Plan-making keeps teachers from being referees, and it has the added benefit of allowing you to say yes to all children.

Children's sense of time is different than adults', so be careful to honor the time limit you agree upon with the children involved. Use a timer to indicate when the toy transfer will take place and alert the children to listen to the sound of the timer going off. Pointing to the hands of the clock face, indicating when the transfer is scheduled, will also work for older children who can tell time.

When children learn to make their own plans, their social skills grow dramatically. Although their first plans may be uneven or unfair, support their attempts, as long as the involved children accept the plan. Later, as skills increase, you can help children make plans that are more fair or equitable.

FOR EXAMPLE...

Three-year-old Taiven is playing with the fire engine, pushing buttons and making the siren wail. His classmate, Matthew, begins to imitate the siren noise. Seeing Matthew's interest, his teacher, Mr. Hassan, says to him, "I think you like the fire truck siren. Do you want to make a plan to get a turn to push the button?" Matthew says in a very quiet voice, "Yes." Mr. Hassan says, "Would you like to make that plan on your own or with my help?" Matthew says quietly, "Help."

Mr. Hassan tells Taiven that Matthew wants to make a plan to get a turn, saying, "Right now, you are pushing the siren button.

In five minutes, Matthew will get to push the siren button. I will remind you when it is time to switch who pushes the button."

After five minutes, Mr. Hassan returns and tells Taiven that it is time to let Matthew push the siren button. When Taiven says "No!," Mr. Hassan asks, "Do you want to let him push the button on your own, or with my help?" Taiven chooses to do it on his own and takes his finger off of the button. Mr. Hassan stays close, reminding Taiven that he can make a plan to push the siren button again if he would like.

SET for Life Language

"Would you like to make a plan for the _____ (truck, sand table, magic wand, etc.)?"

"I can help you make a plan."

HELP CHILDREN LEARN TO REFLECT

Adults usually learn from reviewing events that happen in our lives, making plans to repeat successes or to avoid making the same mistakes in the future. Children are much less likely to reflect on events and learn from them. Teaching children the art of reflection can help them solve and prevent problems. However, they can rarely do this alone. They will need your support to learn how to think back on what happened and to learn from the reflective experience.

It may be hard to reflect right after a conflict, misunderstanding, or emotional meltdown. To benefit from reflection, children need to be calm, so that they can review the situation without being overwhelmed by it. It is perfectly acceptable to allow time between an incident and its resolution and reflection. Waiting until emotions are calmer makes it more likely that the child will be able to examine what happened and come up with alternatives to consider next time. It's okay to wait a few minutes, until the next day, or even until several days later. The important thing is to come back, at some point, to the situation that presented the problem to help the child reflect on what happened.

Before you begin helping a child to reflect, make sure they're ready. Children won't want to talk if they feel like they have been "bad" or that you are mad at them. You can help them to be receptive by starting discussions with something like, "You are not in trouble," or, "I am not angry with you. I think we need to talk about what happened so we can make a plan for what to do next time," or, "I do not think you are bad. I don't like what you did, and I think we can figure out other ways to work this kind of thing out."

When conflicts occur, help children reflect after they have calmed down.

Reflection is not a group activity. Each child who experienced the conflict needs to process and reflect on his or her own, so find a place and time to talk to them individually. Then follow these steps to guide the child through the reflection process. Use the steps when the child is calm and able to think about what happened without big feelings getting in the way.

Start by giving sequence to the events that occurred. Establish what happened and when, from his perspective. When the child is ready to hear you, wonder out loud what could be done differently next time. Throughout the process, identify and validate the feelings that drove the behavior. This does not mean you are validating the behavior. Instead, it helps the child to identify the emotions he was experiencing at that moment, and choose different, more appropriate behaviors that he might use when he has those big feelings again.

The whole reflective process doesn't need to take very long—no more than five minutes, and even less with very young children. It's important to be sure your discussion doesn't take more time than the child's attention span allows him to manage.

Helping Children Reflect

1. Establish that no one is in trouble.
2. Validate feelings.
3. Create a sequence of events (what happened and when).
4. Wonder with the child what could have been done differently.
5. Restate the solutions that the child comes up with.
6. Help generate ideas as needed.
7. Remind the child to use the new ideas the next time the situation arises.

FOR EXAMPLE...

Peter and Julio, both five years old, have a loud argument in the block area. The situation escalates quickly, ending with Julio knocking down Peter's block tower, and Peter retaliating by hitting Julio. Mr. Aguilar separates the boys and helps them take a break from each other while their emotions cool down. The next day, he talks to each boy individually about what happened, after first reassuring them that they are not in trouble for the previous day's conflict.

To Peter, Mr. Aguilar says, "I can understand that you were really angry when Julio knocked over your building. You had worked the whole playtime to get it just the way you wanted it. I understand why you wanted to hit him. Do you think that helped? I wonder what you might do if something like that happens again?"

When he talks to Julio, Mr. Aguilar says, "I think you were feeling frustrated that your structure fell and Peter's was getting so tall. Maybe you were angry with him and felt that he was a better builder than you are. What else could you do if you have those big feelings again?"

Notice how Mr. Aguilar stayed in the supportive, reflective role. He didn't offer advice or solutions. He just continued to ask questions to help each boy consider the situation, what happened, and how they might respond differently if it happens again. If children don't offer solutions, they may still be feeling upset and you might want to try again later rather than offering your own solutions.

SET for Life Language

"Hold on, you are not in trouble."

"I am not angry with you.'"

"I do not think you are bad."

"I do like you and I don't like that you hit."

"I wonder what happened."

"Did you like the way it ended?"

"Do you think it helped to hit (spit, scratch, kick) her?"

"What is another choice you could make?"

"What might help you keep from kicking down block buildings?"

HOW FRIENDSHIPS DEVELOP

Friendship is one of the most important aspects of human life. Developing close, caring relationships with peers takes time. Learning how to make friends and keep friends is an important task of early childhood, and the lessons learned have lifelong implications for success. Early success in peer relationships affects how children view themselves and their place in the world, and it can predict how successful children may be at making friends later in childhood.

The lessons children learn from social relationships with peers in the classroom are different than the ones they learn within their families. With each other, they learn how to join in play, resolve disagreements and conflicts, and maintain relationships. They notice how their social successes compare with others. These self-evaluations influence self-esteem and can help children see themselves as competent and capable.

By around the age of three, children often choose **who** to play with by **what** they are playing with. They choose the toys that are interesting to them, rather than the person who is playing with the toys. Around the age of four, friendship becomes conditional. To play, you must agree to follow the play leader, or risk being rejected as a playmate. Cooperation is the hallmark of five-year-old play. At this age, children often select whom to play with first, and then decide what to play together, negotiating expectations as a group.

To move through these phases, children need to know how to take turns, be attentive to the feelings of others, and be aware of the environment around them. All of these lessons are first learned in relationships with the important adults in their lives. When those relationships are warm and reciprocal, children have a pretty good idea about what good peer relationships might look like.

Building freindships is an important experience during the early childhood years.

However, peer relationships are not always easy. As children become more interested in their peers, they will inevitably make mistakes as they negotiate their growing social world. Play can be derailed when children bump into each other, take each other's toys, lose track of play ideas, or hurt each other. Overall, children tend to get along better with friends they know well. This is another benefit of children and teachers staying together for more than one year. It creates the ideal setting for children to become better friends, giving them lots of time to get to know each other and practice working out conflicts with children they know well.

Conflict plays a big role in how children build relationships, particularly among friends. When children are already friends, they are more likely try to work things out. In fact, conflict among friends can actually support new social skills, as children try to find ways to continue to play together. It gives them experience with negotiations and compromise, and provides opportunities to figure out how to solve their own problems.

Children need the proper tools to build friendships. These include secure relationships with family members, teachers, and other adults to provide a foundation for building friendships. They need social skills, such as the ability to join in play and to cooperate with others to sustain play. They need the ability to be able to communicate clearly, both with gestures and with language. Good observation skills help them to notice when they might need to change their behavior to match the situation. They also need many opportunities to practice building friendships.

Teachers play a key role in helping friendships develop, particularly for children who have trouble being a friend and making friends. When teachers are responsive, friendships and play can mature. When teachers view helping children interact and play successfully as a key teaching role, children are likely to be successful.

TEACHING STRATEGIES TO SUPPORT SOCIAL DEVELOPMENT

TEACH CHILDREN TO USE NAMES

Clear communication is a hallmark of successful relationships. Using names is an important aspect of communicating clearly. Using a name validates the person you are talking with, and it aids in more successful communication. It feels good for children to hear their names used; it makes them feel important. For children on the autistim spectrum and children with developmental delays, this skill is often lacking. Even children who are developing normally sometimes fail to direct their conversation towards the person to whom it is intended. Encourage children to use each other's names in their conversations and communication.

FOR EXAMPLE...

Connor is playing in the sand box with the scoops and bowls with a few other children. He says, "Don't touch that." His teacher, Michelle, asks him, "Connor, who are you talking to?" He replies, "I am talking to you." Michelle then responds, "What's my name?" Connor says, "Michelle." She then remarks to him, "When you use my name, I know you are talking to me."

SET for Life Language

"What's my name?"

"Who are you talking to?"

"His name is Joe."

"You can call him by his name. His name is Sam."

BECOME AN ALLY WITH CHILDREN TO FIGURE THINGS OUT

Instead of solving problems for children, **SET for Life** teachers help children learn how to solve social problems themselves by becoming an **ally**. When you ask questions instead of offering solutions, children have the chance to learn to resolve conflicts on their own and to take charge of their own social problem-solving. Sometimes, they may find solutions you haven't thought of yet. We can't expect children to become good decision-makers without giving them chances to practice making decisions! Children need plenty of opportunities to identify alternatives, decide on solutions, experience what happens, and reflect on their decisions with adult support. Experiencing success helps children feel confident and competent, forming a strong foundation for continuing to improve their social capabilities.

Ally:
A friend, helper, supporter, or collaborator who helps make things happen.

FOR EXAMPLE...

Three-year-old Kiana is having trouble getting the pieces of her puzzle to fit together. In frustration, she throws the pieces on the floor. Her teacher, Ms. Kazumi, comes over, saying, "You look frustrated, Kiana. What happened?" Kiana says, "The puzzle is too hard!" Ms. Kazumi replies, "Let's figure this out together." She sits with Kiana and offers suggestions: "Maybe if you turn it this way it will work better. Do you see where the picture goes together?" Together, they slowly complete the puzzle. Ms. Kazumi congratulates Kiana for figuring it out, as Patricia comes over to the puzzle table. Patricia asks if she can try the puzzle. Ms. Kazumi says, "Maybe Kiana could help you do it. She knows how!"

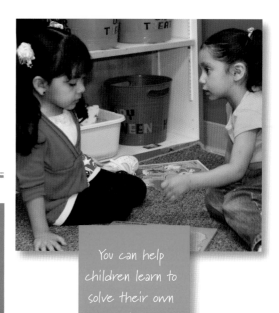

You can help children learn to solve their own problems.

SET for Life Language

"You didn't know how to do that last week and this week you did it."

"I can help you find someone who might know."

"You could ask Alexandra - she likes to paint pictures too."

"What isn't working? What do you think might work?"

"What's your idea? Does Jorge have a different idea?"

"I will help you work it out." (Or find a solution, find a way to do that safely, etc.)

"Two boys want to be first. What do you think we should do?"

"Let's figure this out together."

HELP CHILDREN COMMUNICATE WITH EACH OTHER

Help children identify what they need or want, and then tell each other. For example, when you hear a child screaming "Stop!", help him figure out and say what he really means (e.g., "Stop! There's not enough room for you to play here," or, "I'm angry because you are too close!").

As children are learning social skills, they may need you to provide the language – even the actual words – to express and describe the intent of their feelings. Help children practice communicating clearly with other children because children will often hear messages from a friend more easily than from a teacher.

FOR EXAMPLE...

Juan and Danny are playing with trains on the track. When Juan reaches over and takes Danny's train, Danny responds by hitting Juan with the train he is holding in his hand. Juan screams. Mrs. Michaels comes over. She responds first to Juan, asking, "What happened?" When she feels she has a reasonable idea of what occurred, Mrs. Michaels asks Juan, "What do you want to tell him?" Juan is still too upset to respond, so she models for him one possibility: "Don't hit me, Danny!" Then, she turns to Danny, saying, "I think you were really angry that Juan took your train. What do you want to tell him?" Danny shrugs. Mrs. Michaels provides him with the words: "I was playing with that train, Juan. Don't grab it from me!"

After getting some help making their needs and feelings known, the boys are able to continue playing together. Later, Mrs. Michaels takes a few minutes to discuss with each boy what he can do next time he is playing and something similar happens. She asks Danny how he might get his train back, and reminds him to ask Juan instead of hitting. She helps Juan think of what he can do, instead of grabbing, if he wants to play with the train.

SET for Life Language

"You can tell him, 'Don't hit me!'"

"I think you wanted a turn, and she didn't want to share with you right now. How could you get a turn next time?"

"My turn!"

"I don't like it when you hit me."

"Stop."

"Don't hit my friend!"

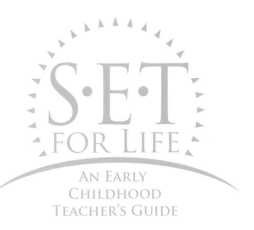

SUMMARY: TEACHING STRATEGIES TO SUPPORT SOCIAL DEVELOPMENT

ENCOURAGE POSITIVE MODELING

- Point out when children use the positive social behaviors you model for them.

  "You figured out that I will come if you raise your hand, even if it takes a few minutes!"

  "You made a plan to share the blocks, and it worked!"

- Use encouragement instead of praise to help children internalize positive behaviors.

  "Your picture has lots of colors!"

  "You worked all morning on that very tall construction!"

HELP CHILDREN LEARN SOCIAL PROBLEM-SOLVING SKILLS

- You can teach children steps to solve the problems they encounter as they negotiate the social world.

  – STEP 1: Calling for Help

  "I can help you figure it out."

  "Hold on! I'm coming!"

  – STEP 2: Trading

  "Ask him to trade trucks with you."

  "Maybe she would trade you the crown for the wand."

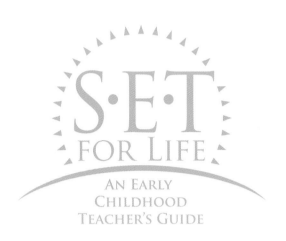

- STEP 3: Taking Turns
  "First Javier, then Michael."
  "You both want to play with the boat. Katelyn, you can have it for five minutes, and then it will be Joshua's turn."
  "I will help you find something to do while you wait for your turn."
- STEP 4: Sharing Resources
  "You can both play with the blocks. Here are some for you, and here are some for Hailey."
  "We have enough dolls for each of you to hold a baby."
- STEP 5: Plan-Making
  "You have a dilemma. What would you like to do about it?"
  "I can help you make a plan."

HELP CHILDREN LEARN TO REFLECT

- Teach children to reflect on conflicts to help them make different choices.
- Validate the feelings behind actions, even if the behaviors were unacceptable.
- Give children time to calm down before helping them to reflect, and reassure them that they are not in trouble.
  "Hold on, you are not in trouble. What made you so angry that you hit Jalissa?"
  "I do like you and I do not like that you pushed."
  "Do you think it helped to kick her? What could you do instead next time someone takes your toy?"
  "How can I help you stop kicking down block buildings?"

TEACHING STRATEGIES TO SUPPORT FRIENDSHIP

TEACH CHILDREN TO USE NAMES

- Using names is an important part of clear communication. Teach children to use the names of the adults and children they are talking to.

  "Who are you talking to?"

  "Her name is Maria."

  "His name is Mr. Chen. You can call him by his name."

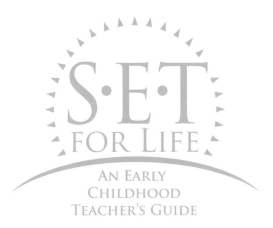

BECOME AN ALLY WITH CHILDREN TO FIGURE THINGS OUT

- An ally is a friend or supporter who helps make things happen. Join with children to figure things out when they encounter social problems.

  "Two children want to be first. What could we do?"

  "I can help you find someone who might know how to do this puzzle."

  "What's your idea? Does Ben have a different idea?"

HELP CHILDREN COMMUNICATE WITH EACH OTHER

- Help children identify what they need or want, and then tell each other directly.

  "You can tell him, 'Don't hit me!'"

  "You can tell her you want a turn on the swings."

  "You told him 'NO!!' You can say, 'It's my turn with the trucks.'"

CHAPTER 7
THE IMPORTANCE OF PLAY

S·E·T
FOR LIFE

AN EARLY
CHILDHOOD
TEACHER'S GUIDE

The way children play can tell us a great deal about all areas of their development. In fact, we often determine where a child is developmentally by watching for certain play behaviors. Because play is so important for the development of young children, it's helpful to know what kinds of play you can expect to see in the children in your classroom.

> "The true object of all human life is play."
>
> G. K. CHESTERTON, WRITER

THE IMPORTANCE OF PLAY

The amount of time children spend in uninterrupted, self-directed play (i.e., when you are not leading or instructing them) has declined tremendously in almost all educational settings, as well as in the home lives of many children. There seems to be a great deal of pressure to replace play with computer use, direct instruction, and highly structured activities that leave no room for the innovation, improvisation, spontaneity, and physicality of child-initiated play. In addition to the loss of social, emotional, and psychological growth, the consequences of declining physical play has led to increasing concern about childhood obesity and related health issues.

Play is a foundational concept that is deeply valued by most early childhood educators. It has many well-documented benefits. Play contributes significantly to development in all areas, including language, self-regulation, creativity, problem-solving, and attention. Imaginary play fills the world of young children. It is the mechanism through which they discover and come to understand the world.

> **Self-Regulation:** *The capacity to regulate or manage emotions, attention, and behavior.*

For children to reap these developmental and learning benefits, play must be freely chosen, initiated, and controlled by children. Different types of play lead to a whole host of fabulous, funny, scary, meaningful, challenging, and fascinating discoveries about the physical, social, and intellectual world. When children have time to explore through play, they develop increasingly sophisticated play skills over time.

Unfortunately, what passes for play these days is often not play at all. Teachers offer children time in activity areas and specify which learning activity can be played. Citing the need to practice skills needed for high stakes testing, the activity is often mathematics, reading readiness, drill and practice, or directed play.

Children lose out on valuable experiences when adults structure their play. In particular, there is a loss in social skill development, and to the benefits of play for children's emotional self-regulation. In today's media-saturated world, children also need a break from electronics and other stimulating digital activities.

Children explore the world through play.

You may recall that Down Time is a critical component of **SET for Life** (see p.33). This opportunity to integrate thinking and experience allows children to learn from various outcomes, to focus on what matters in interactions, and to relax. Self-initiated and self-directed play can be active (shooting basketballs), quiet (reading a book), or some combination (playing dress up in the house center with a small group of friends).

THE RELATIONSHIP BETWEEN PLAY AND SOCIAL DEVELOPMENT

There are two social scientists who are especially important to the way that **SET for Life** approaches play: Jean Piaget and Mildred Parten. These theorists understand play in different ways, but both approaches are useful for understanding the play behavior you see in your classroom and why play is important. A theorist we have already discussed, Lev Vygotsky, continues to contribute to what we know about how children use play to further their own learning.

PIAGET AND PLAY

Jean Piaget was a Swiss psychologist who developed theories about the role of play in development in the mid-1900s. He divided play into three types of play behavior: *practice play*, *symbolic play*, and *play with rules*. Practice play, the most common type of play during the first two years of life, is composed of repetitions of the same movements and actions, both with and without objects. When a baby plays peek-a-boo, hiding his face behind a blanket, over and over again, this is practice play.

> ## Piaget's Three Types of Play
>
> - **Practice play (age 0-2):** Repeating the same actions over and over, like peek-a-boo.
> - **Symbolic play (age 2-7):** Recreating roles and events seen in the real world through pretend play, like playing "house."
> - **Play with rules (age 7-12):** Imposing rules to direct play, like tag or other organized games seen on elementary playgrounds.

Author and early childhood educator, Sue Bredekamp, in her textbook on effective practices, calls this kind of play *functional play*, and notes that the experimentation that occurs during functional play leads to more sophisticated *constructive play*, where children reinterpret and recreate previous play ideas. Blocks, Legos®, and art activities, like drawing, painting, and collage, all allow children to master this reinterpretation process, as they move into Piaget's next phase.

When children move on to symbolic play, they begin to recreate in their play the things they see in the real world. Most children play symbolically between the ages of two and seven. As they begin to develop a sense of themselves as independent from their family members and caregivers, they use play to explore being like these important people, as well as experimenting with being very different from them. Then, as children have more exposure to the larger community around them, they begin trying out the new roles they discover in the wider social world (firefighter, cashier, nurse, shoe salesperson, doctor, grocer, etc.).

Another important aspect of symbolic play is that it allows children to begin to see that one thing can stand in the place of another, (e.g., a block becomes a telephone, when a child uses it that way). This important representational activity is a precursor to future learning, as children learn in due time that numbers, letters, and words represent concepts. This kind of play matures with the use of props, so that children can fully flesh out their ideas while they play.

Play with rules is the last type of play behavior, emerging between ages seven and twelve. During this type of play, children create rules to govern play or to direct the interactions they have with peers. Watch any group of elementary-aged children deciding how to play a game, and you are very likely to see a long and detailed discussion about the rules that will apply and how they will be enforced. Once children begin to negotiate *how* to play, they are close to mastering the social skills they need to sustain play for long periods and to pick up where they left off at a later time.

PARTEN AND PLAY

Mildred Parten, who studied play in the 1930s, had a different way of understanding play, mostly having to do with the ways children interact with each other. She identified the developmental stages of peer play and noted the ages during which each type of play dominates. She also described two types of behavior of children who are not engaged in play: unoccupied and onlooker.

The first stage of peer play is *solitary independent play.* During this stage, children play alone with objects without interacting with others, regardless of how near they may be to each other. *Parallel play* emerges next, with children playing side by side with similar toys, next to each other, but not with each other. In *associative play*, children play with each other, but there is no particular goal or organization to their play. *Cooperative play* is the final, and most sophisticated, form of play. In this stage, children cooperate with others to create play situations, with each child in the group playing an assigned role.

Peer Play: *The play children engage in with each other.*

Children may play in any of these ways at various times during early childhood. During the preschool years, children spend more and more of their playtime in associative and cooperative play. By the early elementary years, play is mostly cooperative, although all types of play behavior are still observed at times.

Examples of Parten's Types of Peer Play

Solitary Independent: Infants play on a mat next to each other, but not interacting or even noticing each other.

Parallel: Toddlers sit near each other, both playing with cars, occasionally looking at each other, yet absorbed in their own activity.

Associative: Young preschoolers chase each other on the playground, with no particular rules about who is chasing and who is trying to get away. Roles change often, and children enter or leave the game without discussing it with each other.

Cooperative: Kindergarteners play "teacher," deciding who will be the teacher, who will be the students, and what the lesson will be, before ever starting to play. Decisions may take time as children discuss and negotiate roles.

As you watch the play of children in your classroom, take note of the kinds of play they are demonstrating. Having this information can help you to offer the right kinds of experiences for each child, to join in play when you are needed, and also to be aware if a child is not trying out more sophisticated play strategies as expected. You can also provide support as children experience rejection when they try to join the play of others, or when their attempts to join in play don't work.

VYGOTSKY AND PLAY

Vygotsky also discussed play. He believed that the extensive use of language required during play is vital to the way that children learn. As children talk, listen to each other, and ask questions, they are actively constructing knowledge and their understanding of the social world. It is the probing, confrontations, disagreements, and provocations that occur during play that make it so meaningful to children's learning.

The teacher's role in play was also expanded by Vygotsky. Listening to conversations, asking open-ended questions that provoke thinking, and participating in conversations are some of the important ways that Vygotsky thought teachers supported children's learning while they play.

TEACHING STRATEGIES TO SUPPORT PLAY

SCHEDULE CHILD-DIRECTED PLAY

The perfect antidote to not enough play is to offer long periods of time in your daily schedule for uninterrupted, child-directed play. Using a block schedule allows teachers to include adequate time for play, and to create opportunities to use all of the ideas suggested by play theorists to build relationships and support learning. It is also a good strategy for managing the multiple demands of individualizing, supervising, and teaching required by today's focus on accountability.

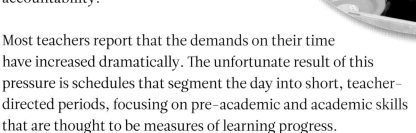

Create blocks of time for child-directed play in well-designed and equipped activity areas.

Most teachers report that the demands on their time have increased dramatically. The unfortunate result of this pressure is schedules that segment the day into short, teacher-directed periods, focusing on pre-academic and academic skills that are thought to be measures of learning progress.

An alternative is to create blocks of time for child-directed play in well-designed and equipped activity areas, so you can focus your time on intentional teaching with children in pairs, triads, and small groups. When the day is viewed this way, teachers find the time to make sure each child gets exactly what they need, not only academically but also emotionally and socially. Several block schedules are included in Appendix F.

FOR EXAMPLE...

Ms. Yuki's multi-age classroom of two to four year olds is set up in seven learning areas that are planned to provide many opportunities for child-directed play. Each morning, children have almost ninety minutes to select an activity of choice, find some playmates, and pursue their play ideas.

During this time, Ms. Yuki has several intentional activities planned for individual children, pairs, and triads. Today, Suri's mother left for a week of traveling, so she knows she will need a little extra time with her. She will make sure Suri gets SET Time with her this morning.

She has also noticed that Justin and Rosalie have been glued to the literacy and writing area. She plans to spend time with these two children and take down their dictation of the meaning of the marks they are making on page after page of paper. And, three children have been building with the trains recently, so Ms. Yuki has selected a nonfiction book on trains to read to them when their train building is complete. While she reads, she will identify the letter "P" when she sees one for Pablo, who has just begun to recognize it.

Ms. Yuki also plans to spend some time during this schedule block observing Talbot while he plays. Yesterday, Talbot and Kamika got into a conflict over who would be the leader during the transition from indoor play to outdoor play, and she wants to see if she can identify the underlying reasons for the upset.

Finally, she will join the children playing in the block area, as time permits this week, to talk about the block shapes and label them. She will also count how many blocks children have used in various constructions. She is hoping that Heather will be able to count to ten using the blocks. She has been interested in counting and she wants to see how long Heather can keep the number-to-object connection going.

PLAY WITH CHILDREN

In the **SET for Life** approach, spending time playing with children is a crucial part of teaching. Children often ask grown-ups to play with them. Say, "Yes," whenever possible. It is one of the most important things you can do to support children's development and learning during the early childhood period.

Joining in play is different that dominating it. When you join in, make sure to take your cues about participation and involvement from the children. Follow their direction and pick up on the play ideas they suggest—let children lead.

JOINTLY ATTEND

Joint attention means spending time with children focusing on the same things. It has many benefits. You get to know children better, making it easier to read and interpret their nonverbal cues. It also helps children learn how to notice the most important details about the things happening around them. For example, if you play checkers with a child and comment on how many checkers are left on the board, instead of whose turn it is, you help her learn that knowing how many checkers are left is important. Children benefit from seeing what you pay attention to and what you ignore when you are with them.

FOR EXAMPLE...

Three-year-old Manuel is fascinated, watching ants crawl down the sidewalk and pick up pieces of apple. Steven, Manuel's teacher, squats down next to him just like Manuel and watches for a few minutes.

When Manuel picks up a leaf and puts in the pathway of the ants to see what happens, Steven says, "What do you think will happen, Manuel?" Manuel replies, "The ants are going in a long line to the apple. The leaf will make them stop." Steven responds, "I wonder how come?" When Manuel doesn't reply, Steven asks, "What do you think they are doing?" Manuel says, "I don't know." They watch a few more minutes and the ants simply walk around the leaf and keep going. Steven asks, "Where do you think they are going with that apple?" Manuel is suddenly excited, saying, "I think they are taking it back to their house to eat it! Let's go find where they are going." Together Steven and Manuel follow the ant trail to where the ants are taking the bits of apple.

Joint Attention: *When two or more people focus on the same thing.*

Joint attention means that both you and the child are focused on the same things—when she is playing with blocks, you also play with blocks. When she notices the movement of a wind chime, you also turn your attention to the chime. As you comment and direct her attention to particular features of the experience (how high blocks can be stacked before they fall, or the way wind chimes get noisier when the wind blows harder), she learns what is relevant, and what can be ignored, even as she stays in charge of the play experience.

The ability to jointly attend is a hallmark of typical development. If it doesn't emerge by toddlerhood, it may be cause for concern and require further assessment. You can use your observations about a lack of joint attention to share your concerns with families and encourage them to talk to their pediatrician or family physician for a referral.

SET for Life Language

"Look up there! What is that bird carrying?"

"You see the trees moving. I wonder why they're doing that."

ENCOURAGE AND ENGAGE IN CONVERSATION WITH CHILDREN

While you are participating in children's play, engage them in conversation, listening carefully to what they have to say. The give-and-take of conversation is new to young children. They are just learning the social expectations of turn-taking in conversation, waiting for a response before responding, and moving on to the next topic. They are exploring how to express what they really mean with a limited vocabulary. When you talk with children, your conversation serves as a model for them to use in future interactions.

Conversations are also a window to a child's experience. Besides offering the pleasure of getting to know children better, time spent conversing with children also helps you gather information about how they respond to different situations, what is on their minds, and topics of interest or curiosity. In the process, you can assess how well their oral communication skills are developing and notice any particular struggles. You can also learn about what children know, what they can do, and how well they are coping with the demands of the classroom. This kind of information is almost impossible to discover without talking with children as they play.

SET for Life Language

"Tell me about what you're working on."

"You are very busy at the art center!"

"Show me what you are doing."

PROVIDE INVITATIONS TO PLAY

Arrange toys and materials to invite play. Cars in a box present a different invitation than cars positioned around a garage; baby dolls in a doll bed or doll carrier suggest different play ideas than a doll sitting in a high chair with a bowl and spoon on the tray. Present available toys in complex, engaging, and even surprising ways to attract children's interest. When interesting toys, materials, and supplies are displayed in intriguing ways, children are drawn to them and will want to play with them.

Provide enough, but not too many, toys and materials. A good variety and selection of age-appropriate toys is essential for early childhood classrooms. Arrange them to invite children to play.

FOR EXAMPLE...
Four-year-old Everitt and Mason almost always choose to play together outdoors, where they run and chase each other on the playground. However, they rarely play together inside. Everitt loves to pretend with knights at the castle and Mason prefers to play with fire trucks.

Extend and expand on children's play ideas with props and related play supports.

Trish, their teacher, notices this and decides to set up an invitation for the boys to play together. She sets up a castle with knights all around it. On top of the castle she has a king, a queen, a princess, and several dogs. She then adds a dragon to the tallest turret. Below, surrounding the castle, she places several fire trucks with firefighter figurines next to them. She puts a blue scarf around the castle as a moat and places a couple of alligators on the blue scarf. She finishes the scene with strips of red and orange construction paper torn into long strips and puts them around the castle as fire. When Everitt and Mason enter the classroom they are immediately drawn to the play scene and both spend the rest of their free choice time there playing together.

EXTEND AND EXPAND CHILDREN'S PLAY IDEAS

When children are developing typically, play comes easily to them. However, some children will need your help to play, either alone or with peers. For very young children or children with developmental delays, the environment can be structured to give them hints or ideas (for example, a barn with animals around it and hay next to it). Invitations from toys, materials, and the environment help children to move into play when they cannot generate ideas themselves.

FOR EXAMPLE...

Mrs. North and several children are playing at the castle. Mrs. North notices that the children are directing their play and comments towards her, so she begins to encourage them to talk to each other instead. She says, "Wow, Anthony's knights are really strong. Maybe they could help Joe's knights get the dragon! That dragon is really trying to get away. Anthony, Joe, what are you going to do?" When the children continue respond to her, she directs them to each other: "Tell Joe," or "Anthony might be interested. Tell him your idea."

Sometimes children need scaffolding with your attention, suggestions, or support to implement their ideas. A child may go to the barn and pick up a horse but not do anything with it. Provide suggestions: "Is the horse hungry or sleepy?" "Does he want a ride in the tractor trailer? Take a look, Peter has a tractor with a trailer. Cassandra has a cow. Does your horse want to talk to her cow?" When a child gets stuck and can't seem to figure out what to do next, (for example, when the answer to a play request is "no"), help her to move on and find something else to do. You might ask what her idea was, or if she has a plan for using the toy she wanted. You might also suggest a different idea or provide a similar, available toy that could substitute for the one she wanted.

SET for Life Language

"I will help you play."

"I will help you play with your friend."

"You might want to ask Derek. He knows the names of all of the trains."

"If you want to play with the castle, you might ask Matthew—he has all of the knight figures."

MORE TEACHING STRATEGIES TO SUPPORT PLAY

Now that you know a variety of ways to engage with children to support play, let's look at some ways you can help children in their play with each other. Even though there may be a great deal of conflict between children, peer play is vital to children's growth and development. Managing conflict is a necessary part of participating in the world in general, and the world of play in particular. Just as children need your assistance to learn new academic skills, they also need your assistance to be successful in their play with peers.

USE CONFLICT AS AN OPPORTUNITY TO TEACH

Conflict is a part of life — we cannot spare ourselves or our children from it. Instead, we need to teach children how to deal with and resolve conflicts as they arise. Children need opportunities to learn and practice negotiation and conflict resolution skills. So, don't put the toys away to prevent arguments. Instead, use conflict as an opportunity to teach.

When you use conflict to teach, it's important to expect some resistance. Over time, as children experience success in negotiating solutions with their peers, and as their conflict resolution skills grow, cooperation will become easier, especially if they know they will have your support while they figure things out.

Conflict can offer valuable moments for teaching and learning.

FOR EXAMPLE...

Three-year-old Lyle and four-year-old Isaac are having trouble sharing the dinosaurs. Lyle had them first, and wants all of them. Their teacher, Miss Nancy, hears their angry voices, and comes over to help. She says, "Lyle, Isaac, what is happening?" Isaac tells her, "He won't let me play!"

Miss Nancy says to Lyle, "Isaac wants to play dinosaurs, too. How can he get some dinosaurs?" When Lyle says, "No," Isaac gets visibly upset. Miss Nancy says to him, "You wanted him to say yes, but he said no. I will help you make a plan."

To Lyle, she says, "You don't want to give Isaac any dinosaurs. Isaac really wants to play with dinosaurs. It is too hard for him not to have any. I can help you find something you can have all of. You may have all the airplanes, since nobody is using them right now." Then she says, "Lyle, choose three dinosaurs for Isaac to play with. You can give them to him on your own or I can help you."

Lyle refuses to give the dinosaurs to Isaac on his own, so Miss Nancy takes three dinosaurs and gives them to Isaac who sits down nearby to play with them. Miss Nancy reminds Lyle that he can have all the airplanes if he wants them and that he still has five dinosaurs. She suggests that perhaps he and Isaac could play together, but Lyle refuses. Miss Nancy then says to Isaac, "When you are finished with the dinosaurs, check with Lyle to see if he wants them back."

SET for Life Language

"What happened?"

"I will help you make a plan."

"You wanted him to say yes and he said no."

"Hold on. You can make a plan to get what you want."

"On your own or with my help?"

HELP CHILDREN STOP DOING THINGS THAT DON'T WORK

Before children can learn new strategies to get their needs met, you sometimes have to help them stop using behaviors that don't work. In many cases, this may mean helping a child to see that, while their behavior is not acceptable, their underlying need or want is perfectly reasonable. Instead of focusing on the behavior, focus on what is driving it. Ally with children to help them get what they want or need. This approach can help children learn new skills that will not only be productive to them, but also be acceptable in the classroom.

Help children find appropriate ways to express their feelings.

After helping the child stop the unacceptable behavior (such as hitting or yelling), talk with the child about what she is trying to accomplish. Then problem-solve together. If the child is too upset or frustrated to come up with solutions independently, it's a good time for you to provide some suggestions that might work. The key to this teaching strategy is to focus the discussion on what is driving the behavior (for example, the child wanting a toy that her friend is playing with), rather than on the behavior itself (grabbing the toy out of her friend's hands). Helping a child to understand why she acted a certain way, and generating more acceptable solutions for the next time, is much more effective than lecturing her about classroom rules.

FOR EXAMPLE...
Five-year-old Abdul sees his classmate Meredith throw herself on the table when she is not the first person Mrs. Brock offers snack to. When he also has to wait for his turn, Abdul throws himself on the table. Mrs. Brock says to Abdul, "You are a different person than Meredith. Throwing yourself on the table will not work. Using your words to tell me what you want will work."

Nadal, a third grader, loses a game that he and Adam are playing. Nadal calls Adam "a stupid moron" and stomps away. Ms. Landry overhears the exchange and calls Nadal over to discuss it. She asks Nadal what happened, and he says, "Adam is a cheater." After talking a little longer, Nadal admits that he didn't like losing and that Adam hadn't cheated. Ms. Landry says, "I think you were disappointed you didn't win." Then, she asks Nadal if he can think of a different way to handle his disappointment when he loses a game. When Nadal can't come up with anything, Ms. Landry wonders if Nadal could ask Adam to play the game again, so he might have a chance to win. Nadal likes this ideas and agrees. Ms. Landry then wonders what will happen if Adam says, "No," or if he loses again. Nadal ponders this, and then tells Ms. Landry that Pierre might play if Adam won't, and that he won't call anybody names if he loses.

Sulemana, a preschooler, is in small group time with four of her classmates. Their teacher, Mrs. O'Halleran, is getting ready to ask children where they want to play during activity time. She turns to Mary, another child in the group, and asks her where she wants to play. Sulemana starts screaming, "Me first, me first!" Mrs. O'Halleran turns to Sulemana and says calmly, "Right now, I'm talking to Mary. When I am finished I will talk to you. It will be your turn next."

SET for Life Language

"You are a different person and throwing yourself on the table won't work. Using your words to tell me what you need will."

"I think you might be wondering if I will change my mind about who gets to go first for snack by pounding your fists on the table. You know how to get snack and that won't work."

"I think you know that name-calling doesn't work."

"When you stop screaming, I'll be able to help you."

ADDRESS NEGATIVE SOCIAL BEHAVIORS

During the early childhood years, children try (and then usually abandon) many negative social behaviors. These behaviors are used for a while, and then fade as they are replaced with more sophisticated skills. Whining, name-calling, threatening, lying, and teasing are some of the most challenging examples of these types of behavior. It is important for teachers to understand these behaviors as attempts to make and keep friends and to recognize the way the social world works, rather than as deviant or bad behavior.

However, these kinds of behaviors are not socially acceptable, no matter how typical they are, and they interrupt play instead of sustaining it. Children will sometimes need your help to stop using the unacceptable behaviors, and to replace them with ideas that work better. Negative social behaviors are opportunities to teach. When your intervention is needed for these behaviors, focus on helping children understand the feelings involved (both theirs and the feelings of others) and finding a solution that works for them, rather than imposing a "one size fits all" solution.

WHINING

Whining is a behavior that usually gets teachers' attention because it is so irritating! Children usually whine for the same reason they taunt or threaten. They tried to be included and it didn't work. They continue whining because it wears adults down and gets them what they want—the teacher's attention.

Children who whine need to work on two skills. First, they need to work on asking for help from a teacher when their attempts to solve a problem aren't working. Often, these problems are ones they can sometimes solve on their own, but this time, they need help. The other skill children need to master is using a normal speaking voice.

Approach whining from the same point of view as you do other negative behaviors. Reflect the child's feelings ("You really wanted to play and didn't get to."), and then help the child pursue his goal another way ("Try again after snack," or, "Ask if you can play with him tomorrow.")

To address the whiny voice, try something like, "I will hear your important words when you can say them in your regular voice." This gentle redirection lets children know that what they say is important to you, that there is a different way to ask besides whining, and that a normal voice will be heard. If the whining continues, then simply use your hand as a stop sign and repeat again: "Regular voice."

> ## SET for Life Language
>
> *"I can hear your words when you use your regular voice."*
>
> *"I can help you when I hear your words in a normal voice."*
>
> *"You are using a ten voice, can you tell me again in a five voice?"*
>
> *"I can tell that you need my help. Tell me in a voice I can understand how you want me to help."*

NAME-CALLING

Name-calling is a negative social behavior many children try out. It emerges as children struggle with ways to be a friend and make friends. Teachers can handle name-calling directly by prompting children to use real names: "His name is John, and you can call him by his name." Then, help children use a similar response to name-calling on their own ("You can tell him, 'My name is Lexi.'") And, don't forget to reflect with the name-caller about how it might feel to be called a name.

> ## SET for Life Language
>
> *"Tell her, 'My name is Maria. You can call me by my name.'"*
>
> *"Jason, how would you feel if Xavier called you an unkind name? What could you do next time you feel angry, instead of using hurtful words?"*
>
> *"Those words are too hard to hear."*

THREATENING

With young children, threatening friends is usually an exclusionary tactic. During the preschool years, we often hear, "You can't play with me," or, "I'm not going to invite you to my birthday party," when children become frustrated with their peers. It is important to recognize this step as progress — children have moved from responding physically when things go wrong (e.g. hitting or pushing) to responding with words. Children who use threats need support for the intense feelings that prompted them, as well as opportunities to replace the threat with better expressions of how they are feeling.

You can rephrase threats, showing children how to identify their feelings and how to express them to their friends. This response is much more effective than forcing children to play together or using punishment to stop the behavior.

Other common childhood threats we often hear include: "I'm gonna tell my mama," "I will kick you." (or kill you, or bite you), "I hate you!", "I'll knock your head off!", or, "I will kick your butt!"

While zero tolerance policies may be necessary with middle and high school students, such policies in early childhood settings or elementary schools may be actually impeding children's ability to identify their underlying feelings and express their emotions accurately and appropriately. A better choice might be to provide teacher facilitation to help children identify the feelings driving their threats, so they say what they really mean. For example, when a four-year-old says, "You can't come to my birthday party," because a peer intrudes on the game she is playing, she really means, "Don't interrupt my game!" Helping her find the words that she really means can be facilitated by a teacher.

When a three-year-old says, "I'm gonna kill you!" to a peer who knocks over his sand castle, he probably really means, "Don't get so close that you knock over my sand castle! That makes me so mad. I don't like it!" Rephrase this comment to help him say what he probably means, rather than focusing on the words that can be labeled threatening.

Help children find the words to say what they really mean.

FOR EXAMPLE...
Pre-kindergarteners George and Aaron are playing together in the block area. When Jose tries to invite Aaron to play cars with him, Mrs.

Scott hears George snarl, "Leave us alone or I'll kick you." Mrs. Scott comes over to the boys. She talks to Jose first, saying, "You really want to play with blocks right now!" He corrects her and says, "No, I asked Aaron to come play cars and George said 'No!'" Next, she turns to George, "You were playing with Aaron. I think you are worried that he will go play with Jose, and then you might feel dissapointed. You can ask Aaron to stay and play with you, or you might decide to invite Jose to join you here at the blocks. Maybe he could bring over some cars. What do you think?"

SET for Life Language

"You seem to be feeling very angry right now. You can tell him, 'I am angry! Leave me alone.'"

"You don't like it when she tells you that you can't play. Try asking if you can play later."

"You stomped your foot. That tells me you are frustrated that your building fell down."

"You said you wanted to kick him. I think you are irritated, and people are not for kicking."

"You said, 'I hate you.' I think you want him to share the cars and he said 'No.' I think you mean that you are super angry that you don't have any cars to play with. I can help you make a plan to get some cars AND those words are too hard to hear."

LYING

When young children lie, it usually reflects their egocentrism. They are not necessarily trying to be deceptive. Often they are telling you what they *wanted* to happen, rather than what really took place. Experts recommend approaching lying without too much discussion about the truth. Instead of punishing young children for being dishonest, restate what really happened. Then help the child move on to solve the problem.

For example, when children fight over toys, one will usually say that the other initiated the conflict, and vise versa. Instead of trying to figure out who is telling the truth, instead say, "It seems that playing together with blocks isn't working for you right now." Then, focus on what needs to happen next. Your intervention should be directed at solving the problem, rather than identifying who is telling the truth. In this situation, you might suggest that the children divide the blocks in half and play in separate areas.

The other thing you can do to help with lying is to avoid giving children the opportunity to be untruthful. When you know a child made a mistake or broke a rule, don't ask them if they did it. State what you see and what needs to be done about it. If a child continues to argue their version of events, simply restate what you've already observed and help them move towards resolution.

FOR EXAMPLE...

Five-year-old Lana has been working at the art center. Mr. Carlos realizes she is now playing in the dramatic play area and the art center is in total disarray. Instead of asking Lana if she made the mess, he tells her, "I see there are lots of supplies still out at the art center where you were working. Let's go clean them up before you move to a different center." When Lana begins to protest that she didn't make the mess, he simply restates, "You are ready to do something else right now, and there are supplies that need picking up. When the art center is clean, you are welcome to pick a different activity."

SET for Life Language

"You wanted it to work out that way and it didn't."

"That sounds like a wish."

"You want it to be your turn and right now it is Julio's turn."

"I think you are hoping that saying it many times will make it true."

TEASING AND BULLYING

Teasing during early childhood usually occurs as a means of control. Teasing is not just kid stuff — it must be addressed. If left alone, children who tease may later feel they have a right to continue teasing others to gain a sense of power over them.

FOR EXAMPLE...

Grant and his big brother Drew are in a multi-age classroom, with many sibling groups. Grant is playing with the architectural blocks in the block area. His big brother, Drew, comes over with a battery-powered car and says, "You can't play with this because you're a baby." Ms. Tamika comes right over to Drew and says, "Drew, you are teasing Grant. I think you know that the toys in the classroom are for all of the children. You are older than Grant AND he can play with the car when he isn't playing with the blocks."

Teasing in early childhood generally is another exclusionary tactic ("Melissa has cooties! She can't play with us."), or sometimes an invitation ("You can't catch me!" while running away, as an invitation to be chased). It can also be an observation with intended consequences of hurting someone's feelings ("Your shirt is ugly," or, "Your hair is dirty.").

Helping children to understand and tolerate differences is one way to reduce teasing and bullying.

However, remember that often young children make inquiries about their observations that come from lack of exposure or understanding. In many cases, they are not intending to be hurtful ("Why is she so fat?" or, "He doesn't have a hand on that arm," or "She's not your mom, she has white skin and you have black skin.") In these situations, help children understand what they are seeing in a matter-of-fact way, and if needed, let them know that their words can be hurtful, even if they're not intended that way.

....

═══

FOR EXAMPLE...

DeShawn runs to his mom as the class exits onto the playground after school is over. Esmeralda watches as DeShawn's mom hugs him and strokes his head. Esmeralda, who has had no exposure to adoption, says out loud to no one in particular, "That can't be DeShawn's mom! She has white skin and he has brown skin."

Ms. Theresa overhears Esmeralda's comment and approaches her. She kneels down close to Esmeralda and says, "DeShawn and his mommy are so happy to see each other! I think you are wondering why their skin is different colors." Esmeralda looks a little shocked that Ms. Theresa has overheard her comment and shyly says, "Yes." Knowing that the Ackermans talk openly about DeShawn's adoption, Ms. Theresa says, "There are lots of ways to make a family. DeShawn's parents adopted him—that means that he has a birth mom and dad AND an adoptive mom and dad. Mr. and Mrs. Ackerman are DeShawn's mom and dad and he is their son. I have a good book that we can read tomorrow that talks about different ways families are made, we will read it at circle time."

Ms. Theresa later calls Esmeralda's parents to tell them about what happened, and that she plans to read the book All Families Are Special *tomorrow at circle time, so the class can see how families are made in all kinds of different ways.*

═══

Teasing can also be a method of one up-ing, in an effort to feel superior ("I have the new Nintendo® and all the games, and you don't have any".) This is a perfect opportunity to help children explore the feelings that underlie the words they are saying. For example, when a child is boasting about possessions, you can simply say, "I think you are proud that you have such nice things. I am wondering what you want to happen when you say that to

176 | SET FOR LIFE

your friends? Do you want them to know about your things, or do you want them to feel bad that they don't have those things? What are you feeling when you say those words?"

Try to read the nonverbal cues that will help you distinguish the intention behind a child's words. You don't want to shame a child (especially if they are just excited, and the boasting is really excitement more than trying to one up another child), yet you can gently help them to see potential consequences for their words.

FOR EXAMPLE...

Nam and Luke are sitting at the lunch table and each pull out their lunch box. Nam has kimchi. Luke pinches his nose and says "Ewww - gross!" as he looks at Nam's lunch, taking out his chicken nuggets. Ms Diane asks Nam if he liked what Luke said and encouraged him to tell Luke, "Don't tease me."

Later on the playground, Luke says to Will and Jake, "Nam eats gross stuff. We aren't going to let him be in our fort. He's too stinky!" Will and Jake, wanting to be Luke's friends, agree and follow Luke's lead pinching their noses chanting, "Nam is a stink bug!"

*Ms. Diane hears the chanting and approaches Nam and asks, "What is happening here, Nam?" He tells her that Luke is making fun of him because he ate kimchi for lunch, and now Will and Jake joining in. Ms. Diane calls Luke, Will, and Jake over. She restates what Nam has said and asks Luke about it. Luke says, "He smells bad because he ate that gross stuff for lunch." Ms. Diane then says to Luke, "I think you don't know a lot about different kinds of foods yet, Luke. There are many different kinds of foods. Kimchi has a strong odor and it tastes very good to some people. You may not like kimchi, **AND** you may not tease him."*

Later that day she creates an opportunity to help Luke and Jake reflect on how their words might have made Nam feel.

For Example...
Bernice, Elizabeth, and Max are playing Sorry® when Bernice draws a Sorry® card and sends Max back to 'Start.' Elizabeth says to Max, "You have to go back! You don't have any pieces on the board now - ha, ha!"

Ms. Margaret, who is nearby says to Max, "Max, what do you want to tell Elizabeth?" Max looks forlorn and doesn't reply. Ms. Margaret then states, "Max, you can tell her, 'Don't tease me!'" Ms. Margaret then adds, "Elizabeth, I think it felt good that Bernice didn't send you back to start, and it is not okay to tease Max."

SET for Life Language

"Teasing is not ok."

"Tell her, don't tease me!"

"That sounds like a tease."

"You may not tease her."

Teasing in young children is different from bullying. Bullying is about contempt, a powerful feeling of dislike toward somebody considered to be inferior. The biases at the foundation of this contempt are often deeply rooted attitudes found in our homes, schools, and society. Any bias or prejudice related to race, gender, sexual orientation, religion, physical attributes, or mental abilities can be used by a bully to validate and justify contempt for an individual child or group of children. It is critical that teachers and caregivers address this behavior as soon as it begins, so unkind patterns do not become ingrained in children's ways of thinking and behaving.

SUMMARY: TEACHING STRATEGIES TO SUPPORT PLAY

The way children play can tell us a great deal about all areas of development. It is also the chief way that children learn during the early childhood years.

SCHEDULE CHILD-DIRECTED PLAY
- Schedule long periods of uninterrupted, child-directed play as a regular part of your day.

PLAY WITH CHILDREN
- Spending time playing with children is a crucial part of teaching. Let children take the lead when you join in their play.
  "Yes, I can play with you!"

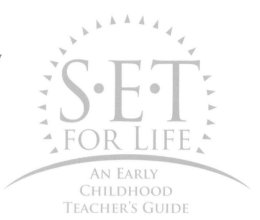

JOINTLY ATTEND
- Spend time with children focusing on the same things
- Children benefit from seeing what you pay attention to, and what you ignore.
  "I see those birds, too! Where do you think they're going?"
  "May I look at this book with you?"

ENCOURAGE AND ENGAGE IN CONVERSATION WITH CHILDREN
- Engaging in conversation with children helps them learn about the give-and-take of communication.
- Engaging in conversation and it serves as a window into a child's experience, skills, and challenges.
  "Tell me about what you're working on."
  "Why did you choose that tool for working in the sand today?"
  "What did you do this weekend, Claudia?"

PROVIDE INVITATIONS TO PLAY
- Provide enough (but not too many) age-appropriate toys and materials.
- Arrange toys in interesting and novel ways to invite children to play.

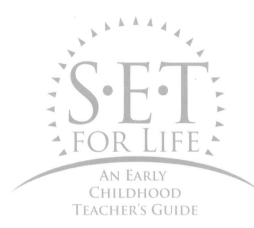

S·E·T
FOR LIFE
AN EARLY
CHILDHOOD
TEACHER'S GUIDE

EXTEND AND EXPAND CHILDREN'S PLAY IDEAS

- Sometimes children will need your help to implement their play ideas. When children get stuck, help them move on and find something else to do.

  "I will help you play with your friend."

  "If you want to play with the castle, you might ask Matthew — he has all of the knights."

TEACHING STRATEGIES TO SUPPORT PEER PLAY

USE CONFLICT AS AN OPPORTUNITY TO TEACH

- Managing conflict is a necessary skill to participate in play and in the wider world. Support children as they work to resolve conflicts as they arise.

  "What happened? What did you want to happen?"

  "You can ask a grown-up to help you."

  "I will help you make a plan to get what you want."

HELP CHILDREN STOP DOING THINGS THAT DON'T WORK

- Before children can learn new ways to get their needs met, you may have to help them stop using behaviors that don't work.
- Focus discussion on the emotions behind the behavior and discuss acceptable ways to deal with those feelings in the future.

  "I think you know name-calling doesn't work."

  "You wanted it to be your turn and it is not your turn. Throwing yourself on the floor won't help."

ADDRESS NEGATIVE SOCIAL BEHAVIORS

It is important to understand negative social behaviors as a normal part of social development. It is equally important to address them and help children make more appropriate choices.

- **Whining**
  - Children who whine need to work on asking for help when they need it, and also to use a normal speaking voice.

"I can hear your words when you use your normal voice."

"It sounds like you need some help. Tell me in a voice I can understand, so that I can figure out how."

- **Name-Calling**
    - Address name-calling by prompting children to use real names, then reflect with the name-caller about how it might feel to be called an unkind name.

        "His name is Jacob. You can call him by his name."

        "Jason, how would you feel if Xavier called you an unkind name? What could you do next time you feel angry, instead of using hurtful words?"

- **Threatening**
    - Help children to rephrase threats to express the feelings behind them.

        "You can just tell her you don't want to play right now."

        "You said you wanted to kick him. I think you are irritated, and people are not for kicking."

- **Lying**
    - When young children lie, they are usually expressing what they wanted to happen. Instead of punishing children for being dishonest, restate what actually occurred, and help children to move on and solve the problem at hand.

        "That sounds like a wish."

        "You wanted it to work out that way and it didn't."

- **Teasing and Bullying**
    - Teasing is not just kid stuff — it must be addressed.
    - Pay careful attention to the meaning behind teasing, so that you can respond appropriately.

        "Leticia's braids are called cornrows and she likes them very much. You have different hair and you may not tease Leticia."

        "You can tell her, 'Don't tease me!'"

CHAPTER 8

UNDERSTAND HOW CHILDREN DEVELOP AND LEARN

S·E·T
FOR LIFE
AN EARLY
CHILDHOOD
TEACHER'S GUIDE

Development and learning are closely connected during early childhood. As children develop new skills, it affects what they learn next and how they learn it. For example, once a baby pulls to a stand, she is able to see things she couldn't see from the floor. All of a sudden, she is interested in the remote control or Mommy's purse, because she has become aware of them. Or, a child who learns to identify the first letter of his name becomes suddenly fascinated by the letters he sees on signs, especially ones that match "his" letter.

In this chapter we will talk about the way children develop and learn and how you can support this process. Learning *how* this happens can help you, so that is where we begin.

DEVELOPMENT AND LEARNING

Many kinds of change take place during the early childhood years. One kind of development is age-related change that occurs as a result of biological maturation (the changes that happen naturally as children get older). Some age related physical changes include cutting teeth, walking, and learning to talk. Age-related development happens quickly. In just a few short years, babies change into toddlers. Soon, they change from preschoolers, full of budding independence, to young school-agers who can do an amazing array of tasks, from reading to riding a bicycle.

We don't often think of learning as a change, but it is. For example, once a child's legs are long enough and strong enough, she can, with experience and instruction, learn to ride a bike. Learning is a change in knowledge and skill that is the result of experience and/or instruction. Throughout early childhood, children learn because they try things out, watch others do interesting things, and are offered age appropriate instruction to learn new knowledge or skills.

Sometimes development leads learning. As language skills develop, babies become more interested in the social world and begin to babble and coo, for example. At other times, it happens

> "No one has yet fully realized the wealth of sympathy, kindness and generosity hidden in the soul of a child. The effort of every true education should be to unlock that treasure."
>
> EMMA GOLDMAN, ACTIVIST

Development:
Age-related, biological change that results from an interaction between maturation and the experiential environment.

Learning:
Knowledge acquired from experience, when growth and development have created the framework for it to occur.

the other way around: learning results in further development. As preschoolers learn how to play organized games, they become interested in understanding how to win, and they begin to develop strategic thinking.

When we understand the connection between development and learning, we are better able to support emerging skills. The new skills children acquire in their first years are critical to their ability to learn more complex skills later on such as reading or mathematics. A good understanding of development and learning helps you to be a better teacher, allowing you to anticipate when to offer particular experiences to support development or instruction to support learning. Even more importantly, it can help you assess whether a child is significantly ahead or behind of typical development and learning, and to make referrals for intervention as needed.

DEVELOPMENTAL THEORY

Which of the following diagrams do you think best represents the way children develop?

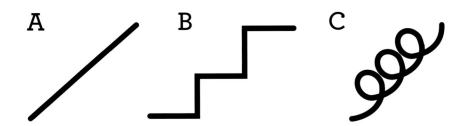

The answer is C. Development is a continuous, though uneven, cycle of ever-increasing skills. Each period of development is often preceded by a brief, sometimes turbulent, period of regression. Developmental theory helps explain the amazing changes that take place during the early childhood years. Let's take a look at the underlying principles behind this theory.

Providing experiences at the right times supports children's development and learning.

PRINCIPLES OF DEVELOPMENTAL THEORY

The first principle of developmental theory is that human development is integrated. All areas of development—physical, emotional, social, and intellectual (including language and cognition) — are linked. Development in one area influences and is influenced by development in another.

The second principle is that development follows a relatively predictable sequence, common to most children. Milestones of development, such as when a baby takes her first steps or when a child learns to read his name, are observable and can be used to track children's progress. This predictability is seen in every area of development. For example, most children learn to write in the same sequence. They begin by scribbling, then move on to making basic shapes, and then, representational images. Soon, they make symbol-like marks, then letters, and then words. Almost all children follow similar developmental patterns in other areas of development during the early childhood years.

The third principle of development is that each child has his or her own individual pattern and timing of growth. This may seem to contradict the previous idea of predictability, but it is important to understand that both are true. Although the developmental sequence—the order in which new skills are acquired—is relatively predictable, individual children's progress through the sequence can vary widely. For example, while some children walk by twelve months, many others walk earlier or later. One child may have the eye-hand coordination to cut with scissors at three years of age, while another may not be able to handle scissors well enough to cut reliably until closer to four, or even five, years of age.

This principle captures the sporadic and uneven nature of development. Developmental growth comes in spurts, and may be more visible in one area than another at different points in a child's life. For example, a child might work on physical development until he can pull to a stand, and then move on to language development (saying "dada" and "mama," for example) before learning to walk. Or, a child might make no observable developmental progress at all for a few weeks or even months, and then all of a sudden make major strides in several areas, seemingly all at once. Each child is unique, and so is his or her development.

This principle also explains why age alone is such an unreliable predictor of developmental stage and can rarely be used to identify or understand the developmental status of an individual child. Many factors, ranging from prenatal experiences to family structure, can influence a child's development.

This is one very important reason there can be such great differences between children who are the same age. However, if a child's development is more than six months behind the typical range, more investigation is warranted. At that point, it is appropriate to share your observations and encourage families to discuss concerns with their health care provider.

Some Factors Affecting Development in Children

- Prenatal and birth experience
- Personality and temperament
- Preferred approach to learning
- Life experiences, both type and variety
- Interests and strengths
- Energy level
- Family structure and background
- Cultural expectations
- Health status

FOR EXAMPLE...

Robert has amazing gross motor skills for a four year old. He can ride a two wheel bike, run like lightning, and slam dunk a basketball. He is quick and agile, yet he has a great deal of difficulty expressing himself verbally. He can't seem to find words and often bolts away if the teacher approaches him to engage in conversation.

Soledad is a talker. At 18 months, she knew hundreds of words and regularly used two and three word sentences. By age two, her language (receptive, expressive, and pragmatic) was advanced. She spoke in sentences, and nearly everything she said was understandable to strangers. At age four, her vocabulary is quite large and she regularly uses words you would not expect to hear from a child her age (such as "synchronized" and "inappropriate").

Deon loves creative art. At age four, he requests and selects working on creative art activities whenever he is given a choice. He likes all kinds of art—crayons, markers, watercolors, pencils, collage making of all kinds. He is not concerned with the final outcome. Instead, he focuses on the process and quantity, producing as many different projects as he can in the time he has in the art area.

Lucy, on the other hand, won't come near the art center. When given a choice, Lucy loves building with blocks. Her buildings are complex, multi-level, and engaging to other children, and she often uses all of the blocks on the shelf in her construction projects. She invites others to watch her build, but if they want to join in, Lucy expects them to follow her rules and directions.

The fourth principle of developmental theory is that development proceeds from the simple to the complex, and from the general to the specific. Simple skills must be acquired before more complex ones can build on them. For example, children typically learn to count things one at a time before they are able make groups of objects and add them together.

Development also proceeds from behavioral knowledge to symbolic or representative knowledge. This simply means that children learn to do things long before they can describe them with words or represent them with pictures or in writing. This explains why children can find the way to their bedrooms long before they can follow a map.

As children master more complex skills, their abilities become more organized and also more internalized. They become more independent, show more self-control, and are more able to match their behavior to the expectations of the people around them.

The fifth principle points to the impact of experience on development. These experiences may be biological, environmental, cultural, social, and interactional. All play a role in determining the way a child develops, impacting both short- and long-term outcomes. For example, most children who are enthusiastic readers have had many positive experiences with books. Children who did not have those early, recurrent, pleasant experiences with books may be less interested, which can have repercussions that last through all of their school years.

Principles of Developmental Theory

- Human development is integrated; all developmental areas are interrelated.

- Growth follows a universal and relatively predictable sequence.

- Each child has an individual pattern and timing of growth within a predictable sequence.

- Development proceeds from the simple to the complex and from the general to the specific.

- The interplay of biological, environmental, cultural, social, and interactional experiences impacts development.

FOR EXAMPLE...

Anne Marie is an enthusiastic, verbal three-year-old. Her parents are professionals and an au pair stays with Anne Marie during the afternoons. Each week, Anne Marie goes to swimming, gymnastics, piano, and art classes. She also works regularly with the au pair writing letters and doing basic addition.

During activity time, Anne Marie never chooses the writing center. If pressed, she gets upset and refuses outright. Mrs. Huang, her pre-K teacher, asks Anne Marie why she doesn't like writing, but Anne Marie doesn't answer. When Mrs. Huang asks the au pair, she seems surprised. The au pair says Anne Marie can trace her letters perfectly at home. Mrs. Huang asks if Anne Marie draws pictures. The au pair tells her that Anne Marie has weekly art lessons where she learns to draw. Mrs. Huang realizes that Anne Marie has had very little opportunity to explore with writing instruments on her own — all of her experience has been guided.

The next day, Mrs. Huang talks with Anne Marie about the writing center. She tells her that at school, she may draw or write any way she likes. She won't have to share her work with anyone unless she wants to, and she can decide if she keeps her work or puts it in the recycling bin. Anne Marie hesitates, but agrees to try. After a few weeks, Anne Marie is scribbling away at the writing center. Freed from instruction, she is able to enjoy writing, practicing skills she acquired on her own, without concern for the outcome or the expectations of others.

Each child's development is unique and influenced by a combination of inborn traits and life experiences.

Another concept in child development is developmental uniqueness, meaning that development is unique to each child. Children mature at different rates, and are able to acquire new skills at different times, and in different ways. For example, nearly all children learn to jump on one foot around the age of four, but the way they learn (watching others, practicing with two feet, or falling down until they figure it out) varies from child to child.

Brain research has shown that there are biological reasons for these differences. When children's brains are developing, the connection of neural pathways (basically the way the brain becomes wired to work) is affected by experience. Because each child's experiences are different, the pattern of connections and neural pathways within their brains are unique. No two brains form and strengthen in exactly the same ways. The combination of biology and experiences makes us who we are.

As you become more familiar with these principles, you will begin to see them at work in your classroom. You'll be better able to recognize the best moments for introducing new experiences, adding context, teaching particular techniques, or encouraging further learning. And, you can help families understand when particular skills are best introduced, explored, or taught. You'll be able to spot possible interruptions or delays in children's development, and amend or modify your approach or curriculum to fit individual children.

FOR EXAMPLE...

Sofia is a spirited five-year-old. Although she was exposed in utero to an unknown variety of toxic substances, she is making rapid progress since her foster care placement at the age of two. Her use of language is average for her age and she is able to play with her friends most of the time without help from adults.

However, being in a group is hard for Sofia. She becomes disruptive, her body moves quickly, and it is difficult for her to calm down once she gets going. Her teacher, Ms. Tsion, hasn't been able to identify what triggers her out-of-control behavior, even though it happens nearly every day. She decides to observe Sofia for a while, writing down her observations, and looking for patterns or clues about the cause of Sofia's difficulties.

During her observation, Ms. Tsion notes that the disruptions usually begin during circle time or during other times when other children are very close to Sofia. For the next week, she decides to have Sofia sit at one end of the circle, and to create a bit of space between Sofia and the child next to her. She also gives Sofia a pillow to hold while she is in circle. Sofia seems calmer and has less disruptive behavior with the new seating arrangement. Although she still has difficulty calming, Sofia becomes less disruptive during circle time.

> ## The Three Components of Developmental Uniqueness
>
> 1. The pattern and timing of development – the pace of development – is unique for each child.
> 2. Growth in one sphere is closely tied to and influenced by development in other areas.
> 3. Development is sporadic and uneven.

TEACHING STRATEGIES TO SUPPORT DEVELOPMENT AND LEARNING

UNDERSTAND AND EMBRACE INDIVIDUAL DIFFERENCES

Humans are complicated, with individual temperaments and unique needs. These differences are good —they make the human condition interesting. At the same time, these differences can make teaching challenging. Being a good teacher means learning what makes each child an individual and valuing and embracing those differences.

It's also important to realize we are not the only ones who see differences. Children see them, too. They respond differently to each other as they explore what works, and change their behavior to fit the different responses they get from others. When teachers point out these natural differences, children get better at seeing and responding to the people around them. Talking about similarities and differences also gives us great opportunities to teach children about tolerance, empathy, and compassion.

FOR EXAMPLE...

Mr. Johnny has a few stability balls in the gross motor area of the classroom. When he has small group time, he encourages Tanner to sit on the ball instead of sitting on the floor. Milly complains that Tanner always gets to sit on a ball and she never does. Mr. Johnny tells Milly, "You are a different person than Tanner. He needs to sit on the ball to be able to pay attention at small group time. You can sit still and pay attention without using the ball. If you'd like to make a plan to use the ball in the gross motor area, I can help you do that. All of the children can use the balls there."

SET for Life Language

"You are a different boy (or girl)."

"Some children need help on the art project. You are able to do the art project without help."

"Children are all different."

"I think you can do it. Celeste is having a hard time listening right now. You are a different girl and you are not having a hard time."

PROVIDE MULTI-SENSORY EXPERIENCES

Learning experiences with multi-sensory dimensions can ensure that all children, regardless of temperament or learning style, are accommodated. This seems like extra work, until you realize that *not* accommodating different styles means you will instead spend plenty of time redirecting and trying to focus the attention of children whose learning styles are not being included. When you plan your interactions with these differences in mind, you will find that both you and the children benefit.

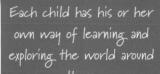

Each child has his or her own way of learning and exploring the world around them.

FOR EXAMPLE...

Mrs. Robbins' kindergarten class is studying frogs. She knows that she has three children that love to talk about what they are studying, two children who are primarily tactile in their approach to learning, one child who has to see what you are talking about to understand it, three who are very active (kinesthetic) learners, one child who approaches all new situations cautiously, and six children who utilize several strategies.

Mrs. Robbins' plans include:
- *an aquarium with several tadpoles and a terrarium with a frog, along with charts and photos of the life cycle of a frog in the science area.*
- *frog costumes with googly eyes in the dramatic play area.*
- *a recording of nighttime frog sounds in the listening area, with nonfiction books about types of frogs in the library area.*
- *the storybook and digital recording of* Frog and Toad, *by Arnold Lobel.*
- *a collection of artistic interpretations of frogs painted and sculpted by artists and naturalists in the art area.*
- *a water table with a collection of plastic frogs, small stones, and lily pads.*
- *a field trip to the local science museum to see a frog exhibit.*

During the study of frogs, children can touch or hold a frog if they want to, wear the frog costume, jump like frogs, hear different stories about frogs, manipulate the plastic frogs in the water table; sketch, paint, and draw frogs, and watch tadpoles lose their tails and grow legs. Each child has an opportunity to learn about frogs in his or her own way. When the class completes a KWL chart two weeks later, Mrs. Robbins finds that all the children have learned quite a lot about frogs and frog behavior.

K	W	L
WHAT DO I **KNOW** ABOUT... FROGS?	WHAT DO I **WANT** TO KNOW ABOUT... FROGS?	WHAT DID I **LEARN** FROM STUDYING ABOUT... FROGS?
Frogs can jump. I like frogs. They have slimy skin. I can chase them around. They like to eat bugs. Tadpoles are baby frogs.	What else do frogs eat? How do frogs get away from predators? Where do frogs live? How long does it take for a tadpole to turn into a frog?	Frogs live all over the world. They like places that are wet and warm. Some frogs blend in, and some are bright colors. Some frogs are poisonous! Frogs eat mosquitoes and all kinds of other insects. Frogs lay their eggs in the water.

MATCH TEACHING AND CURRICULUM TO CHILDREN'S DEVELOPMENTAL STAGE

There is a reason early childhood professionals study child development. Knowing the sequence of how children develop and learn helps you to be a better teacher. When you understand that development is continuous and integrated, that it is an uneven process, and that regressions often precede growth and learning, you can plan activities that match children's needs.

Learning the alphabet is an example of this in action. Infants love the sound of the alphabet song and toddlers may even repeat parts of it. During the preschool years, children learn that writing means something and begin to make marks that mimic adult writing. They are very interested in the first letter of their names and will look for it in books, and in print they see around them. During the pre-kindergarten year, children learn to identify more letters, and connect them to the sounds they make. The following year, most children complete their letter knowledge, and begin to blend sounds into words. This developmental sequence is similar for most children.

Understanding this sequence, and many other developmental sequences like it, helps teachers to offer experiences when children are ready for them, not too early or too late. If you introduce a skill too early, children may be frustrated. If it is too late, they may be bored or uninterested, even if the skill is not one they've mastered yet. If you aren't sure about the right time to bring new experiences into your classroom, look it up.

FOR EXAMPLE...
At fifteen months, Ella loved to draw round and round with a marker that her teacher provided for her while she sat in her high chair. At two years old, she was interested in letters but did not have the fine motor skills to make them. Her teachers saw her interest, and gave her lots of opportunities to explore hand movements and how her movements looked on paper, using crayons, paints, and markers.

By the time she entered preschool at three, Ella had developed enough fine motor control to make letter-like marks. Her preschool teacher encouraged her by making a variety of writing utensils available (crayons, chalk, markers, pencils, pens, and paint brushes). Though her E's often appeared backwards and had extra lines, Ella was delighted to write "her" letter for her name. When she entered pre-kindergarten at four, Ella was able to write her name perfectly, so that it was completely recognizable to her teacher.

EXPECT AND ACCOMMODATE REGRESSION

Neuroscience tells us that regressions precede growth. When children regress, it is usually a sign that they are experiencing a neurological reorganization to accommodate new experiences and skills.

We often make the mistake of treating these regressions as behavioral issues. In fact, they are actually bio-behavioral. The child's brain and body are incredibly busy and sometimes may be overwhelmed by all the changes. She isn't being defiant, difficult, or ornery. Until the reorganization is complete, she is really only able to respond at the regressed level.

Stress or trauma can also cause regression in children. The birth of a new baby, a divorce, a move to a new house or school, or an illness can often cause children to revert to behaviors they had previously given up. When you see regression in your classroom, it's a good time to check in with families and find out if something different or new (a traveling parent or a death of a pet, for example) may be happening at home.

Toileting accidents, night-waking, reverting to baby talk, and whining are all examples of regressive behavior you might see. When they occur, it is important to accept that the child needs sensitive responses that match the regressed level of development. In other words, meet the child where she is. If she is three, but acting like a two-year-old, use teaching strategies that are appropriate to use with a two-year-old.

When the regression is related to stress or trauma, children need even more sensitivity from you. When you are patient and confident that lost skills will re-emerge, children can usually avoid getting stuck at the regressed level of skill.

FOR EXAMPLE...

Eleven-month-old Victoria has been sleeping through the night and taking regular naps since she was six months old. All of a sudden, she begins waking at night and refusing to nap at her usual time. Her mother is exhausted, and her teacher, Ms. Jennie, is frustrated. Victoria had previously been cheerful and easy to comfort, but has become cranky and difficult to soothe. After meeting to talk about Victoria's new struggles, they both decide to take steps to provide Victoria with extra nurturing and a more predictable routine.

Two weeks later, Victoria, who had previously only been pulling to a stand, takes her first steps. The same week, she says her first word. Within days of these developments, Victoria begins sleeping soundly again, and seems back to her usual, happy self.

Three-year-old Harold's mother has been away on a business trip for two days. At school, Harold whines and cries at any small disappointment or frustration. Mrs. Harris lets him climb into her lap, commenting that he might be feeling sad, mad, and worried because Mommy is away. She helps him find comforting things to do to help him feel better, like sitting in the cozy corner with a picture of his mommy, dictating a letter telling her how much he misses her, and drawing a picture to give to her when she comes home. By arrangement, Harold's mother calls at lunchtime to say hello, and to remind him that she will return on Tuesday.

SET for Life Language

"It is hard on you when your parent is away on a trip. He will come back and I will be here to help you until he does."

"One day you will be able to throw the ball really hard again."

"You will figure out how to listen to your body again. You used to be able to and you will be able to do it again another day."

"Someday you will be able to ride a bicycle like your big brother."

RITUALIZE ROUTINES

Routines structure children's lives and help them understand what is to come. Children are more event-oriented than time-oriented. They begin to mentally create order by knowing what comes next. For example, they begin to grasp that circle time comes first, then snack, then playground, etc. When children don't have to be anxious or fearful about what might happen next, they are more likely to relax.

The best routines are ones that follow the same progression every time. This is especially important at times when children need to do what you ask them to do, even if they don't want to. For example, children need predictable routines for arrival and transition into the classroom, transition between activities, and reunion routines at departure time, to name a few.

Use charts or other visual symbols to guide children through routines. This is helpful, both for children and for teachers, and it is particularly useful for children learning a second language or who have other learning or developmental differences. Older children will benefit from being taught how to read and understand these tools on their own, so that they can answer their own questions.

SET for Life Language

"First, wash hands, and then snack."

"We will go outside after snack, just like we always do."

"Grandma comes to pick you up after you take a nap."

"Can you look at the chart and see what comes next?"

PREPARE FOR TRANSITIONS AND CHANGE

Life is a series of transitions. Learning to tolerate and handle them is an important life skill for children. As adults, we often think through what happens next as we move through the day, mentally preparing ourselves for the next activity. ("After I get off work, I'll drop off this package at the post office, and then swing by the grocery store on my way home.")

Young children live in the moment. They don't think ahead unless they are worried about what will happen next. Children need adults to help them prepare for transitions, to create routines that help them understand what will happen next, to offer prompts and reminders about upcoming changes, and to talk out loud about what is happening and what will happen in the future.

This is especially important when there are changes to schedules and routines. If there will be a change from what children are expecting, be sure to let them know in advance. Remind them the day before the change, if possible. For example, "Tomorrow we go to the book fair, so we will not have story time in the library like we usually do. We will have story time again next Wednesday." Then remind them again that day: "Remember, this morning we have the book fair, so no story time in the library."

Children also need reminders that a transition is coming within their regular routines. For most young children, one cue or signal is not enough. Toddlers and preschool children need several reminders before the final notice to help them get ready to transition. A good place to start is with five, two, and one-minute reminders. For example, "In five minutes (then two, then one more minute), it will be time to stop painting at the easel and get ready to pick another place to play." For older children, a countdown timer can be helpful.

Remind children about upcoming transitions to help them get ready. Match the number of reminders to children's developmental age and stage.

If it looks like a child might run out of time to finish playing, help him anticipate what will happen. You might say, "Bobby, you have worked hard to build the train track. I want to let you know we have ten minutes left to play. You might want to add the trains now so you have time to play with them on the great track you built."

Some children need help to get started with the transition process. Go first to the children who need more time to get ready to transition. Then, prepare small groups of children, as they are working or playing, with five, then three, then one minute reminders that a transition is approaching. Then, get the whole group's attention that the transition is beginning (by counting down, for example). Finally, signal that it's time to transition in a noticeable way such as with a song, rhyme, finger play, or chant.

Match the number of choices, prompts, or reminders to the child's developmental age and stage. Routines and reminders should mature as children grow developmentally. Be willing to change and update routines as children get better at tolerating and managing transitions.

It is also important to personalize routines for different children. If one reminder is enough for some children, give those children one reminder. If others need three or four, give them three or four. When children are experiencing stress from life experiences, such as parental job change or a death in the family, provide extra prompts, reminders, and opportunities for choice to help them cope during the stressful time.

MAKE EXPECTATIONS CLEAR

Preparing children for transition or change includes making your expectations clear ahead of time. Telling children in advance of an event how you expect them to respond or behave gives them an opportunity to think about the situation before they are actually in it. This may help to increase compliance when it is time for them to make the transition.

FOR EXAMPLE...

Ms. Hussein is taking her small group to the playground. It is not their usual time to go outside. A broken window in the classroom is being repaired so the children need to leave the room while the repair is being made. On the walk to the playground Ms. Hussein tells the children, "We are going out to the playground for extra recess today while our window is being repaired. When you hear me ring the bell, that means our extra recess time is over and you need to come to the door and line up to go back inside. When you hear the bell, come quickly to the door. I will call roll and you will need to respond, 'I'm here!' so I can be sure no one is left on the playground. Any questions?"

SET for Life Language

"We are going out for 15 minutes. Then you need to line up to come back in."

"After lunch you need to put your artwork away and get your nap mat out."

"Today is different. We will have a visitor in the room and we will continue to have story time on the rug. After the story you may speak to the visitor if you like. During the story, I need your eyes and ears focused on me."

HELP CHILDREN COMPLY WHEN THEY CAN'T DO IT ALONE

Sometimes children need you to stay with them after you remind or prompt them. When compliance doesn't follow, offer your help to comply. Or, count up or down to readiness or to compliance. This strategy gives children a chance to get ready for what is coming and builds in a small delay before they have to cooperate. For example, "I will count to three, then we will start to put the tops on the markers and return them to the basket."

Clear expectations will help your classroom run smoothly.

Some children protest before they comply. Give these children extra time to get ready. Assist with compliance as necessary by using a hand-over-hand approach* or a soft touch to help the child get started.

*This technique looks just like it sounds. Take the child's hand in your hand and pick up the block together. Use this technique in a gentle, supportive way. If the child objects or resists, restate your expectation and ask her to try it on her own. If she still objects, tell her you will leave some of the blocks on the floor for her to pick up later.

FOR EXAMPLE...

Ms. Juarez says, "Harry, we have five more minutes to play and then it will be time to wash up for lunch." Four-year-old Harry says, "NO!" She replies, "You really don't want to stop building with the blocks. You have worked so hard to make your sky scraper. It is not time yet, and in 5 minutes, it will be time to stop. When it's time, I can help you or you can do it by yourself. I will come back when it is time to clean up and you can let me know what you decided — on your own or with my help."

As soon as Ms. Abercrombie counts down for clean up and begins to sing the clean up song, two-and-a-half year old Tate jumps up from the blocks he had been playing with and runs over to the fire truck. Ms. Abercrombie follows him, gets his attention, and says, "It is hard to stop playing AND it is time. Do you want to clean up by yourself or with my help?" Tate says "Help." Ms. Abercrombie takes Tate's hand, walks with him back to the block area, and uses a hand-over-hand technique* to pick up one block and put it where it belongs on the shelf. After helping with one block, she then picks up a block on her own and returns it to the shelf. Tate then picks up a block and puts it away. They continue to take turns putting blocks on the shelf until the area is all picked up.

The Clean Up Song

*"Clean up,
    clean up,
everybody,
    everywhere.*

*Clean up,
    clean up,
everybody,
    do their share."*

SET for Life Language

"In five (then, three, then one) minutes, it will be time to clean up the classroom activity areas and go outside."

"I want to let children know that we have five more minutes for center time and then we will clean up for snack."

"We will read one more story, and then it will be time to go to your rest mats for naptime."

"Can you put down the shovel or do you need my help?"

"Michael, you will have extra time to paint today. When I tell you painting time is over, I need to hear you say, 'Sure, Ms. Becky! No problem!'"

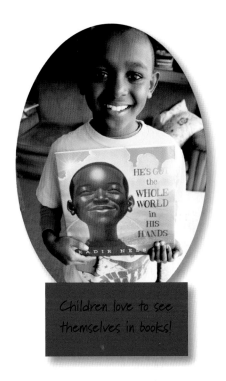

Children love to see themselves in books!

USE BOOKS TO PREPARE CHILDREN FOR DEVELOPMENTAL EXPERIENCES

Children's books have an important role to play in **SET for Life**. Books enrich and expand children's lives, strengthen relationships, and support emerging literacy skills. When young children have many experiences with all kinds of books, they develop a positive attitude toward books, and later, towards reading.

Books can explain developmental changes children are experiencing, along with the developmental experiences they may have at any stage. Common themes in children's books that resonate with young children include:

- posing questions and finding answers.
- the quest for adventure, solutions, or information.
- finding security.
- sharing family experiences.
- understanding interpersonal relationships.
- narrating chronological events.
- explaining developmental experiences.
- exploring emotions and the behaviors that go with them.

Books can also help children deal with and talk about life experiences. A new baby in the house, adoption, a military deployment, same gender parents, separation or divorce, and death of a family member or pet are all examples of topics that can be considered and discussed using children's books.

Characteristics of Good Children's Books

- *interesting and engaging story*
- *familiar subjects*
- *inclusive language*
- *respectful of diversity*
- *free of biases and stereotypes*
- *engaging to the imagination*
- *sensitive to language and cultural values*
- *allow for emotional exploration and reflection*
- *appropriate for the age and stage of audience*

FOR EXAMPLE...

Two-year-old Charlie is expecting a baby brother in a few months. His mother and father have talked a lot about babies and the difference between big boys (who go to sleep in regular beds and eat pasta) and babies (who sleep in cribs and drink from bottles).

Every night, one of his parents reads one of the books that they checked out of the public library about having a baby. One book describes newborns. Another book talks about how it might feel when a new baby comes home. A third talks about a little boy who used to be a baby. Charlie especially likes the one that describes what big brothers can do to help Mommy with the new baby. His mother personalizes this book by using his name as she reads it. The ritual of reading together about the baby helps Charlie anticipate what will happen when the baby is born.

SUMMARY: TEACHING STRATEGIES TO SUPPORT DEVELOPMENT AND LEARNING

Development and learning are closely connected in early childhood. Understanding how children develop can help you offer experiences at the right moments, and extra support when it is needed.

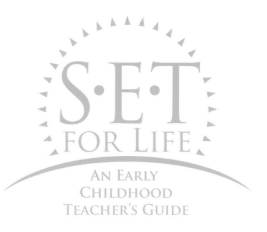

UNDERSTAND AND EMBRACE INDIVIDUAL DIFFERENCES

- When you understand and value differences between individual children, you are better able to meet their needs, and you also serve as a model for tolerance and empathy.

  "Some children need help on the art project. You are able to do the art project without help."

  "You are a different boy (or girl)."

  "Children are all different."

PROVIDE MULTI-SENSORY EXPERIENCES

- Learning experiences with multi-sensory dimensions can ensure that all children, regardless of temperament or learning style, are accommodated.

MATCH TEACHING AND CURRICULUM TO CHILDREN'S DEVELOPMENTAL STAGE

- Understanding typical developmental sequences helps you to offer the right experiences when children are ready for them, not too early or too late.

EXPECT AND ACCOMMODATE REGRESSION

- Regressive behavior is often a sign of developmental growth and reorganization. It can also be a sign of stress or trauma. Observe carefully to figure out the reason for the regression, and ask family members for their input.
- In the meantime, meet the child where he or she is at the moment, with sensitive responses, trusting that as the reorganization completes or the stress resolves, he or she will return to their previous level of development.

  "You will figure out how to listen to your body again. You used to be able to, and you will be able to do it again another day."

  "It's hard when Daddy is deployed. Mommy, Oma, Opa, and I will be here to help while he is away."

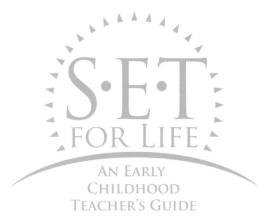

RITUALIZE ROUTINES

- Routines structure children's lives and help them understand what comes next. When children do not feel anxious about what is coming, they are more likely to relax, take risks that lead to learning, and access emerging skills.

  "First, wash hands, then snack."

  "Mommy comes to pick you up after you take a nap."

PREPARE FOR TRANSITIONS AND CHANGE

- Learning to handle transitions is an important life skill. You can help children prepare for transitions by offering plenty of reminders and cues, especially when there is a change in routine.

  "In five minutes, it will be time to pick up and get ready for lunch."

  "Today we have a special visitor, so we will not go to the library. We will go to the library again next weekend. "

MAKE EXPECTATIONS CLEAR

- Telling children in advance of an event how you expect them to respond or behave gives them an opportunity to think about the situation before they are actually in it.

  "We are going outside for 15 minutes. When you hear the bell, you will need to line up to come back inside."

  "When I tell you that art time is over, I need to hear you say, 'Sure! No problem!'"

HELP CHILDREN COMPLY WHEN THEY CAN'T DO IT ALONE

- Sometimes children will need you to stay with them after you remind or prompt them. Allow extra time for protest, and when children do not comply with requests, use a hand-over-hand technique or a gentle touch to get them started.

  "Can you put down the shovel, or do you need my help?"

  "We will read one more story, and then it will be time for naptime."

USE BOOKS TO PREPARE CHILDREN FOR DEVELOPMENTAL CHANGES

- Books can explain developmental changes children are experiencing, as well as discuss events that are common to many children (losing teeth, having a new baby in the family, moving, etc.).

UNDERSTAND LANGUAGE DEVELOPMENT AND COMMUNICATION

Clear communication is a key to building successful relationships. What we say and how we say it shapes all of our relationships, from our deepest friendships to our most casual encounters.

During the early childhood years, children typically go from babbling and communicating with gestures and facial expressions to using grammatically correct sentences and appropriate nonverbal cues. Babies have little understanding of what language means, but in a few short years, they become children who are entering elementary school understanding almost everything they hear. They can use language easily to communicate and get their needs met. As magical as this growth and change seems, language development follows a general developmental principle: It proceeds from the simple to the complex, and from the general to the specific.

For speech and language acquisition, the sequence follows these developmental principles:

- **Motorically simple to motorically complex**; for example, (m) as in *mama* to (kw) as in *queen*. (The earliest sounds children make are usually the ones that require the fewest muscle movements in the mouth.)

- **Acoustically simple to acoustically complex**; for example, (p) as in *pie* to (thr) as in *throw*. (Simple sounds are easier to hear than ones that are more complex or blended.)

- **Visible (simple) to less visible (complex)**; for example, (b) as in *boy* to (r) as in *red*. (It's easier for children to mimic sounds when they can see the movement of the lips of others.)

The sounds children make also develop in a predictable sequence. During the first five years, a child will typically master the following sounds: (m), (b), (j), (n), (w), (d) (p), (h), (v), and (t). Other initial sounds (sounds at the beginning of words) are usually mastered after the fifth year, although, as you have learned, this can occur earlier or later, depending on the child and his or her individual development, experience, and skill level.

The behaviors related to language also follow a fairly predictable developmental pattern. Most children will demonstrate the behaviors described in the chart below, within a few months of the ages given. The chart includes verbal and nonverbal behaviors, because both are important to communication.

Nonverbal Communication: *The parts of communication not related to speech, including body language, gestures, and facial expressions.*

Age	Language Behaviors
0-6 months:	• Responds to familiar voices.
	• Changes cry depending on emotional or physical state (hungry vs. startled).
	• Turns eyes and head toward the source of sound.
	• Is aware of the sounds he makes.
	• Makes soft vowel sounds: uh, ah, etc.
7-10 months:	• Turns head and shoulders toward soft, familiar sounds.
	• Imitates patterns of familiar phrases, using some vowel and consonant patterns (mama, dada, etc.).
	• Practices a variety of sounds and sound combinations.
	• Understands simple phrases, such as, "no," "bye-bye," and his own name.
	• Directs vocalizations toward people and familiar objects.
11-18 months:	• Says first words (dada, mama, "muk" for milk, etc.).
	• Uses several words correctly and consistently.
	• Points or looks to familiar objects when asked to do so.
	• Imitates and jabbers in response to human voice.
	• Frowns when scolded.
	• Imitates sounds he hears (moo, baa baa, vroom, etc.).
	• Expresses physical needs with nonverbal and verbal responses (asking for food or a bottle, pointing to a desired toy).
18-24 months:	• Begins to identify body parts; is able to point to eyes and nose.
	• Uses several meaningful words (may not be articulated correctly, such as "baba" for bottle, "muk" for milk).
	• May use one word to represent several things (*wawa* for, "I want more water," "Look at the water," and "I spilled the water.")
	• Follows simple commands without visual clues ("Pick up the ball!").
	• Enjoys books; likes being read to if book is familiar; will ask to have the same book read again and again.
	• Points to familiar pictures in books or magazines.
	• Develops a sense of "me" and "mine" and says these words.
	• Uses a variety of common words consistently heard in the classroom or at home (usually 10-20 words).
	• Refers to self by name.
	• Puts familiar words together to make simple sentences such as "Daddy work," or "Mommy bye-bye," and, "All gone."
	• Talks mainly about self.
	• Imitates animal or object sounds.
	• Expresses refusal by saying "no."
2-3 years	• Likes listening to music or singing.
	• Sings short songs or says short finger plays.
	• Imitates 3- to 4-word sentences.
	• Reacts to sound by telling what is heard or running to look at the source of the sound.
	• Continues to express refusal by saying "no."
	• Objects to help from others; wants to do it all by himself.

Children's language skills usually develop in a relatively predicatable sequence.

Age	Language Behaviors
3-4 years	• Understands and uses simple verbs.
	• Understands pronouns, prepositions, adverbs, and adjectives (such as "in," "me," "big," "more").
	• Uses plurals ("trucks").
	• Understands contrasts such as yes/no, come/go, run/stop, hot/cold.
	• Uses complete sentences frequently.
	• Answers simple questions from familiar people.
	• Uses "I" and "me."
4-5 years	• Uses sentences that give lots of details.
	• Retells stories; tells stories that stick to the topic.
	• Communicates easily with other adults and children.
	• Begins to notice beginning sounds of words.
	• Uses the same grammar and sentence structure as family members.
	• Reports on past and present experiences.
	• Knows some alphabet letters, particularly those in her own name.
5-6 years	• Has a vocabulary that continues to grow.
	• Corrects most grammatical errors.
	• Uses complex sentences.
	• Creates and tells original stories.
	• Identifies all of the letters in the alphabet (may still confuse a few).
	• Connects letters to the sounds that they make.
	• Begins to sound out words.

From Albrecht, K., & Miller, L.G. (2001). Innovations: Infant and toddler development. Lewisville, NC: Gryphon House. Reprinted with permission. All rights reserved.

As language skills emerge, children's speech becomes easier to understand. Expect about a quarter of the language of 18-24 month old children to be understandable to strangers. This percentage goes up to 60-65% of a three-year-old's language and 75%-90% for four-year-olds. By age five, adults should be able to understand almost everything a child says.

Cultural influence is more visible in language development. The child's language learning style and how they use language is acquired in the context of the family. Some children view language learning as a way to label and identify objects, while others use language as a way to get their needs met and express their feelings. These style differences depend largely on the way adults interact with children in their particular cultural context — another reason why

By elementary school, most children can use language in all kinds of ways.

the observation we stressed in Chapter 3 is so important. Being familiar with a child's family and cultural context will help you support language learning.

Unfortunately, some children will not experience this rapid progress and predictable sequence. If children do not have good language models, or they aren't offered many opportunities to speak and be spoken to, they may have language delays.

Researchers have identified factors that significantly impact language development and learning during the early childhood years. It turns out that the amount of language used by families with their children is important. Families that use more words usually have children with larger vocabularies — a predictor of future academic success. The type of language used is also important. The increase in vocabulary is seen most in families where adults talk to children about complex things (for example, describing what is going on around them and providing explanations, rather than just giving children instructions).

This research highlights the importance of family education about language development. It also means teachers need to know the language acquisition process and notice if it is developing as it should. Although differences in language acquisition are normal, early intervention is important for children who are experiencing language learning delays. For these children, early identification of speech, language, and auditory problems are usually a key to successful intervention.

Receptive Language: *The language children understand, regardless of whether they use it in speech.*

Expressive Language: *The language children use when speaking.*

RECEPTIVE, EXPRESSIVE, AND PRAGMATIC LANGUAGE

Young children have three kinds of language skills. The first is **receptive language**, which refers to the words children understand, regardless of whether they use them when speaking. The second is **expressive language**, meaning the things children can say, the size of the spoken vocabulary, and the way children form sentences. **Pragmatic language** refers to the way children use language in social settings — knowing what to say, when to say it, and how to use language appropriately. As children near the age of three, they have usually developed receptive language skills, and have the expressive language skills required to get many of their needs met.

Pragmatic Language:

Refers to children's ability to use language appropriately with peers and adults; knowing what to say, and how to say it, and making socially appropriate choices about when and how to speak, when to listen, etc...

During the preschool years, children perfect their ability to use language. They learn to use language for different purposes — greeting, promising, instructing, or asking, for example. They also work on learning the rules of communication, such as when to talk and when to listen, or how to read nonverbal cues. One of the hardest pragmatic skills is learning how to change language to fit the situation. Changing the way you ask to be the leader to get others to agree, or asking to play in a way that gets a "yes" answer rather than a "no" are examples of pragmatic language skills at work.

USING SET FOR LIFE LANGUAGE

The **SET for Life** approach comes alive in the classroom in the language teachers use with children. In each chapter, we have provided specific examples of language, and these examples can help you see what **SET for Life** sounds like in action. The way

adults speak to children and to each other has a tremendous impact on the classroom environment. Although classroom size, arrangement, and materials are important, it is the teacher's language that has the greatest influence on how children interact with each other and with their teachers.

The words you choose in your classroom are important. It is the way verbal and emotional messages are communicated that counts. The tone of your voice, your facial expressions, and your body language are all part of the message you send to young children. It is important to make sure that both your words and your nonverbal messages are warm, consistent, and clear.

The vignettes throughout the book are designed to show common situations in classrooms and to help you see how the **SET for Life** approach can be used in real life. In the following vignette notice the emphasis on the teacher's language. As you read the two scenarios, imagine how two-year-old Tommie feels, and think about his teacher's language.

FOR EXAMPLE...

Two-year-old Tommie is sitting in the manipulative area. There are six bins of toys on a low shelf, and one by one, he picks up each bin and dumps its contents on the floor. Soon, all of the bins are empty and the toys are in a jumble on the floor.

His teacher, Sonya, is frustrated. She stands over him with her hands on her hips, and yells, "I've told you a million times that you need to play with one set of manipulatives at a time. Why can't you listen to me? The other children listen. I am very mad at you! I'm going to stand right here until you pick up every single one of the toys." Tommie gets up and runs away from the manipulative center. Sonya follows and grabs him by the arm, dragging him back to the pile of toys.

Tommie starts wailing loudly. Sonya doesn't know what to do next so she sends Tommie to go get a tissue. The toys stay in a pile until lunchtime, when Sonya gets two children who like to pick up toys to help her clean up the area.

Now, let's apply some of the **SET for Life** teaching strategies and language you have learned to this situation. Notice how small changes can turn the same scenario into a teachable moment and a positive interaction.

CHAPTER 9

FOR EXAMPLE...

Two- year-old Tommie has just dumped the contents of six bins of manipulatives into a pile on the floor. His teacher, Sonya, comes over and sits down next to him. Tommie jumps up and runs away. She follows him and gently takes his hand and walks back over to the manipulative area. "You are not in trouble, Tommie. I am interested in the toys you have here on the floor. All of the toys are in a pile. What's your idea?" Tommie shrugs.

Smiling, Sonya says, "I think it was fun to dump all of the containers on the floor." Tommie grins and nods. Sonya asks Tommie, "Which toys are you going to play with now?" Again, he jumps up, heading for another area in the classroom. Sonya follows him again and gently takes him by the hand. She kneels down and says to Tommie, "I think that there were too many toys on the floor for you to choose what to play with. I'll help you put some of them away, so that you can choose." Tommie walks back to the manipulative area, and with Sonya's help, begins picking up some of the toys and putting them in the bins. As he works, he finds his favorite motor bike and a few small cars. Sonya notices his interest, and says, "You like the motorcycle and the cars. I'll help you finish picking up the rest of the toys so you can play with the ones you like."

As they pick up the rest of the toys, they find two more motorcycles and several more cars. Sonya points out that when there aren't so many toys on the floor, it's easier to find the ones you want to play with. She offers to get Tommie a special bin for the motorcycles and cars, so that he can find them next time, without dumping all the toys on the floor. Tommie likes this idea and happily loads up the bin when Sonya brings it to him.

Notice the different feeling between the first vignette and the second. In the first, both Tommie and Sonya ended up upset and frustrated, and neither one learned anything that might help them the next time something similar happened. In the second vignette, Sonya did not get upset and react to Tommie's dumping activity. She recognized that toddlers love to dump things out and that they aren't so good at picking things up. Her careful observation helped her figure out what interested Tommie (cars and motorcycles), and why he was dumping out the toys (he was looking for his favorite toys). She also noticed that he is easily overwhelmed when he can't find what he is looking for. She helped Tommie stay in the manipulative center, scaffolding his limited skill in picking up his own messes by helping him to get started. While she didn't allow the cars and motorcycles to distract him from cleaning up, she did recognize his interest and helped him find a solution that didn't involve dumping out all the toys next time.

You might be thinking, "But it took so much time!" You're right, but Tommie was going to take Sonya's time either way. She could either deal with Tommie's frustration and his emotional outburst; or she could spend her time helping Tommie understand his own motivation, developing a plan to help him get his needs met, and helping him stay under control as the problem was solved.

As you begin to use the **SET for Life** teaching strategies and language, it will get easier to identify a child's motivation and emotional needs, and for him to use the **SET for Life** skills on his own. It takes practice, but it will begin to feel more natural with time. The change starts with language. So, practice using **SET for Life** language and see where it leads you. A table of helpful words and phrases can be found in Appendix G. Feel free to post it in your classroom so that you can refer to it when needed.

TEACHING STRATEGIES TO SUPPORT CHILDREN'S LANGUAGE DEVELOPMENT AND COMMUNICATION

ENGAGE IN CONVERSATION WITH CHILDREN

While you are participating in children's play, engage them in conversation, and listen carefully to what they have to say. The give and take of social communication is relatively new to children in the early childhood stage. They are just learning the social expectations of turn-taking in conversation, waiting for a response before moving on to the next topic, and how to express what they really mean with a fairly limited vocabulary.

Conversations are also a window into children's experiences. As you talk with them, you can discover bits and pieces of information about how they respond to different situations, what is on their minds, and topics of high interest or curiosity. In addition, you can assess their level of success in oral communication. You may also gather data about what children know, what they can do, and how they feel. This kind of information is hard to come by unless you participate with children as they play.

ENCOURAGE EYE CONTACT

Eye contact is an important indicator that children are forming social and emotional connections. When you are talking with or to a child, make and hold eye contact. When children talk to you, help them make eye contact with you. This is particularly important for children who are having development difficulties or have been identified as needing special intervention. Focusing children's attention on looking at you reminds them to be where they are, along with helping you to be sure that you have their attention. Gentle reminders may be in order; for example, "Tatum, let me see your eyes so I know that you hear my words."

> *Taking the time to get the child's full attention before you start talking ensures that they will be ready to actually listen to what you have to say.*

Ask children to look at you when you are talking to them— helping them with physical cues such as pointing to your nose or chin, holding a desired object close to your face as you talk about it, or gently tilting their head or chin in the direction of your face. For some children a tactile cue is helpful, such as a pat on the arm. Wait until eye contact is established—don't continue talking until it is.

When you ask children to look at you, it tells them that what you are saying is important. When you look at children when they talk to you, it tells them that what *they* are saying is important. Reciprocity in eye contact is a hallmark of successful social interactions—learned predominantly by experiencing reciprocal eye contact.

Making and keeping eye contact is particularly important when children need directions, redirection, a change of activity, or a change of behavior. Stopping what they are doing long enough to make eye contact isn't easy for children. When they are busy playing, the cues from others are often missed or ignored. Taking the time to get the child's full attention before you start talking ensures he or she will be ready to actually listen to what you have to say. Teachers need to continue supporting this skill until it is a spontaneous response, one that the child uses without physical or verbal prompting.

Eye contact is a key part of communication.

FOR EXAMPLE...

Dominic is excited upon his arrival and Kay kneels at the door and says "Hello Dominic. It is good to see you." Dominic pushes on the door. Kay says to Dominic, "Take a look. I'm right here." Then she gently touches his face on both sides and says, "Right here, Dominic."

He turns his face to her, but doesn't make eye contact. She points to her eyes and says, "My eyes are right here. Take a look." He does and says, "Hi, Kay."

SET for Life Language

"Let me see your eyes."

"I'm right here." (pointing to chin or nose)

"Take a look."

"Look at my eyes!"

"You are not in trouble. I have something important to tell you."

"When I see your eyes, I'll know you are ready to listen."

USE LANGUAGE STIMULATION TECHNIQUES

The way that you talk to children can go a long way in helping them develop important language skills. The field of speech and language pathology offers several indirect language stimulation techniques that you can use to help children. What follows is a brief description of several of these important techniques and suggestions for ways you can incorporate them into your classroom dialogue.

DESCRIPTION

Description involves narrating or describing what is going on in the child's world by putting word labels on things. In short, your job is to explain to a child what he or she is seeing. For example, if a child looks toward the door as a parent enters the room, you might say, "That's Jenny's mother. She must be here to pick up Jenny." Or, when it is almost time for a transition, you might say, "In five minutes, it will be time to wash hands so we can eat lunch," describing what will happen and when. This strategy is especially useful for helping children under three develop a working vocabulary.

Here are some examples of description:

"That squirrel just dashed up the tree!"

"Lydia's grandmother is here. She is going to read us a story today."

"After lunch, it will be time to put your shoes in your cubbies and lay down for nap."

"In five minutes, it will be time to go outside."

PARALLEL TALK

Parallel talk uses short phrases that focus on what a child is doing at that moment. These phrases usually begin with *you* –

Describing what you see helps children add vocabulary and improve their communication skills.

for example, "You are playing with the cars and the trucks." Focusing on the action helps the child put word labels on what they are doing. Even more importantly, it connects the word labels into a complete sentence describing the action. Using this technique as you observe children at play also shows that you are interested and involved as you watch.

Here are some examples of parallel talk:

"You are carrying a lot of stuffed animals!"

"You picked the pirate's outfit today."

"You are digging in the sand."

SELF TALK

Self talk focuses on the teacher's actions, labeling and describing what you are doing. Use self talk by starting your sentences with *I*. For example, you might say to a child who is getting tired, "I am turning off the lights so you can rest." Self talk is particularly helpful in preparing children for transitions. When you announce transitions with self talk, you help children get ready for them ahead of time, which can make changing activities easier. Use self talk by saying things like, "In ten more minutes, I will put the mats down for naptime." Self talk helps children understand what you are doing and more importantly, why.

Here are some examples of self talk:

"I am cleaning up the table because it is almost time for snack."

"I am warming up your bottle because I think your tummy is hungry."

"I am putting all your artwork in your cubby, so it will be ready when Mommy gets here."

Description
Explains or describes what is happening in child's world, what they might be seeing. "That is Jose's grandmother. He is picking Jose up today."

Parallel Talk
Describes child's actions. "You are using the red paint, Biruk."

Self Talk
Talks about teacher's actions. "I am wiping the tables so we can get ready for snack."

Expansion
Restates what the child has said. Lamar says, "Milk!" Teacher says, "You'd like more milk, Lamar."

EXPANSION

Expansion is a technique to use as children's language skills grow. It takes what the child says and expands on it, sometimes adding to what the child says. For example, when a toddler says, "cracker," you might say, "You want another graham cracker," or, "Jason would like another saltine cracker, please," expanding what Jason says into a complete, grammatically correct sentence. When a child in your class says, "Time to go bye-bye," you might say, "It's time to get your things and go home now," restating what the child says in a complete and expanded sentence.

Here are some examples of expansion:

When Claire says, "Milk," the teacher responds, "You want milk."

Logan says, "Go bye-bye," the teacher replies, "You are ready to go home now."

Sophie screams, "NO, MAGGIE!!" The teacher says, "I think you mean, 'No, Maggie, don't touch my snack.'"

Notice that these previous techniques (description, parallel talk, self talk, and expansion) require nothing of the child. When we use these techniques, we don't ask children to repeat what we have said, or respond in any other way. Instead, these techniques allow us to add to the child's language skills and encourage their language development. They are also very useful when you are observing children as they play, as you try to identify the emotional meaning of children's behavior, and as you talk with children during SET Time.

HELP CHILDREN BUILD VOCABULARY

Children's expressive vocabulary grows to over 10,000 words by the end of the early childhood period. This growth is important because vocabulary size can often predict how successful a child will be in school later on. Here are some strategies for building vocabulary in your classroom:

- *Provide word labels for things in the environment.* Increase the sophistication of the labels as children age. For example, when you are on a walk, start by pointing out birds, clouds, trees, and other features of the environment. Then, add more detailed information: "That's a blue bird; that one is called a mockingbird. That one's a crow."

- *Use pictures to enhance and expand vocabulary.* Continuing with the bird example, post pictures of different species of birds along with their written names so that you can point out and use these new vocabulary words. Exposing children to words is a great literacy activity, whether they use them expressively or not.

- *Play word games with children.* Children love to play with language. Encourage and expand on this interest by enjoying word games, too. Change the initial letter of a child's name (Baitlin instead of Caitlin). Or, use sequential initial sounds ("Aitlin, Baitlin, Caitlin") to explore initial sounds.

- *Chant, repeat rhymes and finger plays, and sing songs.* All of these activities help to grow vocabulary.

- *Add vocabulary words to your curriculum plan.* Focus your attention on new words and share the words you have identified for vocabulary development with family members.

READ NONVERBAL CUES AND CAREFULLY INTERPRET VERBAL CUES

Learning to read and interpret nonverbal and verbal cues accurately is an important teaching skill. Interpreting a baby's cries the right way, by responding with a warmed bottle or a snack when a baby is hungry, or providing a cuddle for a child who is startled or hurt, allows children to perfect communication skills. Prompt response to distress also helps children develop a sense of trust that their needs will be met.

Paying attention to non-verbal cues will help you meet children's needs.

Until children develop more expressive language, reading non-verbal cues is important. Once children develop receptive language skills (meaning they understand what is being said to them, even if they don't verbally respond), you can ask them to show or take you to what they want, if you aren't sure what they are trying to tell you. Family members can be a valuable resource in understanding an individual child's cues, too, so don't forget to ask them if you are having trouble figuring out a child's needs or desires.

FOR EXAMPLE...

Three-year-old Christopher continually puts his cup on his head midway through lunch. He doesn't say anything; he just puts his empty cup on his head. Mrs. Bart was concerned it may lead to others doing the same. She asks Christopher what it means when he put his cup on his head. Christopher responds, "More water." Mrs. Bart tells Christopher that he can use her name and ask for more water when he needs it.

During pick-up time, Mrs. Bart asks Christopher's mother about his putting his cup on his head. His mother tells Mrs. Bart that, in his previous school, he had been instructed to do this. There were many more children in that class, and his teacher had asked children to put their cup on their head if they wanted more water, since she could not tell one child's voice from another when they were all clamoring for her attention. Before lunch the next day, Mrs. Bart talks with Christopher again, telling him she understands why he was putting his cup on his head, and reinforcing that at this school, he can just use words.

SET for Life Language

"Show me what snack you'd like."

"I don't understand – can you show me?"

"That really scared you! I will hold you until you feel better."

"You look sleepy. I think you are ready for a nap."

TALK ABOUT WHAT WILL HAPPEN NEXT

As each transition in the classroom approaches talk about what has already happened and what will come next. Focus on what is important to the child, whether it is Mommy coming back or being first in line. Then, as the transition unfolds, continue to talk about what will happen next: "First you will clean up the blocks, and then you will wash your hands. After you wash hands, you will have a snack, and then we will go outside." This kind of language helps children understand the sequence of upcoming events and prepare themselves for transitions.

FOR EXAMPLE...

Eliza, a four-year-old pre-kindergartner, is adjusting to a new schedule after her parents' separation a month ago. Eliza continually asks her teacher, "Who's picking me up?" as she attempts to figure out where she will be going after school. After finding out more about the new custody arrangement from Eliza's parents, Mrs. Schwartz begins a routine of telling Eliza at the beginning and the end of the day who will pick her up and when she will see her parents.

She also put a calendar in Eliza's cubby with a picture on each day of which family member she will be staying with for the evening. As Eliza enters the room, Mrs. Schwartz says to her, "Good morning, Eliza. Today is Wednesday, Daddy drops you off at school and Aunt Suzie picks you up. You will see Daddy before dinner when he picks you up at Aunt Suzie's."

Jennifer, a preschool teacher, reflects with three-year-old Eli, about an event that occurred the previous day. "Eli, yesterday you had a very hard time leaving your block construction. Today, I will give you two extra reminders about when activity time will end. When it's time put blocks away, I will help you take a picture of your construction so you can remember what you created, and maybe it won't be so hard to stop."

> ## SET for Life Language
>
> *"Now we are having lunch. We will go outside to the playground next."*
>
> *"First we are going to play, then we will do work."*
>
> *"After you finish your art project, you will have time to read in the cozy corner."*
>
> *"Today is different. First we have story, and then snack, because the firefighters are coming to show us their truck. We usually have snack first."*
>
> *"After playground time, children will go home early today. Teachers have meetings and there is no school this afternoon."*
>
> *"In five (then three, then one) more minutes, it will be time to stop playing. (Or go outside, say goodbye, listen to a story, clean up and go home, etc.)"*

TEACH CHILDREN HOW TO USE LANGUAGE TO GET THEIR NEEDS MET

Children have a hard time finding just the right words or phrases to get their needs met. Using any words can help, but using the right words is much more effective. When children don't have the right words, provide them. When you find two children pulling on opposite ends of a toy, you can say, "Julie, you can tell Leslie, 'Hand me that toy, please.'" To a frustrated child, you might say, "Jackie, instead of throwing the pencil and calling it stupid, you can ask a teacher for help."

Often early childhood teachers are heard saying "Use your words." This is not a bad phrase, but it doesn't provide a solution when children don't know the words to use or can't access them as quickly as they are needed. So, rather than saying, "Use your words," to an angry child who is yelling at his friend, model a better choice to help them resolve their conflict: "Ian, you are really angry at Rebecca. You can tell her in a different way, and I think she will be able to hear your words." When children use inappropriate words (e.g., "you stupid idiot"), tell the child, "Those words are too hard to hear. Try these words instead."

HELP CHILDREN USE LANGUAGE TO DEAL DIRECTLY WITH EACH OTHER

There are many times when children turn to their teachers to help them solve problems. Sometimes, they don't need your intervention, just your support to help them deal with the issue at hand. When children turn to you for help, refer the child back to the situation and become an ally with them to solve the problem. If they can't work it out, you'll be close by to help them or to intervene if necessary. For example, when a child comes to you because a friend has taken a toy from her, ask her, "What do you want to do about that?" If she doesn't have any ideas, you might say, "Tell him that's your toy." Then, use your language to support expectations for behavior: "Johnny, Sara has something to tell you. Take a look. This is important to her. Please listen."

While children want to please their caregivers and look to you for approval, peer relationships become more important as they get older. A message from a friend will have much more of an impact than you saying the same thing. For example, when Wyatt hits Braden, it will be much more powerful if Braden can say, "Don't hit me!" for himself. Stay close by to provide support if necessary. Once children are accustomed to speaking for themselves, allow them to work it out as best they can, before stepping in. With your support and encouragement, over time, children will learn to speak up for themselves and resolve conflicts without prompting or help.

> ### SET for Life Language
>
> "Tell her, 'Leave me alone!'"
>
> "Her name is Ellen. You can call her by her name."
>
> "You can tell him 'No.'"
>
> "You can tell her you want the toy."
>
> "I'll help you talk to him."
>
> "You can ask for a grown-up's help."

FOR EXAMPLE...

There is one pair of wings in the dress-up area and three children want them. They are tugging at the wings and yelling at each other. Mrs. Gonzales intervenes, saying, "It looks like you all want the wings. Let's see if you can all get what you want." Then she takes the wings and says, "I will hold on to these while the three of you decide what to do."

Each child says, "I want to go first!" Mrs. Gonzales says, "Not everyone can go first. What other ideas do you have?" Jelisa says, "I don't want to play." Mrs. Gonzales says, "Hold on, Jelisa. You wanted to play with the wings and I can help you get a turn to play. Wings are for all of the children."

Audrey offers, "First me, then you, then you." Mrs. Gonzales asks the other girls what they think of Audrey's idea. "I want to go first," says Sara, "but I'll go second." "So," the teacher says, "Audrey will go first and Sara will go second." Turning to Jelisa, she says, "What about you Jelisa?" "I'll go second, too," says Jelisa.

Mrs. Gonzales restates the solution for the three children (without correcting the numerical order—just reporting the children's solution): "Audrey will go first, Sara will go second, and then Jelisa will go second. Is that right?" The children nod. The teacher hands the wings to Audrey. "Remember, Sara is next, and after her, give the wings to Jelisa. You found a solution!" Then she turns to Sara and Jelisa and says, "I can help you find something to do until it is your turn with the wings."

SET for Life Language

"Ask him. He might say yes or he might say no."

"Let's make a plan for all of the children to get a turn."

"These toys are for everyone to play with. You can work it out together."

"Tell Josh what you would like him to do."

"Addie, Janice has something to tell you. Please listen to her important words."

"You can solve this problem. I will help you if you need me."

LIMIT UNRELATED CONVERSATIONS AND EXTENDED NEGOTIATION
Capable, verbal children sometimes use their language skills to keep teacher attention focused on them. Anxious children, who won't talk in groups or in structured play situations, may compensate by dominating conversation during unstructured

times. These children need help to understand that the strategy they are using doesn't remove their worries, even if it provides them with temporary relief. Help them find appropriate places and times to talk without dominating conversations or negotiating endlessly.

Learning when and how to express themselves is an especially important skill for children on the autism spectrum. These children sometimes miss cues telling them if anyone else is interested in what has captured their attention. Help these children notice environmental clues, focus on the relevant features of conversation, and keep discussions on topic.

FOR EXAMPLE...

Ross is fascinated by clouds. He talks about the different kinds of clouds continuously. Other children, who are not so interested, begin to avoid him. When Ross gets stuck on the subject of clouds, his teacher, Mr. Thomas, redirects him by gently affirming his interest, and then helping him to find an appropriate way to play. He says, "Ross, you really like clouds and you know a lot about them. During recess we can look at the clouds together and you can tell me about them. Right now I will help you find a friend to play with. Who would you like to play with?" Mr. Thomas then walks Ross over to the blocks, where Jeremiah is playing. After a few moments, Ross begins to talk about clouds again. Mr. Thomas reminds him of the plan to talk about clouds outdoors and then offers a visual cue. He says, "Put your cloud talk in this box so you can hold onto it until later."

Miranda talks all the time. She is especially insistent on telling her teacher, Ms. Ledoux, what to do while she is trying to talk with the other children about snack. Ms. Ledoux says, "Miranda, I hear that you have lots of ideas, and right now I am talking with children about snack. I need you to listen to my words."

"Maybe you are worried I am going to forget something. You would like to be in charge of reminding me. It is not your worry and I will take care of snack." In this way, Ms. Ledoux acknowledges Miranda, helps her hold her ideas until a more appropriate time, and also names Miranda's worry.

SET for Life Language

"I'll talk to you about a snack when all of the toys are put away."

"I'll talk to you about more snacks after story."

"I'm going to stop you; we are talking about clean up, not toys."

"I will let you know when you can go outside." (Or get your shoes on, take out the paints, and etc.).

"I would like to hear your important words later. Now, we are talking about counting."

"Right now, I'm talking about naptime."

ASSESS CHILDREN'S LANGUAGE DEVELOPMENT

Because of how important early language acquisition and vocabulary are to future success, teachers need to know where children are in their language development. The best way to ensure that language is developing normally is to complete a normative language assessment on a regular basis for each child in the program. Ideally, these assessments should be completed quarterly for children under the age of three, and at least twice a year after that. The assessment should include checking for developmental milestones, as well as monitoring the growth of receptive language (understood words) and expressive language (what words children say).

Using a normative language assessment can help you identify children who may be struggling, and might benefit from additional intervention. Your observations are even more important for children new to your program, especially if you don't know much about their prior experiences. You can find a language checklist on p. 209-210.

If a child's language behaviors fall six months behind his or her chronological age, don't wait. Schedule a family conference and suggest that the family consult with their pediatrician, a speech and language pathologist, or an audiologist for an evaluation.

Know where children are in their language development.

BE AWARE OF FAMILY CULTURE AND HOME LANGUAGE

Culture is an important part of our lives, but it is often invisible and internal. The best way to learn about a family's particular cultural expectations is to ask them directly. It's important to know things like nonverbal expectations (eye contact, deference to adults, what information is considered private, what is considered public, when, where, and how much talking is appropriate, the right ways to physically approach other family members, etc.).

Teachers also need to be aware of their own culture and how it might interact or possibly conflict with the cultural expectations of families. When cultural differences are accepted as variations, instead of seen as problematic or wrong, biases and stereotyping may be avoided.

FOR EXAMPLE...

Ms. Whitaker is welcoming the Buck Elk family into the classroom on their first day. She tries to make small talk, but Mrs. Buck Elk doesn't seem to want to chat and is hesitant to disclose much information about their family or her daughter Dakota's previous experiences with school. When she asks Mrs. Buck Elk how many other children she has, Mrs. Buck Elk replies, "Oh, I have a few."

Puzzled by this interaction, and wondering if she had done something to offend Mrs. Buck Elk, Ms. Whitaker asks Mrs. Many Horses, a Lakota coworker, for her thoughts. Mrs. Many Horses explains that culturally, Lakota people often spend less time in small talk and family matters are considered private. Ms. Whitaker realizes she will need to spend more time building her relationship with Dakota and her family before she can expect a willingness to share further.

SUPPORT SECOND LANGUAGE ACQUISITION

Growing up in families where more than one language is spoken is becoming more and more common. One in five families speaks a language other than English at home and almost 20% of children in the U.S. are learning two languages at once.

Are there any benefits to being bi- or even trilingual? The answer to this question is yes. There are real advantages for children who learn two or more languages at once during early childhood. Research shows that children who learn to speak two or more languages have improved overall school performance and are successful students at all levels of their education. They have better problem-solving skills and score higher on standardized tests. The advantages carry into adulthood, opening additional career opportunities in an increasingly global economy.

Can children learn two languages at once? Of course they can. And, more importantly, some linguists think that the earlier we are exposed to a second language, the easier it is for us to learn it.

Learning a second language happens in stages, much like learning in other areas. However, as you can see in the chart that follows, the process is a fairly complex one. Although some children may move through these stages more quickly than others, second language learning takes time. These children will need extra support from you as learning a new language can be both frustrating and tiring.

Stages of Second Language Learning

Stage 1: **Continued home language use**—Initially, children will use the language spoken at home in the school setting, even if no one else at school is speaking that language. During this stage, teachers should try to use the needs-meeting words they have learned from families (e.g. hello, goodbye, eat, more, potty, etc.).

Stage 2: **Nonverbal period**— Soon, children stop speaking either language for a while, as they listen and interact with children and adults in the second language. Accept this silence, and continue using description, self-talk, and parallel talk with the child. Simplify the language you use when you are giving instructions during this time, and slow down your pace of speech.

Stage 3: **Early language production**—Next, some second language speaking begins—usually words in isolation or simple phrases. Use pictures and objects, labeling them in both languages, to help children build their vocabulary.

Stage 4: **Speech emergence**—As children learn vocabulary and the structure of the new language, they will begin talking more with classmates and peers who speak that language. They will also begin to understand more of what others are saying. Support children in talking to each other and interpret/translate when needed.

Stage 5: **Fluency**—Soon children are speaking the second language fairly fluently, occasioning switching between the two known languages (called code-switching). This skill indicates a fairly high level of fluency in both languages. This is a great time to create opportunities for children to teach each other.

Stage 6: **Advanced language proficiency** emerges after plenty of language exposure (both oral and written), and lots of opportunities within relationships to talk and write. Find places in the classroom for the child's home language to be used specifically, by, for example, providing a basket of books in that language in the library area.

Adapted from Nemeth, K. (2012). Basics of supporting dual language learners: An introduction for educators of children from birth through age 8. Washington, DC: National Association for the Education of Young Children. Reprinted with permission. All rights reserved.

There are many misconceptions about dual language learning. While many people believe that mere exposure is enough to help children learn a foreign language (watching television shows that include Spanish vocabulary, for example), the truth is that watching is not enough.

On the other side of the argument, some educators and families worry that learning two languages at once will confuse children. This is not the case. In addition, there is no evidence that learning two languages at once results in language delays. In fact, the benefits of learning second (or third!) languages in childhood can last a lifetime.

What can you do to help children learn two languages? First of all, communicate with families. Learn about the child's home language experiences and ask about the family's expectations as their child learns a second language. If children are learning two languages at once, particularly during the early childhood years, working together with families will help you ensure that children have the best possible experiences in both languages. Asking families to teach you some important words in their home language, ones than can help their child get his or her needs met (especially vocabulary related to eating, toileting, sleep, and pain), can be helpful within the context of your classroom. It will also strengthen your relationship with the family.

In your classroom, use pictures, objects, and real events to link the language the child knows to the language the child is learning. These teaching strategies are not only helpful to the child who is learning a new language — they also enrich the vocabulary of other children in the classroom, and help them develop curiosity about other languages. Here are some ways you can incorporate children's home language into your classroom environment:

- Have families label photographs in the home language, and share how to pronounce the words phonetically.
- Provide books in the child's first language and second language.
- Ask families to translate songs, rhymes, and finger plays, and share them so everyone can learn.
- Have families make audio recordings children can listen to in the listening center.
- Listen to audio books in children's second languages.
- Add first-word dictionaries in multiple languages to your library.
- Learn needs-meeting words, written phonetically, so you can use them with the child in the classroom.

SUMMARY: TEACHING STRATEGIES TO SUPPORT CHILDREN'S LANGUAGE DEVELOPMENT AND COMMUNICATION

Clear communication is a key to building successful relationships. The way you use language in your classroom sets the tone for all your interactions with children. Teaching children to use language successfully can help them succeed in all aspects of their lives.

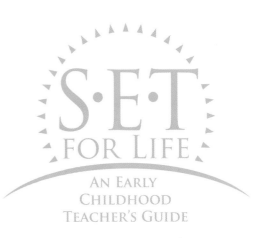

Exposure to language via digital media is not enough to build second language skills.

ENGAGE IN CONVERSATION WITH CHILDREN

- Talking with children helps you assess how their language skills are progressing, as well as gain insight into their experiences, interests, and skills.

ENCOURAGE EYE CONTACT

- Eye contact is an important indicator that children are forming emotional and social connections. Ask children to look at you when you are talking to them, and make eye contact with them when they talk to you, so they know you are listening.

  "Let me see your eyes."

  "When I see your eyes, I'll know you are ready to listen."

USE LANGUAGE STIMULATION TECHNIQUES

- The following language stimulation techniques can help children develop the language skills they need to be successful. Note that they require nothing of the child.
  - **Description**

    "There is a bird building a nest in that tree!"

    "That is Michael's stepmother. She brought him to school today."
  - **Parallel Talk**

    "You are wearing a green shirt and blue pants today."

    "You have all the cars lined up in a row."

S·E·T FOR LIFE
AN EARLY CHILDHOOD TEACHER'S GUIDE

- **Self Talk**
  "I am washing my hands so I can fix snack for all the children."
  "I am wearing my rubber boots because it is raining today."
- **Expansion**
  When a child says, "Up!", you respond with, "You want me to pick you up!"

HELP CHILDREN BUILD VOCABULARY

- Incorporate new vocabulary into your curriculum and classroom, providing both spoken and written labels for the things that children see.

READ NONVERBAL CUES AND CAREFULLY INTERPRET VERBAL CUES

- Learning to read and interpret nonverbal and verbal cues accurately is an important teaching skill that supports children's development.
  "I don't understand. Can you show me?"
  "That really scared you! I can hold you until you feel better."
  "You look sleepy. I think you will feel better after naptime."

TALK ABOUT WHAT WILL HAPPEN NEXT

- As transitions approach, talk about what has already happened and what will come next. This kind of language helps children prepare for transitions.
  "Now we are having snack. Next we will go outside, and then your mommy will be here to pick you up."
  "After you finish picking up the blocks, you can choose a book to read."

TEACH CHILDREN HOW TO USE LANGUAGE TO GET NEEDS MET

- Children sometimes have a hard time finding just the right words or phrases to get their needs met. Provide the words for them, when they aren't able to say what they mean.

    "I think Julie will be able to hear your words when you use a friendly voice."

    "Those words are too hard to hear. Try these words instead."

    "I can help you talk to him."

HELP CHILDREN TO USE LANGUAGE TO DEAL DIRECTLY WITH EACH OTHER

- Sometimes, children don't need your intervention to solve a problem — they just need your support. Ally with them to solve problems. Messages from a peer are often much stronger than messages delivered by a teacher.

    "You can tell him, 'Don't hit me!'"

    "Lucy, Andrew has something to tell you. Please listen to his important words."

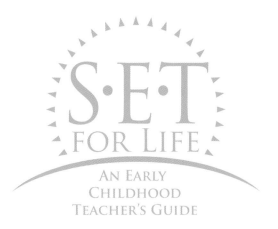

LIMIT UNRELATED CONVERSATIONS AND EXTENDED NEGOTIATION

- Some children will use language to demand your attention or to relieve anxiety. Help them to find appropriate times and places to talk.

    "I'll talk to you about snack when toys are put away."

    "I would like to hear your important words, and right now we are talking about counting."

ASSESS CHILDREN'S LANGUAGE DEVELOPMENT

- Teachers need to know where children are in their language development, confirming that it is progressing as expected. You can use the Language Behaviors Checklist on p. 209, or other checklists obtained from pediatricians, child development specialists, or speech and language professionals.
- If a child's language falls more than six months behind his or her chronological age, consult with his or her family, and seek further assessment and/or intervention.

BE AWARE OF FAMILY CULTURE AND HOME LANGUAGE

- Be aware of the home culture of the families you serve and consider your own culture, as well.
- Recognize, validate, and accommodate cultural differences in your classroom.

SUPPORT SECOND LANGUAGE ACQUISITION

- The benefits of learning two or more languages during childhood can last a lifetime.
- Support children by being aware of the stages of second language acquisition (see chart on p. 231) by learning needs-meeting words in their first language and incorporating the home language into your classroom.

CREATE A CLASSROOM WITH A SUPPORTIVE ENVIRONMENT

S·E·T
FOR LIFE

AN EARLY
CHILDHOOD
TEACHER'S GUIDE

The classroom often becomes a home away from home for children – they can spend much of their day in this environment. The way it is arranged and equipped will predict how well it functions as both an educational environment and a place to experience relationships.

HOW THE ENVIRONMENT CONTRIBUTES TO SOCIAL-EMOTIONAL DEVELOPMENT

The teachers in the world-famous early childhood settings of Reggio Emilia in northern Italy tell us that the environment is the third teacher — it can amplify the ability of the teachers to support children's experiences. In the **SET for Life** approach, the environment, particularly the emotional environment of the classroom, sets the tone for everything else we want to happen with young children. Without a positive, warm, and supportive emotional environment, children are less likely to be able to succeed in learning the academic skills we are trying to teach them.

The **SET for Life** classroom aims to create an atmosphere where children feel safe and secure. The most important component of the emotional environment is your warm regard toward all children. Viewing children as competent, capable, and able to learn is the right mindset. Each child in your classroom needs to feel welcomed, wanted, and recognized by you as a special individual.

No matter what, welcome each child with a smile and a warm greeting. Start each day with a clean slate, leaving yesterday's experiences (positive and negative) behind. Make sure a plan for meaningful and appropriate activities is complete, and that family members are welcome partners in the educational process. On this firm foundation, **SET for Life** teaching strategies add tools and techniques to your skill set, helping you support children's continued social and emotional growth and development.

> *"Learn to use ten minutes intelligently. It will pay you huge dividends."*
>
> WILLIAM A. IRWIN, PROFESSOR

MASLOW'S HIERARCHY OF NEEDS

Another theorist, Abraham Maslow, helps us understand the importance of the environment in supporting emotional and social growth. He was a psychologist who believed, among other things, that human beings naturally strive to achieve their fullest potential. He is best known for his conceptualization of a hierarchy of needs. These needs span across a person's lifetime, but here, we will focus on the needs that pertain most to children. His theory proposes that basic needs are arranged in a hierarchical order. The lowest level of needs must be met before higher order needs can be addressed, and before a person can achieve his or her full potential.

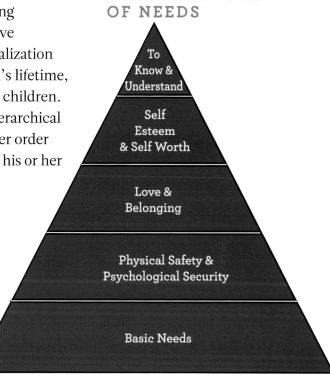

MASLOW'S HIERARCHY OF NEEDS

The first level of needs is related to basic physical survival and well-being. Food, water, clothing, shelter, hygiene, and health care are examples of basic needs of this level.

The second level of needs relates to physical safety and and psychological security. This includes safety from physical dangers, and the meeting of psychological needs, such as the need for warm, loving touch and responsive nurturing from caregivers.

The need for love and belonging form the third level of the hierarchy. Emotional support from a limited number of consistent, responsive adults, and healthy interactions with other children are both required to meet this need. This is a reciprocal need – children need to both give and receive love and acceptance to achieve this level of development.

The fourth level of the needs hierarchy is the need for self-esteem and self-worth. It's easy to see why the need for love and belonging would need to be present before this fourth level can be addressed. When children have the emotional support they need, they feel good about themselves and valued for their unique abilities.

Finally, the need to know and understand is the fifth level of Maslow's Hierarchy of Needs. This is the level that allows learning to take place! Human beings cannot get to this level until needs have been met at all of the other levels. This is yet another reason teachers must be deeply invested in the emotional and physical well-being of the children in their care.

This theory also illustrates why the classroom furniture, arrangement, toys and materials, as well as the attention and responses of thoughtful teachers, are so important. Careful attention to these details can create a sense of security and trust for children. Each time children experience a new environment, their first concern is about safety and security. According to Maslow, when children feel safe and secure, they are more likely to move into the next stage of the hierarchy.

It is important to realize that all people move up and down this pyramid in response to events in their lives. It is not unusual for children to regress if lower level needs are threatened. For example, if a child is suddenly threatened physically by disease, his need level will revert from the third level (the need for love) to the first level (the need for physical safety), until that need for survival and well-being is once again satisfied. Sensitive teachers can support children experiencing these regressions, knowing that once their lower level needs are met, children will once again begin operating at a higher level. A child experiencing physical or emotional stress needs extra nurturing and compassion (and perhaps a modified curriculum), until their more primary needs are met.

When children experience stressors like serious illness, they may experience regression until their need for physical saftey and security is met.

THE FUNDAMENTALS OF CLASSROOM ENVIRONMENT

SET for Life classrooms may look very similar to typical early childhood classrooms, but there are some important differences. These differences change your focus from simply managing children's learning and behavior, to supporting their developing skills, both emotional and academic. This focus will help you build relationships with individual children—the relationships that serve as the foundation of the **SET for Life** approach. Varied and interesting learning centers or activity areas are the primary strategy for building a **SET for Life** classroom. Each of the following components provides different opportunities for play and learning, and as many as possible should be incorporated into your classroom.

Art Area: Art activities for young children are opportunities for open-ended exploration, personal expression, and fun. In this activity area, children use a variety of art materials such as paper, crayons, play dough, paste or glue, magazines for cutting, collage items, and watercolor and tempera paints in trays with brushes. An easel, complete with paint cups and a good paper supply, should always be available in this area. Add a full-length mirror to the wall nearby so that children can watch what they are doing in the art center, as well as check out one of their favorite subjects — themselves!

Art activities for young children are opportunities for open-ended exploration, personal expression, and fun.

For younger children, stock art areas with a limited variety of supplies. Teachers should take time to introduce children to new materials and show them how to use them appropriately. As children grow, art areas can be more completely stocked, so older preschoolers can use their own ideas and imagination to combine art media and techniques.

Art is a messy activity. Arrange the art area near the sink on a surface that can be easily cleaned. If you don't have a sink nearby, provide towels and spray bottles for clean-up. The art area may also be may be a combination of areas. An easel in a well-lit location, a work table or two for children to complete their creations, and shelves to store materials are the usual components. Place a closed storage unit nearby to keep extra supplies and store recycled materials.

Sensory Area: Sensory experiences heighten children's awareness of the world around them by stimulating the senses. Sensory awareness becomes more complex, coordinated, and organized during the preschool years, as children have many experiences with touching, tasting, smelling, and listening. In the **SET for Life** classroom, soothing sensory experiences like sand and water are a mainstay. Provide a sensory table in the classroom that can be used with a variety of sensory materials.

Sensory experiences offer children opportunities to practice a wide variety of skills, from fine motor skills to hygiene. They also serve as a much needed break from the intensity of a busy classroom.

Children learn important health and safety skills in this area, as they practice washing their hands before they go to the sensory table and help teachers clean and sanitize tables, bins, and materials after use. Other skills are supported, as well. As children learn to coordinate small muscles of the hand and arm with small muscles of the eye, they perfect fine motor skills. Attention to detail, such as noticing what sensory materials smell like, how they feel, or the sounds materials make when manipulated, increase children's ability to receive and process information from the physical world, enhancing readiness for literacy, reading, and mathematical understanding. This area also provides opportunities to practice noticing and responding to emotional and social cues from friends and teachers.

Over-stimulation is an issue to consider in planning and placing the sensory activity area. The materials are stimulating enough that few additional cues from the environment are needed. In particular, keep the wall space and area around the sensory center uncluttered and undecorated.

Finally, the sensory center is an ideal place to put a bottle of hand lotion — the perfect sensory experience for one. When children need help to regain self-control, taking a quiet moment to rub lotion on their hands may help.

Store sensory materials in closed containers, near the area where they are to be used. Use small, non-skid mats to catch spills, and keep a supply of towels on hand to keep the area dry. Appropriate clean-up equipment is important — be sure to include handheld brooms, dustpans, sponges, and paper towels. Clean-up should be a shared job that children practice doing together.

Educators have different views of what materials are appropriate for use at sensory tables. Some suggest that only non-food items should be used, while others find that some food items (dried beans, pasta, and rice, for example) are an inexpensive source of sensory experiences. When deciding what to use as sensory materials, consider the families you serve, available resources, children's experiences, and the expectations and experiences of the community and cultures you work with.

Dramatic Play Area: In this area, children develop communication skills, learn to be leaders and followers, practice cooperation skills, and play out the roles that interest them from their social community. This area encourages play that emerges from children's lives, homes, and cultural context. It is one of the most spontaneous and natural play settings in the classroom, where children are free to play, feel, and act on their ideas and interests. Children need dramatic play spaces and props that allow them to express the complete range of emotions they feel — not just the positive ones. They need practice to learn acceptable ways of acting out anger, fear, hostility, eagerness, as well as empathy, altruism, curiosity, and so on. This is the place where they practice the roles they see adults performing in the real world. They also begin to separate what is real from what isn't, and start to understand when and how to switch from fantasy to reality.

Plan interesting and changing dramatic play centers. Play along with children, facilitating and enhancing their experiences. And, spend lots of time observing children as they play, watching for emerging interests, new abilities being practiced, and for ideas about what play themes can be expanded or supported.

Dramatic play lets children explore all kinds of possibilities!

Science/Discovery Area: Young children are curious about the world in which they live. They want to find out what is in it and how things work. They enjoy exploring new things in the environment. Include quality science experiences and opportunities for children to observe and manipulate materials. If possible, provide a class pet (such as a fish, gerbil, mouse, or rabbit) that is approved by appropriate regulatory agencies. This is an area that should change throughout the year.

A class pet can be a great addition to your science area.

You should also plan a way for children to add their discoveries to this area. Some ways you might do this is by providing a bug box for holding interesting insects, and magnifying glasses and a children's microscope to provide different views of objects.

Literacy/Writing Area: In this area, children have opportunities to practice and experiment with reading and writing activities. The physical arrangement of this area should include two separate components. The first is a library area, where a good variety of children's books and written resources are displayed in attractive and inviting ways. A book rack that displays books with the covers facing out is typically the foundation of the children's library, and can be supplemented with bookshelves to store books that are not in use. Consider having several different kinds of seating available for children near the books. A rocking chair gives a child the chance to look at books all by him or herself and creates a way to be with books without interruption from others. Cushions and pillows give children the opportunity to relax and look at books together, as well as on their own.

The second component is a sturdy table that sits 3-6 children, depending on your group's size. A well-stocked shelf unit needs to be close to the table. Fill it with a good collection of age-appropriate materials, such as crayons, markers, colored pencils, chalk, and other writing and drawing tools. Paper is essential to this area. Paper can be stored in stacking bins and should be of various sizes and textures. Don't forget to add a roll of craft paper so that children can use it when large amounts of paper are needed for their writing projects. This area is a resource area, where children come to find the tools they need to express themselves through drawing or writing.

Blocks/Construction Area: Putting things together, taking things apart, building with unit blocks and other kinds of blocks, figuring out how parts relate to the whole, discovering one-to-one correspondence, and creating and manipulating groups of objects, are all facilitated by activities and experiences in the Blocks/Construction area. Additionally, building and constructing, destroying constructions, and building them again are powerful opportunities for children to experience control over their lives.

As a teacher, you play an important role supporting the exploration of materials and bridging old skills to new skills during construction and block play. Add literacy activities to this area by posting architecturally interesting photographs, providing books related to construction, and adding a way for children to sketch their constructions, either before or after they are made (e.g., an easel, clipboards, post-it paper on the wall, or a camera for taking photographs). Adding play supports to give building projects purpose also supports learning in this area. Cars, construction vehicles, space shuttles, airplanes and train tracks are all things to consider!

Math/Manipulative Area: As children's fine motor skills improve, they become interested in the manipulation of different types of hands-on materials, such as puzzles, Duplos®, linking rings,

> Building and constructing, destroying constructions, and building them again are powerful opportunities for children to experience control over their lives.

and cards. Grouping, sorting, matching, and ordering activities are beginning math skills that will prepare children for the more formal math skills that develop later.

You play an important role in introducing new materials and mathematical concepts, helping children learn to use the materials safely (e.g., reminding children that toys are not for their mouths, asking them to take mouthed toys to a dirty toy bin for washing, or asking children to wash toys and return them to storage) and expanding learning by counting, sorting, grouping, and building patterns as children play. When mathematical concepts are discussed as children play, they develop a common mathematical language that can be used as they explore the world around them.

In the math/manipulatives area, children learn mathmatical concepts through play.

TEACHING STRATEGIES FOR CREATING A CLASSROOM WITH A SUPPORTIVE ENVIRONMENT

STAY CLOSE
If you are in a classroom by yourself, stay visible at all times so children can find you if they need you, as well as reference you visually as they move around the classroom. If you are in the classroom with other adults, distribute yourselves around the classroom, making sure children are never too far away from a teacher.

PAY CLOSE ATTENTION TO STAFFING AND GROUPING
Large group sizes are particularly problematic for children in early childhood programs. Even if you have a large number of children in the classroom, there are ways to reduce the size of the groups in which children are expected to work and play. Group size can be lowered by dividing children into small groups, or by having part of the group play outside or in a multipurpose room while the other half is in the classroom.

It may be too hard for a child to wait for four other children to finish playing with a toy before she can have a turn. But, if you lower the number of children in the group to two, the wait is much shorter and she can be more successful. Ask young children to participate in large group settings as rarely as possible. It is just too difficult for them – not to mention hard on you, as a teacher!

CREATE A SENSE OF CALM AND BELONGING

A supportive environment begins by creating a sense of calm, even amid the high activity level that is normal for groups of young children. Use carpets, curtains, and other soft elements to absorb sounds and keep the classroom from being too noisy. Include pillows, floor cushions, and stuffed animals, to make the environment more home-like and familiar. Keep noise levels low by designing the classroom's activity areas to spread children throughout the available space. Provide a variety of both quiet and active experiences for children.

Having a place to keep personal things safe also helps children to feel secure and safe. Classrooms should have a cubby with each child's photo and name on it, a set of hooks to provide a place for coats, boots, extra clothing, security items from home, art projects, and notes between home and school. Keep family photographs in the cubby covered with clear contact paper, so children can look at them when they feel the need to reconnect. Maslow's theory suggests that photos of important people, objects brought from home, and places to safely store personal things contribute to a child and his or her family's sense of belonging in your classroom.

ESTABLISH A PREDICTABLE ENVIRONMENT

Children need a predictable environment that includes both new and familiar features. To provide predictability, arrange a wide variety of toys and materials on low shelves in clear containers, labeled with pictures and words. Make sure enough toys and materials are available without cluttering up the display space. Novelty can be provided with mirrors, art projects, music, sensory experiences, sand and water play activities, and texture experiences.

When you need to make changes to your classroom set-up, make them a little at a time, instead of all at once. Make sure that most of the classroom looks familiar to children, reassuring them that the classroom will be as expected when they return the next day.

MAINTAIN AND MANAGE PREDICTABLE SCHEDULES

Keeping schedules predictable requires more than just a good written schedule posted on the bulletin board, although that is a good place to begin. For young children, the daily routine needs to be fairly stable; the same thing should happen in much the same way, day in and day out. The pattern of the schedule should be reinforced by reminders, visual cues, and teacher talk.

Use pictures to help children understand schedules in a concrete way. A handmade, laminated book of photos of the children participating in each activity across the day is a great tool. For children with language and/or developmental delays, photographs or illustrations can decrease frustration, providing them with the tools for understanding when the language used may be too difficult for them.

SET for Life Language

"First we wash our hands, then we have snack, then we play outside."

"Let's look at the schedule on the wall to see what happens next."

"Yes, your mom will be here after your nap."

"First story time, then you can look for a library book."

CREATE WAYS TO DECREASE AND INCREASE STIMULATION

When considering how much stimulation to provide in your classroom, keep balance as your goal. Provide soothing activity choices such as sand, water, and sensory play, as well as creative activities using paint, clay, play dough, markers, and other alternatives to active, physical play.

Decreasing or increasing the amount of light in the classroom can help adjust the level of stimulation in your classroom at any given time. Consider using a variety of ways to light your classroom, including various types of light bulbs in lamps, and both fluorescent and full-spectrum lighting for the whole room. Adding quiet music, or removing all background noise and replacing it with sounds of nature, are additional examples. Consider all the senses to create a feeling of harmony and balance in your classroom.

OFFER PLACES TO REGAIN COMPOSURE

During the early childhood years, children have intense emotions, and as you have learned, they are still working on regulating these powerful feelings. They need places in the classroom where they can go to regain composure and calm down when they are upset. Make these spaces welcoming, soft, and comforting. Separate these areas from other activities, and equip them with comfortable chairs, pillows, and other soothing props.

Create areas for quiet in your classroom.

FOR EXAMPLE...

Alex has been diagnosed with an autism spectrum disorder. He is a bright, verbal 6-year-old who tries very hard to engage with his peers. However, his feelings are sometimes hurt, and it is difficult for Alex to manage his emotions when he feels he has been wronged. His teacher, Ms. Carrier, has learned that it is best to give Alex cool down time in the cozy corner, away from his peers, when there has been an altercation. She gives him as much time as he needs to calm down. Ms. Carrier then asks him to talk about what happened with the other classmates who were involved. This gives Alex time to get out of the emotion of the moment and re-group, reflect, and generally, be more rational when he rejoins the group.

CREATE PLACES TO BE ALONE, WITH THE TEACHER, AND WITH FRIENDS

Early childhood classrooms are stimulating places, sometimes too much so. Children need places in the classroom where they can get away from the hustle and bustle. Use shelf units, area carpets, dividers, pillows, and rugs to create places to play without interruption, and provide a sometimes much needed break from interaction and stimulation.

Create places for children to be near teachers.

Your classroom environment should allow for close communication and frequent face-to-face contact between you and the children in your care. This intimacy helps create a feeling of security, supporting emerging relationships between children and teachers. It should include places where children can be near teachers. Provide adult-sized furniture that encourages sitting side by side, room on the teacher's lap, or space to sit next to each other on the floor.

Also, provide places where children can be with friends, selecting their own level of involvement. Some children initiate involvement. Others prefer to watch friends at play before joining in. Some children can play with more than one friend, easily joining groups of children already playing, while others need the special experience of being the only playmate. An environment that provides many activity areas, and a variety of interesting things to do, will enhance children's opportunities to be with and play with friends, as well as accommodate different temperaments and play preferences.

It's important to be sure that the environment also supports children's ability to *play* with friends. Provide duplicates of popular toys, so children can play together with the same or similar toys and materials. (It is not necessary to have exactly the same toy — popular toys can be duplicated with ones that have similar play characteristics, so there are always additional toys to select if a favorite one is in use.) Make sure there are enough toys — sharing is not possible when resources are too scarce.

When there are plenty of toys and materials to go around, children are less likely to have play interrupted because of conflicts over materials. You might also consider duplicating popular activity areas, if space allows. Two block/construction areas or two sensory areas will keep children from having to wait too long to get to play in a favorite area with their friends.

CLEARLY DEFINE SPACES AND MAINTAIN ORDER

Ordered and predictable environments help children understand what to do. Order helps children make sense of their physical world and understand that there are different expectations for behavior in different areas of the classroom.

For young children, this means having a place for everything, such as a chair for every child at the table, a place to put your personal things (such as a cubby or a locker), and places to put the toys you are playing with when you are through with them. It also means having everything in its place; for example, being sure that crayons are returned to the art shelf, so they can be found the next time someone wants to use them. In order for children to learn to find the things they want and to pick up after themselves, they need an orderly, predictable classroom environment to begin with.

Create order by having a place for everything.

MAKE TOYS AND MATERIALS ACCESSIBLE TO CHILDREN

Young children learn through exploration. Because of this, they are constantly exploring their environment. Carefully plan the classroom to take maximum advantage of the child's natural desire to explore and learn. The environment must be intellectually stimulating, encouraging children to become involved with interesting objects and activities.

Children need to be able to go to shelves and choose things that interest them. Toys and materials that are piled together or in toy boxes don't offer cues as to how to use and play with them. Display toys separately, with just a few on each shelf. When given a choice among appropriate options, children usually choose toys that are just right for their own stage of development.

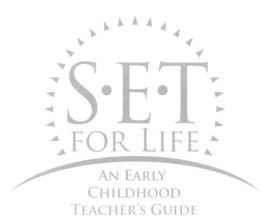

SUMMARY: TEACHING STRATEGIES FOR CREATE A CLASSROOM WITH A SUPPORTIVE ENVIRONMENT

The classroom becomes a home away from home for children. A warm, supportive, and positive environment sets the tone for everything else we want to happen with young children.

STAY CLOSE

- Stay visible at all times, so children can find you when they need you.

PAY CLOSE ATTENTION TO STAFFING AND GROUPING

- Group size can be lowered by dividing children into small groups. Less waiting time and more individualized attention can create a more harmonious classroom.
- Ask young children to participate in large group settings as infrequently as possible.

CREATE A SENSE OF CALM AND BELONGING

- A supportive environment begins by creating a sense of calm, even amid the high activity level that is normal for groups of young children. Keep noise levels low by providing soft surfaces, like pillows and carpets. Spread children throughout the available space, offering both quiet and active experiences.
- Provide each child with his or her own space to keep personal items.

ESTABLISH A PREDICTABLE ENVIRONMENT

- To provide predictability, display toys on low shelves in clear, labeled containers, offering enough toys and materials for all of the children, but without cluttering up the space.
- When you need to change your classroom space, do it a little at a time, so that most of the classroom continues to feel familiar to children.

MAINTAIN AND MANAGE PREDICTABLE SCHEDULES

- For young children, daily routines need to be fairly stable, with the same things happening day after day.
- Provide pictures and photographs to help children understand schedules in a concrete way.

    "Let's look at the schedule and see what comes next."

    "First story time, then you can look for a library book."

CREATE WAYS TO DECREASE AND INCREASE STIMULATION

- When considering how much stimulation to provide in your classroom, keep balance as your goal. Consider all of the senses and adjust noise levels, lighting, and available activities as needed.

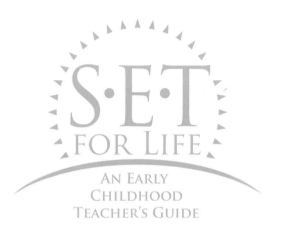

OFFER PLACES TO REGAIN COMPOSURE

- Children need places to regain composure and calm down when they are upset. Make these spaces welcoming, soft, and comforting. Separate them from other activities.

CREATE PLACES TO BE ALONE, WITH THE TEACHER, AND WITH FRIENDS

- Children need places where they can get away from the activity of a busy classroom. Use shelf units, dividers, area rugs, and pillows to create places for children to play alone when they need a break.
- The classroom should also provide many opportunities for face-to-face contact between you and children. Adult-sized furniture where children can sit on your lap or by your side, or time to sit together on the floor, gives them this time.
- Provide places where children can be with friends, selecting their own level of involvement in activities.

CLEARLY DEFINE SPACES AND MAINTAIN ORDER

- Order helps children make sense of their physical world and understand that there are different expectations for behavior in different areas of the classroom.
- In order for children to learn to find things they want and to pick up after themselves, they need an orderly, predictable classroom environment to begin with.

MAKE TOYS AND MATERIALS ACCESSIBLE TO CHILDREN

- Children learn through exploration. Children need to be able to go to shelves and choose things that interest them.
- When given a choice among appropriate options, children usually choose toys that are just right for their own stage of development.

MANAGE NORMAL AND CHALLENGING BEHAVIORS

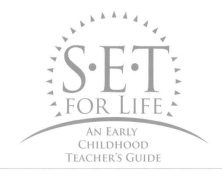

S·E·T
FOR LIFE
AN EARLY
CHILDHOOD
TEACHER'S GUIDE

In this chapter, we will learn about self-control, how it comes about and how you can help children learn this key developmental skill. We will also look at anger and aggression, providing classroom strategies to manage angry feelings and aggressive behaviors. Using these strategies can help children gain emotional and social skills, as well as create a more peaceful classroom environment for everyone.

MORE ABOUT SELF-REGULATION AND SELF-CONTROL

As we discussed in Chapter 5, children's emerging self-control is of particular interest to teachers. Gaining self-control means that children are making progress in self-regulation, and that they are beginning to understand and accept the expectations that others have for their behavior. We often mistakenly approach self-control as a guidance or discipline issue — gaining self-control is actually a developmental task (just like learning to jump, ride a bike, or read).

It helps to understand that the development of self-control happens along a continuum, moving from external adult control, to adult-assisted self-control, to independent self-control. At each point on the continuum, self-control is supported or influenced by important adults in the child's life. Self-control begins outside the child and then moves inside. This process is called internalization.

Children need adult support at all of the points on the continuum to maintain self-control, especially during the toddler and early preschool years. In order to gain self-control, children need to learn four key skills:

> • *To control emotional and physical impulses.*
> • *To tolerate frustration.*
> • *To delay gratification.*
> • *To make and implement plans.*

We will take a look at each one of these skills, and discuss ways you can support children in acquiring them in the context of your classroom.

> "Problems call forth our courage and our wisdom, indeed they create our courage and wisdom. It is only because of problems that we grow. It is for this reason that wise people learn not to dread but actually welcome problems."
>
> M. SCOTT PECK
> PSYCHIATRIST

When a child in your classroom is struggling with inappropriate behavior, devote some observation time to discover if any of these four aspects of self-control may need more development and support. You can use the teaching strategies that follow in this chapter to help them build the skills they need to manage their behavior and their emotions in the classroom.

Controlling impulses, tolerating frustration, delaying gratification, and making plans all lead to increases in self-control. As children develop these four skills, the number of meltdowns, tantrums, and conflicts diminish. But success is not guaranteed. It takes an intentional teacher to help children learn how to use social problem-solving skills in the classroom. Typically, children begin to develop these skills around the age of three, although though they don't perfect using them on their own until around age eight. In the years between three and eight, children are sometimes able to access the self-control they need, but they won't be able to do it all the time. In the meantime, they will continue to need your support.

LEARNING TO CONTROL IMPULSES

Learning to control emotional and physical impulses is part of learning self-control. This developmental task is learned within the relationships with the adults who help children control their emotional and physical responses. These important adults do this by encouraging children to hold in their minds the idea of what they want to happen. Once children are able to decide what they want to happen, visualize what it might look like, and then keep that idea in their minds, they gradually become better able to control their impulses.

Maintaining a safe environment, both emotionally and physically, comes first. When children are out of control, we must help them stop when they aren't able to stop themselves, set clear limits, apply consequences, and allow them to have experiences with natural consequences. (In Chapter 2, we discussed setting appropriate limits on p.39.)

FOR EXAMPLE...

James is a curious and energetic four-year-old boy. He is actively engaged in learning and enjoys rough-and-tumble play. He is an intense child and his teacher, Mrs. Montoya, has noticed that his parents seem reluctant to set limits for him. In the classroom, James requires a good deal of her attention to maintain appropriate behavior. He has a hard time hearing 'no.' His difficulty with self-regulation makes it hard for him to stay focused on the task at hand, and he moves quickly from one task to another without completing them, even when he's able to do the requested task. Mrs. Montoya feels James is not performing as well as he could, so she decides to make a concerted effort to help him manage himself in the classroom and complete his work. She gives him extra one-on-one time during tasks and helps him stay in one area until he finishes the task at hand. He is reluctant, but with Mrs. Montoya's help, he can do it.

Learning to tolerate frustration is an important skill.

TOLERATING FRUSTRATION

Tolerating frustration is difficult for young children. (It's hard for adults, too!) Children feel frustrated when there is a difference between what they want and what actually happens. Sometimes the frustration comes from not having the necessary skills to accomplish something, like wanting to make a bicycle go but not being able to make it happen. Other times, frustration comes from wanting something you know you can't have, such as a cookie before dinner. Either way, tolerating these experiences without falling apart is part of the emerging self-control process.

In previous chapters, we have already discussed some ways to help children tolerate frustration. Some of those strategies include preparing children for transition (p. 199), ritualizing routines (p. 198), and using children's books to discuss the experience of frustration and explore ways to manage it (p. 121 and 203). All of those strategies can be used to support children as they learn to tolerate frustration.

DELAYING GRATIFICATION

Delaying gratification means postponing participation in a pleasurable activity or experience. *Egocentrism* in young children makes them want almost everything *now*, as soon as the thought occurs to them. Learning to experience and recover from not getting what you want is an important emotional skill.

Waiting is part of everyday social experience—waiting to be line leader, waiting to get your turn, or waiting for your birthday. But don't expect young children to wait or delay gratification without your support. Make waiting easier by talking children through the waiting process, supporting it by being close and with gentle touch, and by having enough adults available to help children wait successfully.

Egocentrism:
Viewing everything in relation to oneself (in other words, why we say children think the world revolves around them – in their minds, it does!)

MAKING AND IMPLEMENTING PLANS

A final skill needed for the development of self-control is the ability to make and implement a plan to get what you want or to solve a problem. The ability to make a plan indicates a giant leap in understanding of the social and physical world, as it involves thinking of ways to make things happen, and then keeping track of those ideas long enough to implement them. As children learn that you can get what you want if you can control impulses long enough to make a plan, tolerate the frustration of waiting for the plan to work, and delay gratification until the plan is implemented, it becomes easier for them to navigate the social and emotional world.

TEACHING STRATEGIES TO SUPPORT SELF-REGULATION AND SELF-CONTROL

USE PHYSICAL PROXIMITY AND TOUCH

Staying close is the best tool to help children control impulses. When you are close by, you can support children with non-verbal cues (such as nods and smiles), verbal cues (like providing suggestions of what might work), or physical support (holding the child back with a hand on his shoulder before he acts on his impulse, giving him a moment to think about what might work).

Be aware of the children in your classroom who seem to need extra support to control their impulses, and stay near them during times when they might act without thinking. Helping before their behavior becomes a problem gives children practice with impulse control.

FOR EXAMPLE...

Three-year-old Melanie is happily playing with a drum in the sandbox. She bangs with the drumstick, enjoying the big noise she makes. Jalen, also three, runs toward Melanie. Ms. Butler, their teacher, follows quickly behind him. Just as Jalen reaches for the drumstick in Melanie's hand, Ms. Butler puts her hand on Jalen's shoulder, saying to him, "Hold on Jalen! I think you want a turn with the drum. Right now Melanie is using it. I can help you get a turn."

HELP CHILDREN NOTICE WHEN THEY ARE BEGINNING TO LOSE CONTROL

Young children don't always realize they are losing control. Emotions surface quickly and can overwhelm children before they are aware of what is happening. You can help children identify what is happening and help them control the impulse to act in a way that is unacceptable in the classroom. When you see a potential conflict developing, move in to help before it becomes a crisis.

When you notice a child who looks like they are losing control, ask for more information: "This looks like it could be hard. How are you feeling?" You might comment on physical changes, noticing that his face looks red, or that her hands are moving very fast. You can also narrate an unfolding situation, commenting, "He is really close to you, and sometimes you don't like your friends so close." Helping children to be aware of their escalating emotions gives them more tools to cope, and opportunities to ask for help.

FOR EXAMPLE...

Brooke is moving toward LaShonda, reaching for the magic wand in LaShonda's hand. Her teacher, Mrs. Washington, quickly moves close, saying, "I think you want a turn with the magic wand that LaShonda has. I can help you ask for a turn and make a plan to get one." Brooke doesn't respond to the prompt to ask on her own, so Mrs. Washington models how to ask: "LaShonda, Brooke would like a turn with the wand."

When LaShonda says, "No," Mrs. Washington says, "You don't want to share the wand. Right now it is your turn, and in five minutes, it will be Brooke's turn." Then, she helps Brooke find something to do until it is her turn, asking, "What do you want to play with while you are waiting for your turn with the wand?"

When it is time for Brooke's turn, LaShonda does not want to give her the wand. Mrs. Washington says to her, "It is hard to give up the wand when you are having fun, and it is Brooke's turn. Can you give it to her yourself or do you need my help?" LaShonda throws the wand on the floor in front of Brooke and stomps away. Mrs. Washington follows her and says, "I don't think you want to give Brooke the wand. You were really having fun with it. I can help you get another turn if you would like to play with it again. You know that throwing toys is not ok. I will help you hand the wand to Brooke instead of throwing it on the floor."

SET for Life Language

"I can help you figure this out."

"This looks very hard. How are you feeling?"

"Your hands are in tight fists – looks like you are feeling angry."

"If you need my help, I can help you."

SCAFFOLD EMERGING CONTROL

When situations arise when children do not want to do what is asked of them (sharing a toy, or stopping a favorite activity, for example), give them the choice of complying on their own or with your help. Sometimes, children need hands-on, physical support to accomplish their goals, or to do what is expected or required of them. At other times, they need reminders that they can do it, with support from an adult or on their own. Sometimes, just the reminder can help make it happen.

FOR EXAMPLE...

Eight-year-old Thomas is working on his Lego® ship when Mrs. Oxenbury gives a five minute reminder before clean-up time. When the five minutes are up, she tells children to put away their manipulatives to get ready for the music teacher. Thomas continues to build without looking up. Mrs. Oxenbury helps other children in naming their particular clean up jobs, then walks over to Thomas, saying, "Thomas, I know you worked hard on your Legos® and I think you heard me call clean up time. Can you stop building and put the Legos® away by yourself, or do you need my help?" Thomas reluctantly places the Legos® in the bin and heads back to his desk to get ready for music.

In the same classroom, seven-year-old Michaela is doing math on the computer when Mrs. Oxenbury calls for clean-up. After Mrs. Oxenbury sees that Thomas puts away the Legos®, she walks over to Michaela and says to her, "Michaela, I think you heard that free time is over and it is time to go to your desk for music now." Michaela responds, "I know, I know - just a minute. I only have two left to get to the next level!" Mrs. Oxenbury empathizes, "Oh shucks, you were almost finished and now you have to stop. Can you turn it off by yourself or do you need my help?" Michaela responds again with, "Wait! Just two more, pleeeeeese!"

Mrs. Oxenbury says, "By yourself or with my help?" Michaela again attempts to persuade Ms. Oxenbury to let her continue, saying, "I promise I'll stop when I get to the next level!" Mrs. Oxenbury repeats, "By yourself or with my help?" Michaela whines and crosses her arms. Mrs. Oxenbury says, "It looks like you are choosing my help," and reaches over to turn off the computer. Michaela stomps angrily to her desk. Mrs. Oxenbury says, "I know it was hard to stop, Michaela, and you will have another turn on Tuesday."

SET for Life Language

"Can you give Hope a turn on your own, or do you need my help?"

"Center time is over now. Would you like to turn off the computer on your own, or would you like my help?"

"You wanted more time on the swings, and it is time for lunch. We will have more outdoor time later. Would you like to hold my hand, or walk to the door on your own?"

VALIDATE CHILDREN'S FEELINGS OF FRUSTRATION

Begin by validating that the feelings of frustration a child has are okay. It is normal for people to be upset, angry, and frustrated. In Chapter 5, we explored the importance of recognizing and validating feelings. (You can turn back to page 106 for more of that discussion.) Sometimes, just knowing that an adult hears that a situation is frustrating can help a child to cope.

SET for Life Language

"It is hard to learn how to ride a bicycle! You look frustrated."

"I see that you are frustrated with your zipper. Would you like my help?"

. . . .

HELP CHILDREN BUILD SKILLS TO TOLERATE FRUSTRATION

When frustration arises from lack of skill, help children break the skill down into components and practice what they can do. Then, help them continue the activity or interaction with your support.

Wonder with the child about why things aren't working, and again, validate his or her feelings of frustration. Next, explore some options for success (e.g., finishing the task with teacher help, watching a child who already knows how to do a certain task, or working to complete the task while you verbally describe the steps). Finally, share in the child's success — celebrate with them when they stick with a frustrating task long enough to complete it!

_____

FOR EXAMPLE...

Jack and Javier, both five years old, are at the woodworking center. Jack uses the hammer with ease. Javier is struggling to do the same, but he holds the hammer handle at the very end and can't get a good grip. Javier throws the hammer to the floor, yelling, "This is a stupid hammer!" His teacher, Mrs. Chen comes over. She says to Javier, "You sound really frustrated! What is happening?"

Javier immediately apologizes, and Mrs. Chen reassures him, "You are not in trouble. Tell me what happened." He tells her that the hammer won't work, and she sympathizes, saying how hard it is when you can't get something to work the way you want it to. She asks Javier to show her how the hammer isn't working. She sees that a better grip would help Javier be more successful, so she shows him how to place his hands lower on the handle. Javier tries a few times with her encouragement. After three tries, he succeeds at hitting the nail. Javier beams proudly. Mrs. Chen comments to Jack, "Look Jack! Javier figured it out!"

_____

SET for Life Language

"Shucks! It didn't work the way you wanted it to work."

"It is hard to want to do it and not be able to do it."

TEACHING STRATEGIES TO HELP CHILDREN LEARN TO DELAY GRATIFICATION

NAME WHAT IS GOING ON

Give words to children's waiting experience so they recognize the situation. Tell them what is happening, so they understand that what they are doing has a name: "Right now, you are waiting."

Playing turn-taking games helps children practice waiting.

Comment on the emotions that may be present, as well: "You are waiting and I can tell you are not happy about it. Soon it will be your turn." Then, comment on what the child is doing that is appropriate: "You are able to wait even when you don't want to!" Validate for children that waiting is hard and sometimes frustrating. When children "feel felt," they are often better able to access the self-control they already have.

SET for Life Language

"You are waiting."

*"It is hard to wait **and** you can do it."*

PLAN CURRICULUM ACTIVITIES TO TEACH CHILDREN HOW TO WAIT

There are ways that teachers can help children develop their waiting skills within the context of curriculum. This begins with very young infants and toddlers, when we recognize that they are not yet able to wait, and we don't ask them to wait to have their physical needs met. When they feel certain that their basic needs will be met as babies, children will be better able to wait when they are older.

Young toddlers can practice waiting with simple turn-taking games, like rolling a ball back and forth. Preschoolers can further improve their waiting skills with simple games that require them to take turns and wait just a moment, with board games like Candy Land and active games like Red Light/Green Light.

For older children, you can develop curriculum that requires plan making, such as drawing a plan for an outdoor garden before planting it, or collecting a certain number of objects before starting an art project using them.

SUPPORT WAITING

Support waiting, providing assistance if necessary. Hold the child's hands as you remind her she can wait. Tell her, "I can help you wait." Hand signals such as a hand held up like a stop sign, a touch (a hand on the shoulder), or a reminder (pointing out on the clock how many more minutes until a child's turn) are examples of different ways to support waiting.

Your physical support can help children wait.

You can also support waiting by helping children think of other things to do while they wait for what they want. For example, when a child is waiting for a turn with the swing, ask her if she would like to run two laps, find a friend to play tag, or dig with a shovel in the sandbox while she waits. Be sure to let the child know that you will remember to get her when it is her turn. This will help alleviate any anxiety about you forgetting. When you make these kinds of promises, be sure to follow through, even if it requires that you write reminders or set timers for yourself!

FOR EXAMPLE...

Three-year-old Tony moves toward Kate, who is happily pushing buttons on the toy cash register. Miss Amy, seeing that Tony also wants to play with the cash register, comes over to help Tony make a plan. She encourages him to choose something to play with while he is waiting, since it is too hard for both children if he stays and hovers over Kate.

When he can't make a decision, Miss Amy suggests some ideas and guides him away from Kate. When he tries to go back over to the cash register, she puts a hand on his shoulder and reminds him that he is waiting, points to the clock, and tells him that she will not forget to let

him know when it is his turn. When he still heads toward Kate, she
gently holds onto him and reminds him that she will help him wait if it
is too hard to wait by himself.

SET for Life Language

"I can help you find something to do while you wait."

"I can help you get a turn after Jonah."

"Soon it will be your turn."

"Wait!"

TEACHING STRATEGIES TO HELP CHILDREN MAKE AND IMPLEMENT PLANS

SUGGEST PLAN-MAKING AS A SOLUTION TO CONFLICT

In Chapter 7, we introduced plan-making as a step in social problem-solving. Plan-making is also an effective way to resolve conflict. Teach children the language of plan-making so they can make plans with each other, at first with support, then independently. When there is conflict over toys/materials, encourage children to use the phrase, "I want to make a plan for ____." Once it becomes a common phrase in the classroom, children will be able to negotiate with each other and to make plans to get what they want.

FOR EXAMPLE...
Three-year-old Laquisha has the baby stroller and Elias (age 2 ½)
wants it. Elias grabs the stroller from Laquisha and runs away with
it. Laquisha melts into tears. Mrs. Wise goes first to Laquisha and
acknowledges her feelings, and then asks what happened. She then
goes to Elias and says, "It looks like you really want a turn with the
stroller. Let's make a plan for you to get one." She helps him return the

stroller to Laquisha, telling him, "Right now it is Laquisha's turn with the stroller, and in five minutes it will be your turn." She then helps Elias find something to play with while he waits for his turn.

In five minutes, Mrs. Wise tells Laquisha that it is now Elias' turn with the stroller. Mrs. Wise asks if Laquisha would like to give the stroller to him on her own, or if she would like help. Laquisha is still angry but she gives the stroller begrudgingly to Mrs. Wise, glaring at Elias. Mrs. Wise acknowledges that Laquisha is still feeling angry that she has to give up the stroller and takes the stroller over to Elias. She returns to ask Laquisha if she would like another turn with the stroller after Elias. Laquisha says, "Yes." Mrs. Wise says "Right now it is Elias' turn, and in five minutes it will be your turn again." While they are waiting, she talks with Laquisha about how hard it felt to have the stroller jerked away by Elias, and how it may also feel hard that he now has a turn with it. Then, Mrs. Wise then helps Laquisha find something else to play with while she waits to get the stroller back.

SET for Life Language

"You can make a plan for it."

"Tell her you would like to make a plan."

"You can tell her, I'm next."

"You can tell him, I want a turn in five minutes."

"You can tell her, you can have it in five minutes."

USE A PLAN BOARD TO DOCUMENT PLANS

Consider using a small plan board in the classroom to allow children to visually document their plans. When children see their wishes or desires written down, they know they are heard, and feel validated. It also serves as a reminder, so children don't worry that adults will forget. Children know that adults often forget things that are important to them, sometimes on purpose as a way of distracting a child, and sometimes from just being overwhelmed or busy. When children can make requests, have them fully heard, and see their plans written down and then followed, they feel understood and valued.

A plan board can be incorporated into a morning meeting (to make plans for where they will play), or into a good-bye routine (to make plans for what they will do tomorrow or the next time they are at school), giving voice to children's ideas and letting them know the importance of their choices. Provide children with opportunities to make choices among acceptable options. For example, they may be allowed to choose toys or games for inside or outside time, or pick what books they would like to read at story time. An extra benefit of plan boards for preschoolers is that it enhances early literacy skills, as children begin to practice identifying names and spelling simple words.

MANAGE ANGER AND AGGRESSION

Media coverage of the violence seen in school children is frequent. To be able to help children learn to deal with anger, it is important to understand what it is, how children learn to manage it, and how to prevent anger from leading to aggression.

Anger: *Feelings of resentful displeasure caused by what is perceived as unjust, mean, or insulting.*

Aggression: *Any behavior that injures or diminishes a person or thing, or destroys property.*

Anger is a normal human emotion that every person feels during his or her life. In and of itself, anger is not bad. It is how people deal with anger that often gives it a bad name. In this section, we'll talk about the difference between anger and aggression, the different kinds of aggression, and some ways that you can help children learn to manage anger in healthy and productive ways.

TYPES OF AGGRESSION

While aggression is defined as any behavior that injures or diminishes a person or living thing, or damages or destroys property, there are different types of aggression. We will discuss three different types here: *accidental aggression*, *instrumental aggression*, and *hostile aggression*.

Accidental aggression occurs during the process of sensory exploration, play, or interactions. It is not intended to hurt others. Children often bump into each other, knock over play materials, crawl over hands, and accidentally run into each other as they play. When these acts are **not** intentional, they are called accidental aggression.

You can address this type of aggression by identifying things that are accidental for children (e.g., "Oh shucks, Omar bumped into you. I don't think he meant to bump you, he was just moving fast. You can ask him to slow down.") Naming the incident as an accident also helps the child who caused the incident to be aware of his impact, even if it he didn't do it on purpose.

Instrumental aggression is aggression aimed at getting something a child wants, such as a toy, a turn, or the attention of a teacher. Typically, instrumental aggression has no deliberate intent to hurt the other person. When one child pushes another out of your lap, she is not trying to hurt the other child. She is, however, intending to take the other child's place in your lap. In this instance, a teacher could respond by picking up the pushed child and asking him to say *no* to the child who pushed him. Then tell the child who pushed that she can ask for a turn to sit on your lap.

Types of Agression

Accidental aggression —aggression that is not intended to hurt.
Example: Alice is in such a rush to get to the door for outside time, she knocks Kenny over as she runs past.

Instrumental aggression — aggression aimed at getting something you want.
Example: Javi pushes Ally out of Ms. Christy's lap, because he wants to be held.

Hostile aggression — aggression intended to harm another person.
Example: Jacob and Landon can't agree whose turn it is on the slide. Landon pushes Jacob to the ground and yells, "You're stupid!"

Hostile aggression is aggression that is intended to harm another person. There are usually two types: *overt aggression* and *relational aggression*. *Overt aggression* is physical aggression that is intentional. The child who wants a toy and bites or hits the child who has it so he will drop it, then runs away with the toy, is exhibiting overt aggression. This type of aggression seems to bother teachers the most. Research shows that overt aggression peaks between two and three years of age, and then declines during the preschool years as children learn to use language to solve problems, think about what might happen next, and gain the ability to delay gratification.

Relational aggression is designed to modify relationships between peers or between children and adults. Relational aggression occurs as children gain an understanding of other children's motivations and discover that they are often in conflict with their own motivations. Some examples of relational aggression include when children call their friends mean names, or attempt to exclude them from play. While it is very common in the early preschool years, teachers still need to address this kind of aggression, along with all other kinds, and help children make different, more appropriate choices.

Two Types of Hostile Aggression

Overt Aggression: Physical aggression that is intentional and focused. Usually declines as children acquire language to solve problems.

Example: Jacob pushes Emily down so that she will let him have the shovel she is playing with.

Relational Aggression: Verbal aggression intended to modify relationships.

Example: Yolie wants the fairy wings that Emma is wearing. She tells Emma that she won't be her friend anymore if Emma doesn't give her the wings.

HOW AGGRESSION DEVELOPS

The way aggression develops in children is complex, and it's influenced by the things children see in their families, among their peers, in society, and in the media. Aggression develops within families when children are exposed to violent and aggressive behaviors or when they see solutions to problems addressed in aggressive ways. Then, children model the behaviors they see to solve their own social problems. Families learn many of their behaviors for coping from the culture, community, and society in which they live. When a culture or community accepts violence as normal, aggressive behaviors tend to increase.

Peers also influence aggression, as children try on behaviors they see in the other children around them. When they experience aggressive behaviors with their peers, either by being on the receiving end of aggression or just by observing it around them, they may use those same behaviors to try to work out problems in their own friendships. When these behaviors succeed in getting them what they want, it reinforces the aggressive cycle. This is one of the most important reasons that teachers must address and redirect aggression in the classroom. The more children use aggression, the more natural it feels to them, and the more likely they will be to use it again in the future.

Children also learn aggressive behaviors from observing them in broadcast, print, and video media. Because young children are not good at distinguishing fantasy from reality or understanding cause and effect, they focus on one aspect of a situation at a time. Violence on television has very little context for them — they are only aware of the aggressive act, and miss both the causes and the consequences of those acts. As a result, the many acts of violence and aggression in cartoons, commercials, video, and television programming can have a profound influence on children. From these sources, children can learn that fighting is an acceptable way to solve problems, that conflict is normal, that violence is fun and exciting, and that the world is a dangerous place, where fighting is necessary.

For most children, some aggression is normal—a by-product of growing, becoming in control of and responsible for one's behavior, and of being in a group of peers at school. Children construct their knowledge about how to respond to aggression, as well as what to do when aggression doesn't work for them, by watching others. They usually move along a continuum of aggressive behaviors as their understanding and skills become more sophisticated, as the graphic on the next page illustrates.

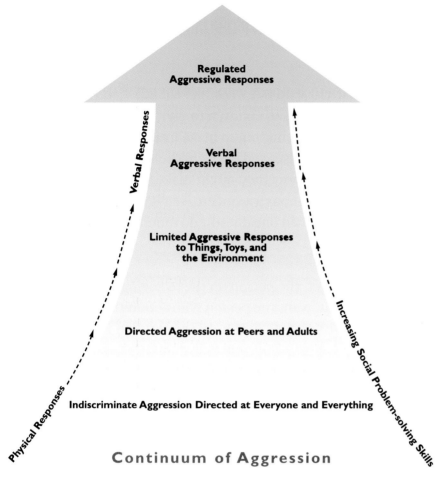

Continuum of Aggression

From Albrecht, K., & Miller, L.G. (2001). Innovations: Infant and toddler development. Lewisville, NC: Gryphon House. Reprinted with permission. All rights reserved.

At the bottom of the arrow are aggressive responses that are directed at everyone and everything in the child's environment, both people and things. As children get a little older, they usually direct their aggressive behaviors at others, the adults and peers around them. The next point is aggression that is limited to things— the toys and the environment. Finally, children learn to control their aggressive behavior, and to use words and language as the means of expressing aggression. At each point on this continuum, children can learn other strategies to cope with and solve their problems. Learning non-aggressive strategies and being taught problem-solving skills can help children replace aggression with more emotionally appropriate and socially acceptable behaviors.

TEACHING STRATEGIES TO HELP CHILDREN MANAGE ANGER AND AGGRESSION

DON'T ASK CHILDREN TO APOLOGIZE WHEN THEY ARE NOT REALLY SORRY

What is the point of asking children to say, "*I'm sorry,*" when they aren't? Don't ask children to make insincere apologies. Forced apologies are false, and both children and adults know it. Instead, ask them how they might make amends when the recipient is ready. Although a sincere, self-generated apology can be very healing, a forced one doesn't do much good for any of the children involved.

Right after a conflict, the person on the receiving end of the aggression may not want the person who committed the act to make it better. It's okay to wait until the emotion is less intense. It doesn't really matter when you talk about it. It only matters that you do talk about it eventually.

With preschool children, use the incident as a basis for a small group discussion making sure that the person who committed the act is not maligned as a "bad guy". Discuss what occurred in a matter-of-fact way with the children who were involved. Ask each one if anything like that ever happened to them (as perpetrator or victim) and how they felt about it. Check in with the children who were involved about how they are feeling now. While some of those feelings may still be present, it's likely that they'll be less intense.

Then, talk about how to make a plan, how to get a toy that you want, and what to do if someone hurts you. Or help children write a book about the episode and use it in the future with other children who resort to aggression. Children's own experiences are incredible sources for learning!

Talk to children about their intense emotions.

SET for Life Language

"Right now she doesn't want to hear your words."

"He is not ready yet. He is still feeling sad and mad."

"You don't look so angry anymore."

"Are you still mad?"

"How could you help Melissa to feel better?"

ACKNOWLEDGE, COMMUNICATE, TARGET

Children are not born knowing how to handle anger; they must be taught how to manage this powerful emotion. Most adults are quick to respond to inappropriate behavior with, *Don't!* It is more helpful to first respond to the emotion that is driving the behavior. One effective teaching strategy for helping children to deal with strong emotions is play therapy's three-step technique of setting limits, known as **A.C.T.**:

A – Acknowledge the feeling. (*"You are very mad!"*)
C – Communicate the limit. (*"You may not hit another child!"*)
T – Target an acceptable alternative. (*"I can get you a pillow to hit."*)

Behavior is generally driven by emotion. If the emotion is acknowledged, a person is more likely to feel understood. Once you have acknowledged and named the child's emotion, then communicate the limit ("You may not hit me"), and follow up with what the child **can** do to express the emotion. Children are more physical, and experience emotion with an intensity that most adults have forgotten. They may need to **do** something to release the feeling of anger, sadness, etc. Help them find ways to appropriately express these feelings.

FOR EXAMPLE...
*Marshall, an energetic five-year-old is jumping from the slide into the sandpit. Ms. Olivia says to Marshall, (**A**) "I see you have lots of energy and you are excited to be outdoors. (**C**) The slide is for sliding, not jumping. (**T**) You may jump on the grassy hill."*

*Three-year-old Maria grabs a shovel from another three-year-old, Abdul, in the sand pit. Abdul shoves Maria to the ground to get it back. Mrs. Chambers quickly moves to Maria and helps her sit up. Mrs. Chambers helps Maria to tell Abdul, "Don't push me!" Then, Mrs. Chambers helps Abdul tell Maria, "Don't take my shovel!" Afterwards, she empathizes with Abdul about having something grabbed from his hand. She **acknowledges** that he was angry, **communicates** that shoving is not allowed, and **targets** another option for his anger if it were to happen again, such as saying loudly to Maria, "That is mine! Don't take it!".*

SET for Life Language

"You are very angry, Sierra! Children are not for hitting. If you need to hit, I can find something safe to hit."

"I see you are frustrated, Joseph. Those words are too hard to hear. You can tell him you are angry, you may not call him that. You may call him by his name."

USE PREVENTION WHENEVER POSSIBLE

Whenever possible, stop aggressive acts before they happen. When you hear conflict escalating, it is time to move close to the children who are involved. Tell the children that you see them getting angry or aggressive: "Hold on! I think you are getting mad enough to hit." State what you see and hear, and wonder with the children what can be done. Make it clear what is and isn't acceptable: "You can be upset with each other, and you may not hit."

> ## SET for Life Language
>
> *"Hold on! I think you are getting mad enough to hit!"*
>
> *"You can be angry at Olivia, and you may not push her."*

USE REFLECTION WHEN PREVENTION FAILS

As we discussed in Chapter 6, reflection can be a very useful tool in the classroom. Despite your best efforts, it is inevitable that aggression will sometimes occur in any group of children. When it does, give children time for emotions to calm down. Then, help children to reflect and make a plan for the next time: "I wonder what you could do next time so that this won't happen again." Let them know you can help if they can't solve problems on their own: "If you ask a teacher for help, it might work out better than trying to handle it on your own with your fists when a friend says *no* and you want them to say *yes*."

> ## SET for Life Language
>
> *"Next time, I wonder if you could ask a teacher for help before you use your fists."*
>
> *"When you took the ball from Samuel, what happened? What could you do next time?"*
>
> *"What happened with the red truck?"*
>
> *"Why do you think that happened?"*
>
> *"What did you hope would happen?"*

DIRECT CHILDREN TOWARDS NATURAL CONSEQUENCES

Often there are natural consequences to actions that can provide valuable lessons. When children resort to pushing, pulling, or grabbing, they often don't get the results that they are hoping for. You can help them learn from these experiences by pointing out the natural consequences of their actions, calmly and without judgment. Then, help children think of what they might do next time instead.

FOR EXAMPLE...

Hope and Kristin are playing in the dramatic play area in their preschool classroom. Both girls want the doll that Ms. Kinimaka had placed in the high chair. Hope grabs the doll by the head, Kristin latches onto the legs, and they both pull, each trying to yank the doll out of the other girl's hands. Suddenly, the head of the doll pops off. Ms. Kinimaka calmly takes the doll pieces from each girl's hands. She puts them on a shelf for later repair, saying, "Wow! Look what happened! It seems like that didn't work for either of you to get the doll to play with. I wonder what else you might try next time."

HELP CHILDREN THINK OF ALTERNATIVE SOLUTIONS AND MAKE AMENDS

Children often act impulsively because they do not see other options. Help them to think before they act by talking with them about situations that have occurred both with individual children, in small groups, and as a class. Talk together with children about events, and give them the opportunity to come up with a variety of solutions to problems that occur in the classroom. When you put these difficult topics on the table for discussion, it becomes clear to everyone that all topics are okay to talk about.

FOR EXAMPLE...

Five-year-old Chloe has brought her bunny, Snowball, for Show and Tell. Her classmate, Jacob, in trying to pet the bunny, opens the cage and Snowball escapes. The bunny scurries around the room, terrified by all the chaos as the children scamper to try to catch it. Mrs. Harper finally gets the children calmed and Chloe catches and returns Snowball to the cage. Chloe is furious with Jacob and yells at him. Jacob bursts into tears. Mrs. Harper first consoles Chloe, reassuring her that Snowball is alright. She then directs her attention to Jacob.

As she talks to Jacob, Mrs. Harper learns that he had a bunny that died last year. Jacob was so excited about Snowball that he wanted to pet it before it was Show and Tell time. Mrs. Harper empathizes with his loss and his desire to pet Snowball. She then asks him what else he could do. He says, "Ask." Mrs. Harper agrees that this is a better plan. She then calls Chloe over and asks Jacob to tell Chloe what happened.

Chloe listens to Jacob's story. She has some empathy, but is still upset that Snowball was out. Mrs. Harper acknowledges her fear that something might have happened to Snowball. Jacob is able to hear Chloe's fear and says he is sorry. Chloe softens a bit and says "Ok, just don't do it again." Jacob agrees that he won't open the cage again. Mrs. Harper wonders out loud if Chloe would be willing to allow Jacob to pet Snowball later, as long as they are careful to make sure Snowball is safe. Chloe says, "Yes," and Jacob is delighted.

Later that day, Mrs. Harper has everyone sit in the circle for a class discussion about what happened. She is careful not to make Jacob the bad guy or the victim (the poor guy whose rabbit died), but goes over what happened and what went wrong. The class then discusses how to ask for things you want, and how to make plans to get them.

SUMMARY: TEACHING STRATEGIES TO MANAGE NORMAL AND CHALLENGING BEHAVIOR

Self-control and self-regulation are developmental skills. You can support this development, managing challenging behaviors in supportive ways that help children make more appropriate choices in the future. Learning to control impulses, tolerate frustration, delay gratification, and make and implement plans are all important learning tasks for young children. Teaching children to manage anger and control aggression are important teacher tasks.

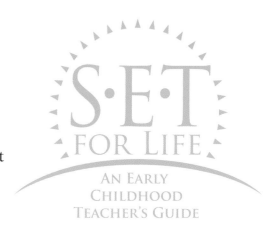

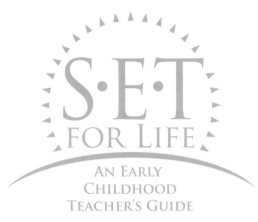

USE PHYSICAL PROXIMITY AND TOUCH

- Staying close is the best tool to help children control impulses. Provide verbal and nonverbal cues and physical support to help children think before they act.

HELP CHILDREN NOTICE WHEN THEY ARE LOSING CONTROL

- When you see a potential conflict developing, move into help before it becomes a crisis.

  "This looks very hard. How are you feeling?"

  "Your hands are in tight fists – it looks like you are feeling angry."

SCAFFOLD EMERGING CONTROL

- Give children the choice of complying on their own, or with your help.

  "Can you give Hope a turn on your own, or do you need my help?"

  "Outdoor time is over now. Would you like to hold my hand, or walk to the door by yourself?"

VALIDATE CHILDREN'S FEELINGS OF FRUSTRATION

- It is normal for people to get upset, angry, or frustrated. Help children "feel felt" when they experience these emotions.

  "I see you are frustrated with your zipper. Would you like my help?"

  "That didn't work like you thought it would. That's frustrating!"

HELP CHILDREN BUILD SKILLS TO TOLERATE FRUSTRATION

- Help children break skills down into components and practice the parts that they can do.

  "I wonder how you could get that block tower as high as you want it?"

  "I wonder if you could put the baby's clothes on if you put one leg in at a time."

TEACHING STRATEGIES TO HELP CHILDREN LEARN TO DELAY GRATIFICATION

NAME IT
- Give words to children's waiting experience, so they understand that what they are doing has a name.
    - *"You are waiting."*
    - *"It's hard to wait and you can do it."*

PLAN CURRICULUM ACTIVITIES TO TEACH CHILDREN HOW TO WAIT
- Children can practice waiting with simple turn-taking games, like rolling a ball back and forth or playing board games.

SUPPORT WAITING
- Provide physical support for waiting when it is needed. Gently hold the child's hands or shoulders, reminding him that he can wait.
    - *"I can help you get a turn after Jonah."*
    - *"I can help you find something to do while you wait."*

TEACHING STRATEGIES TO HELP CHILDREN MAKE AND IMPLEMENT PLANS

SUGGEST PLAN-MAKING A SOLUTION TO CONFLICT
- Teach children the language of plan-making so they can make plans with each other.
    - *"Right now it's Jessie's turn with the stroller. Would you like to make a plan to get a turn?"*
    - *"Tell him you want to make a plan for a turn on the swing."*

USE A PLAN BOARD TO DOCUMENT PLANS
- When children see their wishes and plans written down, they know they are heard and that their desires are valued.

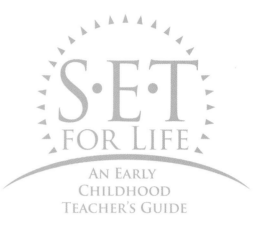

TEACHING STRATEGIES TO HELP CHILDREN MANAGE ANGER AND AGRESSION

DON'T ASK CHILDREN TO APOLOGIZE WHEN THEY ARE NOT REALLY SORRY

- Forced apologies benefit no one. Instead, help children find ways to make amends when the recipient is ready.

  "He's not ready yet. He is still feeling mad and sad."

  "Melissa's feelings are hurt. I wonder how you could help her feel better?"

ACKNOWLEDGE, COMMUNICATE, TARGET (ACT)

- **A**cknowledge the emotion behind the inappropriate behavior.
- **C**ommunicate the limit.
- **T**arget an acceptable alternative.

  "You are very angry! You may not hit Landon. I can find you something safe to hit."

USE PREVENTION WHENEVER POSSIBLE

- When you hear conflict escalating, move in close to the children who are involved. State what you see and hear, and wonder with children what could be done.

  "Hold on! I think you are getting angry enough to hit!"

  "What could you do when you want to get a turn?"

USE REFLECTION WHEN PREVENTION FAILS

- After emotions calm down, help children reflect and make a plan for next time.

  "When you took the truck from Samuel, what happened? What did you want to happen? What could you do next time instead?"

DIRECT CHILDREN TOWARDS NATURAL CONSEQUENCES

- Often, the natural consequences of actions can provide valuable lessons.

    "You were both pulling on the robot, and it broke. What can we do now?"

HELP CHILDREN THINK OF ALTERNATIVE SOLUTIONS AND MAKE AMENDS

- Help children to think before they act by talking with them about situations that have occurred. Talking about difficult topics makes it clear that it is okay to discuss them.

    "What could you do next time there are too many children waiting for the slide?"

    "Lola is feeling sad. I wonder if you could help."

PARTNER WITH FAMILIES

S·E·T
FOR LIFE
AN EARLY
CHILDHOOD
TEACHER'S GUIDE

. . . .

The challenges facing today's families mean that helping all children grow up healthy and successful can't be accomplished in isolation. In order to succeed, children need positive experiences in all the places they spend time. When teachers partner with families to support children's growth and development, everyone benefits.

"To make progress in any field, you have to take action. But the success of the action you take depends entirely on how you think beforehand."

JOHN C. MAXWELL,
AUTHOR

WHY PARTNERING WITH FAMILIES IS IMPORTANT

Partnering with families is important—even necessary—for children to fully benefit from early educational experiences. Just being in out-of-home settings requires that children contend with some level of stress because they are separated from the people they know best. This inevitable stress affects individual children differently—some children are highly impacted while others seem to manage it without difficulty. Yet even children who seem to manage such stress well may be affected by it and just not show it. Stress can be managed better by all of the parties involved if the family, school, and teacher are on the same page and readily share information with one another.

The benefits of such partnerships are well documented. Children, families, teachers, and programs *all* benefit. Children experience the greatest long term benefits when their families start participating in school settings during the early childhood years. These families are more likely to continue to participate in their child's schooling as their child gets older. Educational settings change frequently during children's lives as they move from early childhood settings to high school settings. Families are the enduring link between these changing venues.

Children whose families are involved in their school experiences are often more motivated to fully participate, have improved self-esteem, experience greater continuity between home and school, and make more significant gains in academic performance and skill development. But perhaps the greatest benefit to children is their teacher's improved abilities to match teaching strategies to the child's development, abilities, learning style, and interests.

When their families actively share what they know about their children, teachers can be much more effective in individualizing the curriculum to fit the child.

There are benefits for families, too. They gain a greater understanding of their child's educational needs and individual differences, and they get a clearer view of their child's developmental skills and abilities. Families also have the opportunity to develop more flexible child-rearing attitudes, based on information shared with them by their child's teachers, and can gain access to additional resources and services when they need them. Research also indicates that family involvement impacts children's overall school readiness because it improves the alignment between the experiences at home and the ones at school. This alignment increases the success in achieving goals that schools and families both agree are important.

It also turns out that family wellness is also positively influenced by family/school partnerships. When early childhood programs work with families to identify and address their needs, changes in parenting result and families feel more capable of fulfilling their role as first teacher.

Teachers benefit when partnerships work, too. Job satisfaction goes up and personal fulfillment increases. In particular, teachers report that it is easier to create meaningful curriculum tied to what individual children need when families are involved.

There are even benefits for schools or programs — when families are connected to their children's schools, there is greater consistency between home and school in overall educational goals, and much greater compliance with policies and procedures. Finally, involved parents are more likely to be advocates for early childhood programs and to support increases in community resources that benefit them.

Before we talk about the characteristics of partnerships, let's take a look at two theoretical viewpoints that lay the foundation for partnering. The first is ecological systems theory. The second is family systems theory. Both theories will help you understand why partnering with families is complex, dynamic, and essential.

ECOLOGICAL SYSTEMS THEORY OF HUMAN DEVELOPMENT

The ecological systems theory of human development, proposed by Urie Bronfenbrenner, suggests that development is influenced by the complex social systems in which the child and his or her family operates. Four systems of influence were identified— the microsystem, the mesosystem, the exosystem, and the macrosystem.

Microsystem: The smallest circle, consisting of the child's immediate family, and including their history, values, and cultural practices.

Mesosystem: The next larger circle, including the child's extended family, neighborhood, and school, as well the ethnicity, religion, race, socio-economic status with which the child and his or her family identify.

Exosystem: The child's larger community, including important social groups, local government, and religious organizations. The media is also a part of this system.

Macrosystem: The broader society in which the child lives, including its health and education priorities, government policies, demographic trends, and available technology. The priority given to children and families can usually be seen within this system.

Ecological systems theory helps us consider the way families and early childhood programs interact, communicate, and connect. When a family arrives at school, they bring with them all of the unique contexts in which they have experienced the social and cultural world. These factors are important to consider

for all families, and particularly important to consider when working with immigrant families and families who have recently relocated. Although these families are now living in a new culture and place, where they come from and their previous experiences will continue to influence and affect them. Your program also has its own unique context that is a part of larger systems. Values, educational beliefs, program requirements, families, neighborhoods, social and cultural expectations, and economic resources shape it.

It is no surprise that families come with unique points of view, skills, stresses, and dreams for their children and their education. The challenge for teachers and schools is to cherish differences, while also finding common ground to support families in serving as their child's primary educators.

Programs can embrace a more ecological model by focusing on the child in the context of the family. The experiences that families have had will impact how they relate to you, the ways they receive your feedback or suggestions, and how they fit into your program. Viewing the child as a part of a family unit (whatever its composition or size) allows a greater opportunity to impact children and families. When you take this perspective, the program itself also benefits, as you are able to match your approach to the needs and expectations of the families you serve.

Ecological systems theory helps us consider the way families and early childhood programs interact, communicate, and connect.

From an ecological systems' perspective, everyone a child knows, everything they do, and every experience they have, influences her life. And, each of these influences impact how the next experience will be received and further influence her life. This interactional view reminds early childhood educators that we must be aware of the long-term impact we have on young children. As we interact with, teach, and support children's learning and development, everything we do will leave an impression and influence the child. We have to be planful about how that influence builds by making interactions intentional and purposeful.

FOR EXAMPLE...

Grace is the youngest of four children. When she was fifteen months old, her mother, Susan, was sent to prison for illegal drug possession. During their mother's incarceration, Grace's Aunt Caren cared for the children, and other than a few short visits to the prison, they had very little contact with their mother. Shortly after Grace turned four, her mother was scheduled for release from prison.

Grace's primary teacher, Mrs. Ashoka, has known her since she began school as a two-year-old, and has reached out to Aunt Caren and Susan to help them make a plan for Grace and her siblings as they transition back to their mother's care. Grace has little memory of her mother, but she has pictures and her siblings' stories that give her some ideas. Nevertheless, her primary attachment figure at this time is Aunt Caren.

By sharing her knowledge of attachment and children's emotional development, Mrs. Ashoka helps Aunt Caren and Susan understand that Grace and her siblings might have some difficulty with the transition. Mrs. Ashoka proposes a transitional plan, where both women continue to provide care for Grace and her siblings, as they adjust to being back with Susan. With Aunt Caren and Susan's help, she creates a book for Grace, showing her progression from baby to preschooler, including photos and stories from her family and caregivers. The book explains her mother's absence and return in language Grace can understand, and validates the importance of all the people who love and care for her.

Mrs. Ashoka spends some extra time with Susan, sharing the many things Grace has accomplished at school, showing her Grace's artwork and photographs of Grace at school. She helps her to understand that while Grace is no longer a baby, she still needs her mother's love and support. With Mrs. Ashoka's help, Grace's transition back to her mother goes smoothly. Grace still has strong feelings for Aunt Caren and she regularly has special time with her. And, she is increasingly reconnecting with her mother as her primary caregiver. By not expecting anyone in this family to transition quickly to the new arrangement, the whole family is functioning more effectively.

FAMILY SYSTEMS THEORY

Family systems theory extends the ideas you learned about ecological systems theory and suggests that teachers view the family as a unit. In this way, teachers can focus their observations and interactions on the family's behavior, rather than on the behavior of any one individual. This theory helps us prevent placing blame by reminding us of the interconnectedness of the family. It also helps teachers plan curriculum that incorporates who children are individually, as well as who they are within their families.

Family systems theory reminds us to keep our focus on family strengths rather than focusing on a family's weaknesses. This requires us to be good observers of the dynamics of family interaction and to make efforts to get to know and develop partnerships with the entire family.

FOR EXAMPLE...

Serita's mother, Mrs. Avelar, is highly emotional about her daughter's safety. She has many fears that Serita will be injured, hurt, or threatened in some way by her participation in the pre-k program at her neighborhood school. Her anxiety is palpable when she brings Serita in for her first day to settle into her new classroom.

Serita's teacher, Ms. Baldini, immediately picks up on Mrs. Avelar's anxiety and assures her that she can stay and watch until she is comfortable with Serita's progress in adjusting to school. She finds her a comfortable place to sit in the classroom and helps her settle in as she gets the day started. After the first week of school is over, Ms. Baldini invites Mrs. Avelar and her husband to a conference with her to make a plan for addressing their concerns about Serita's safety.

When they meet, Mr. Avelar dismisses his wife's concerns about Serita and says he is confident that she is adjusting to school. He suggests that Ms. Baldini communicate only with him about any issues that arise while Serita is at school.

Ms. Baldini notices Mrs. Avelar's anxiety rising. She asks a series of questions designed to determine whom she should talk to about which issues and how the family should be contacted. Mr. Avelar quickly answers that he is the person who should be contacted regardless of the issue and that a phone call is all that is needed. Ms. Baldini agrees to contact him directly. However, she then she turns to Mrs. Avelar, asking her how information should be shared with her. Given the opportunity to respond, Mrs. Avelar asks Ms. Baldini to send a written note to the family in addition to the phone call. Ms. Baldini recognizes that Mrs. Avelar will miss information if it is only shared verbally with Mr. Avelar and agrees to written notes, as well.

By recognizing the dynamics of the Avelar family (Serita's father views himself as the family leader, and her mother is anxious that she won't know what is going on at school because of this), Ms. Baldini responds to the family's behavior rather than siding with one or the other family member. Despite her own personal discomfort with the apparent power imbalance between Serita's parents, Ms. Baldini's response ensures that Serita has the best opportunity for success in her classroom. In addition, the extra effort to call Serita's father and write a note to her mother is validation that both are valued and recognized for the roles they play within their family.

WHAT GOOD FAMILY PARTNERSHIPS LOOK LIKE

A great deal of information is available about the characteristics of family/school partnerships. The following characteristics are essential:

> • *Mutual respect and trust between all parties.*
> • *Recognition of each person's knowledge, expertise, and perspective.*
> • *Shared power and decision-making.*
> • *Open and ongoing two-way communication.*

As you consider the following teaching strategies, keep these characteristics in mind. They are designed to lead you and the families you serve toward partnerships by improving the structural supports for these four characteristics.

TEACHING STRATEGIES FOR PARTNERING WITH FAMILIES

CREATE ENVIRONMENTS THAT WELCOME FAMILIES

Classrooms are the teacher's domain. While parents and other family members come in and out relatively quickly, it is the place where you spend your whole day. Parents may or may not feel comfortable there, but it should be a goal to make your classroom a welcoming place for the important adults in children's lives.

A good place to start is to create places for adults to comfortably "be" in the classroom. This may mean having an area that has adult-sized furniture, leaving a clear pathway from the door to the child's cubby area, or providing a place to put purses, keys, or personal items while family members are reconnecting with their children. Pair these kinds of accommodations with a stated and written "open door" policy. Explain clearly and often that family members are a part of the classroom, not just visitors. Formalize your welcome by having a family sign-in book located near the adult-size furniture so you and families can recognize the frequency and importance of their visits.

The way you design and decorate your classroom can also help families to feel welcome—familiar faces and photos of children invite families into the classroom. Post photos of parents, children, and families throughout the environment, making sure that the images of families posted represent the diversity of the families enrolled your program and in the wider community. You might also ask families to share photographs.

Your classroom environment should welcome, support, and reflect a diversity of families, including biological, adoptive, divorced, foster, and LGBT families, traditional families, grandparents raising grandchildren, immigrant families, transracial families, single parent families, and blended families. The pictures you post on your wall should represent this kind of diversity, as well as a variety of skin colors and ethnicities. Books related to a variety of cultures and family structures should be on the bookshelf and read to children with regularity.

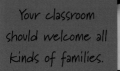

Your classroom should welcome all kinds of families.

FOR EXAMPLE...

Mrs. Scott is a pre-kindergarten teacher with a diverse classroom. One of the families in her classroom was partially formed by adoption. Mr. and Mrs. Harris are white. They have a biological son, Ethan, in Mrs. Scott's class, and a younger daughter, Hirute, who was adopted from Ethiopia, in another classroom. One day, just after Ethan arrives, Erica, asks Ethan who that "brown girl" is. Ethan response is matter-of-fact: "That's my sister." Erica challenges him, saying, "How can she be your sister? You're white!" Mrs. Scott, in the same matter-of-fact tone says, "You noticed that Ethan's sister has a different color of skin. Ethan's sister is from Ethiopia—that's why her skin is brown. Families are made in many ways."

The next time she sees Mrs. Harris, she asks if she might be interested in sharing some information about Ethiopia with the class, and also adds Norma Simon's All Kinds of Families *to her lesson plan to help discuss different kinds of families.*

Parents often feel insecure in their role as their child's first and most important teachers. Some family members try to read everything possible on child rearing and development to overcome their feelings of uncertainty and inadequacy. Others ask many questions, seeking input from a wide variety of sources. Still others may try to defer parenting decisions to their child's teacher.

Respect for parents as their child's most important teacher will allow teachers to work together with parents to support young children as they grow and learn.

DEVELOP TWO-WAY, OPEN COMMUNICATION

Frequent communication between parents and teachers is an important part of creating partnerships. No two families communicate in the same way, so you'll need to use multiple methods to make sure every family is reached. Using a variety of methods also reinforces your messages, increasing the chances that families will receive the information you need them to have.

Help children understand that families come in all colors, shapes, and sizes.

Plan to have both written and oral communication systems. Written systems help families get information to you, and provide you with a straightforward way to let families know how things are going at school. Written systems can be as simple as a spiral bound notebook in which families and teachers write sequential notes to each other as needed, or as detailed as a daily or weekly communication log. An example of a communication log is included in Appendix H. Exchanging information creates a platform for you to accurately anticipate and interpret children's needs, and for families to get information about what the child's day at school was like. Events in the child's day can be recorded and shared in written format—addressing potential problems, such as the teacher missing a chance to communicate with a family at pick-up time because of schedule differences.

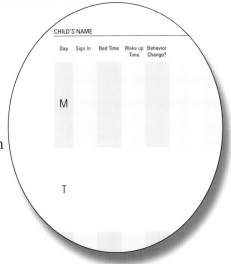

Digital strategies, such as social networking and email, offer even more chances to put information families might need into writing. And, these strategies allow families to access the information at a time when they are not responsible for transitioning their child into or out of the classroom. This ability to access information at a convenient moment is one of the reasons families and early childhood programs have embraced these new technologies.

Some additional methods of communication to consider are listed in the green box on this page. One caveat: It is important for programs to have a media use policy when they take advantage of electronic media, and to be sure that each family's safety, privacy, and comfort levels are respected.

One size does not fit all when it comes to communication. Remember that communicating isn't just about talking or sending newsletters or notes home to families — it includes nonverbal communication, as well. Becoming a good observer, asking open-ended questions, and paying attention to the nonverbal cues coming from families, can help you understand their particular comfort level. Don't forget to be sensitive to cultural factors that may influence families as well.

Family Communication Strategies

- home visits
- family orientation meetings
- family-teacher conferences
- child-led conferences
- parent support meetings
- discussion boards
- teacher blogs
- secure web cams
- program or classroom newsletters
- monthly/annual calendar of events
- sign in books
- notes sent home
- Twitter
- Facebook
- Text messages

FOR EXAMPLE...
Laurie and her husband John have three children at Smaller Scholars. Carrie is in the kindergarten program, Cory is in the toddler program, and new baby Christopher is in the infant room. Laurie and John are very laid back parents, and only require feedback or communication from the school or teacher when they need to do something or one of their children needs something. Beyond that, they are fine with a note about an accident or minor injury, and don't ask for much information about what their children are doing or how they are developing.

This all changes when the family begins to get notes from the teacher, Mr. Lamar, about Carrie scratching, pulling hair, and spitting at her friends and the teacher. A face-to-face conference reveals that Carrie has developed an allergy to peanut oil. Further conversation uncovers that John has been stopping for donuts on the way to school when he is running late on the days he drops off the children. Quickly, a connection between donuts (fried in peanut oil) and Carrie's behavior emerges. The family promises no more donuts on the way to school, and Laurie asks Mr. Lamar to let her know if Carrie repeats the behaviors, so she can talk to John, and see if there is a reason. They agree to connect again in a week. A quick note from Mr. Lamar to Laurie and John at the end of the week confirms their theory—there are no more behavior outbursts from Carrie.

The Chens are a new family at Smaller Scholars. Their only son, three-year-old Jeffrey, has just joined the preschool classroom because his father, who has been caring for him at home, is returning to work. A conversation with them reveals that Jeffrey's father speaks Cantonese to him at home and his mother speaks English to him. Jeffrey is very fluent in Cantonese, but has less expressive and receptive understanding in English.

The Chens are very concerned about how Jeffrey will cope with an all English-speaking classroom. They want to be kept informed about how he is doing. The teacher, Ms. Gretchen, and the Chens agree to talk every evening for a few weeks about Jeffrey's day, either in person or through written notes. They also exchange email addresses and agree to keep in touch that way, if they aren't able to talk face to face.

These examples illustrate the different needs of different families. Although it may seem more complicated initially, individualizing communication to particular families allows you to use your energy more efficiently, ensuring that every family has their needs met, and helping your classroom to run more smoothly.

HELP FAMILIES ESTABLISH ARRIVAL AND DEPARTURE ROUTINES

The way the day begins and ends for children is so important. It sets the tone for the day and supports not only adjustment to school, but also how the day proceeds for the child. Families play an important role in these transitions. When they establish a predictable way to separate and reunite, it promotes a feeling of well-being and security for children.

There are many ways to separate and reunite—as many variations as there are family configurations. Here is one example that might work. Encourage families to come into the room, talk a minute with you, and assist their child in putting his or her things away. Next, help the child begin to settle in by offering a toy to play with or a book to read. Don't rush the separation process. It may take ten minutes or more to get ready for the family member to leave.

When it is time to leave, encourage families to get your attention to help the transition go well. When a teacher is nearby, the child can turn to you for help in completing the separation. Encourage families to always say goodbye and remind their child when they will return.

Help families do the same upon their return. Instead of rushing off to gather the child's belongings to go home, help families cherish the reuniting process. Ask them to spend a few minutes getting reconnected before they gather the child's belongings to leave. Remind parents that it is not uncommon for their child to ignore them for a minute or two after they arrive. Encourage them to sit down and watch what the child is doing, giving the child time to finish what they are working on and get ready to leave.

Predictable arrival and departure routines benefit children, families, and teachers.

If you are teaching in a pre-kindergarten program in an elementary school, your separation and reunion routine might look very different from one described above. Nevertheless, a predictable routine will still provide security and help both you and the children in your classroom with the transition.

PROBLEM-SOLVE WITH FAMILIES

Regardless of support, communication, and shared knowledge, it is inevitable that conflicts will sometimes arise. When they do, it is important to first turn to the common ground that exists (i.e. your mutual commitment to the child or children involved), and find a way to address both your concerns and the concerns of the family.

Janis Keyser, author of *From Parents to Partners*, suggests a five step process to address conflicts or disagreements. Here are her steps for solving problems with families:

1. Listen to the family's concern, asking open-ended questions to be sure you understand the concern or issue completely. Below are some examples of ways to keep the conversation going until you really understand what the family member is saying.

> *"I think I get it, but say a little more."*
> *"What do you think was on his mind when he lost control?"*
> *"How do you handle similar situations?"*
> *"How do you want to proceed from here?"*
> *"Can we think together about what we should do?"*

2. Empathize and find common ground. Use this conversation to figure out each other's perspective and to share your experience and opinions.

3. Define the specific problem, then brainstorm or invite solutions.

4. Choose a strategy to try, make a plan, and agree to check back by a specific date. Be sure to make a note in your personal calendar, so you don't forget.

5. Thank the family for talking with you and working together to address their concern.

FOR EXAMPLE...

Alfonso is eighteen months old and just beginning a three-day program. His mother, Olivia, seemed confident of his readiness during parent orientation. However, each day after drop off, his teacher Ms. Jacobsen, notices that Olivia lingers in the hallway. She also sees Olivia peeking in the classroom window during the school day at unexpected times, like during music class.

A month into school, Alfonso is doing very well, but Olivia is still peeking into the classroom at odd times during the day, and often lingers rather than leaving once Alfonso makes the transition to the classroom. This is becoming disruptive for Alfonso, who sometimes begins to cry for his mother when he sees her unexpectedly. It is upsetting for Ms. Jacobsen, too, because she doesn't understand Olivia's unexpected appearances.

Ms. Jacobsen asks Olivia to come in for a conference. She begins by talking about how well Alfonso's transition into the classroom has gone, and invites Olivia to share her thoughts. Olivia is glad that Alfonso is doing so well, but to Ms. Jacobsen's surprise, she then asks if a child named Gracie attends the same class. Ms. Jacobsen replies, "Why do you ask?" Olivia explains that she saw Gracie hit Alfonso at the park. She is worried that Alfonso might be hurt at school, and that he might not ask his teacher for help because of his limited language skills and calm temperament.

Problem solve with families to find common ground and explore solutions.

After assuring Olivia that she has never seen another child hurt Alfonso at school, Ms. Jacobsen suggests they make a plan to make be sure Alfonso is safe and to address his mother's fears. She asks if Olivia might be interested in volunteering as a classroom helper at the start of the day. This way, she will be in the classroom to see how Alfonso is doing, and also see how Ms. Jacobsen deals with classroom safety issues and conflict between children. Olivia eagerly agrees.

During volunteer training, Olivia learns about the school's guidance and discipline policy and the ways teachers help children learn to solve problems. She also learns more about how the curriculum is designed to support children's social and emotional development over time.

Olivia and Ms. Jacobsen decide to meet in a few weeks and discuss continuing, altering, or ceasing Olivia's classroom job, based on how comfortable Olivia is feeling at that time. After six weeks, Olivia tells Ms. Jacobsen that she feels confident that her son is safe at school. However, she is happy to continue volunteering, if her help is still needed!

These problem-solving steps are not hard. The difficulty comes in making sure you work your way through them instead of getting upset, telling the family what you want them to do, or having them do the same to you. When families share their perspective, listen to yours, and help you come up with a solutions for a situation, the likelihood that the situation will be resolved to the satisfaction of all parties increases.

Problem-solving that takes two perspectives is an example of the best outcome of partnering. Instead of a win/lose situation, problem-solving in this way results in win/win situations. Neither partner feels ignored or compromised. Both partners get to think through the impact of their ideas on each other as they consider the possible solutions. This results in new insight into the perspectives and allows both teachers and families to apply the experience of problem-solving to future challenges.

EXPLAIN WHAT YOU ARE DOING WHEN YOU MODEL SET FOR LIFE TEACHING STRATEGIES AND USE SET FOR LIFE LANGUAGE

Some of the most helpful conversations between parents and teachers are not about what families should be doing, but about what teachers are doing and why. One of the purposes of this book is to increase your understanding of child development, with specific emphasis on emotional and social development. We provide teaching strategies, so that you can explain to families why you do what you do. When you keep the focus on what you are trying and what is working at school, families are less likely to feel that you are blaming them for challenges that arise with their child in the classroom.

A terrific way to help families understand the **SET for Life** approach is to use **SET For Life** teaching strategies and language in your classroom when families are present. During arrival and departure times, when family members are visiting your classroom, and during planned observation sessions by parents in the classroom, you have an opportunity to help families see successful strategies at work and hear the **SET for Life** language that accompanies them. Once families have observed these effective strategies, you will be able to open a discussion about the strategies you choose to use with their child and share the reasons for your choices.

FOR EXAMPLE...

Ms. Cho is helping three-year-old Brian gather up his things and get ready to go home — his father has just arrived to pick him up. As she puts his artwork in his backpack, she notices that he has put a few of the classroom's dinosaurs in his bag. This is not the first time Brian has tried to take toys from school home with him. She kneels down next to Brian with the bag and says, "Brian, you put some of the dinosaurs in your back pack. You really love to play with them. I think you are worried that you might not get to play with them tomorrow. I can help you make a plan to get a turn, and these dinosaurs stay here at school."

She reassures Brian that he is not in trouble, and then asks his father if he has a few minutes to wait, so that she and Brian can make a plan for the next day. Before they leave, Ms. Cho takes the dinosaurs out of Brian's backpack, and together they find a safe place to put them, so he will be able to find them in the morning. Then, they talk about how he can make sure he gets to play with the dinosaurs and what he might do if someone else has them when he wants them.

After the plan is made and Brian sees that his teacher understands his motives for taking the dinosaurs, he is ready to go home with his dad without worrying about getting to play with them the next day. His dad got to see Ms. Cho offer Brian a way to get what he really wanted in an acceptable way. Both Brian and his dad benefit from seeing the process of looking for intent in behavior and problem-solving without blaming, confrontation, or conflict.

SHARE RESOURCES

Either in your classroom, or in your larger facility, provide a family resource library that includes books, articles, and pamphlets to read and perhaps a computer, so that families can search and find information pertaining to their children and the community. In addition, you might want to have a copy or two of *Social Emotional Tools for Life: An Early Childhood Teacher's Guide to Supporting Strong Emotional Foundations and Successful Social Relationships*, so you can share them.

At times, you may serve as the family's link to community resources and services. If you aren't sure about who can help and how to get in touch with social services and community resources, you will want to find out.

HELP FAMILIES PLAN AND IMPLEMENT PREDICTABLE SCHEDULES AT HOME

Predictable routines come naturally for some families. For others, life can be too challenging or unpredictable to build routines into their lifestyles. Regardless of the family's place on this continuum, your support to help them implement more predictable schedules at home will support their child's experience at school. Routines help children know what will happen next, relieve anxiety and concerns caused by life's inevitable ups and downs, and give children the security they need to focus on whatever task is at hand.

You can raise awareness about the importance of routines by asking families during the enrollment process to share a typical daily schedule with you. As they talk through the events that make up their child's daily experience, you'll get an idea about how predictable the routines are. Sometimes, this is all that is needed to help families realize the benefits of working towards a more predictable schedule. Here are a few questions to help explore each family's daily schedule and level of predictability. They are also helpful in giving you the information you need to align children's school experiences with their home life.

QUESTIONS TO ASK TO EXPLORE SCHEDULE PREDICTABILITY

1. *Tell me about your child's typical day. What does her schedule look like from the time she wakes up in the morning until she goes to sleep at night?*
2. *What is the easiest part of the day?*
3. *How can I help when you have planned or unexpected changes in your routine?*
4. *What part of the day is the most challenging? What influences whether that time is easy or not?*
5. *How can I help when you have planned or unexpected changes in your routine?*
6. *How can I help you maintain your typical family schedule?*

In addition, consider sharing information about the importance of routines with families. Include articles in your newsletter, create a way for families to share tips and ideas for maintaining routines with each other, and discuss challenges related to routines during family meetings and conferences.

SUMMARY: TEACHING STRATEGIES FOR PARTNERING WITH FAMILIES

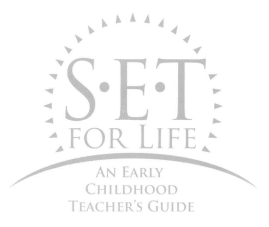

Children need positive experiences in all the places they spend time. When teachers partner with families to support children's growth and development, everyone benefits.

CREATE CLASSROOM ENVIRONMENTS THAT WELCOME FAMILIES
- Create places in your classroom for families to comfortably be.
- Ensure that your classroom reflects and welcomes the diversity of families in your classroom and in the wider community.

DEVELOP TWO-WAY, OPEN COMMUNICATION
- Frequent, individualized communication between parents and teachers is an important part of creating partnerships.

HELP FAMILIES ESTABLISH ARRIVAL AND DEPARTURE ROUTINES
- Create predictable routines for arrival and departure.
- Encourage families to take time to help their children settle in at the beginning of the day, and to spend a few moments reconnecting at the end of the day.

PROBLEM-SOLVE WITH FAMILIES
- When conflicts arise between teachers and families, find a way to address both your concerns and the concerns of the family.

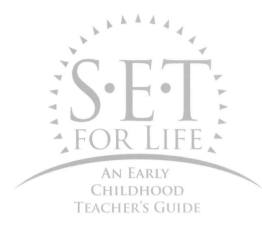

EXPLAIN WHAT YOU ARE DOING WHEN YOU MODEL SET FOR LIFE TEACHING STRATEGIES AND LANGUAGE

- When you focus on what you are trying (and why), and what is working in the classroom, families won't feel like you are blaming them for challenges that arise with their children.
- Use departure and arrival times, as well as scheduled observation times, to model **SET for Life** strategies.

SHARE RESOURCES

- In your classroom, or in your larger facility, provide a family resource library that includes books, articles, and other materials to help families find information pertaining to their children and the community.

HELP FAMILIES PLAN AND IMPLEMENT PREDICTABLE SCHEDULES AT HOME

- You can raise awareness about the importance of routines by asking families during the enrollment process to share a typical daily schedule with you. This information can help you align children's school experiences with their home life.

APPENDICES

S·E·T
FOR LIFE

AN EARLY
CHILDHOOD
TEACHER'S GUIDE

Family Diamond

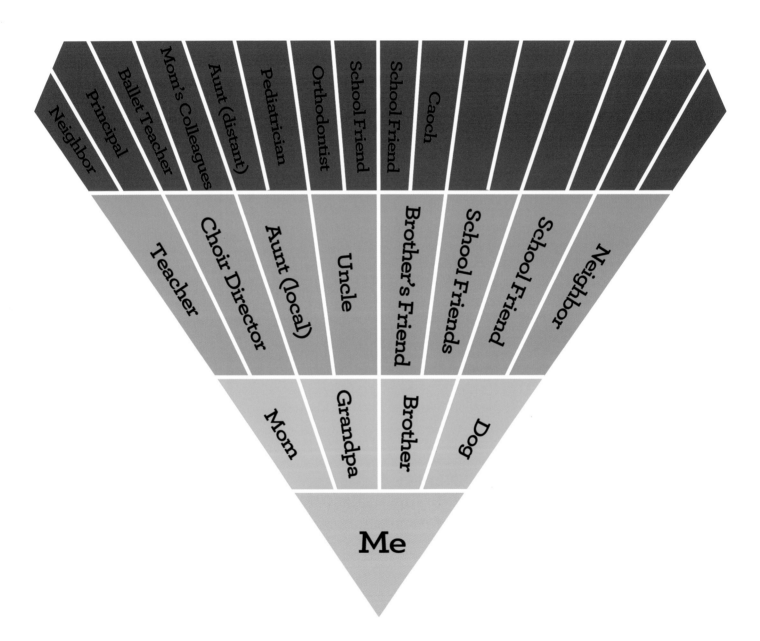

Family Diamond

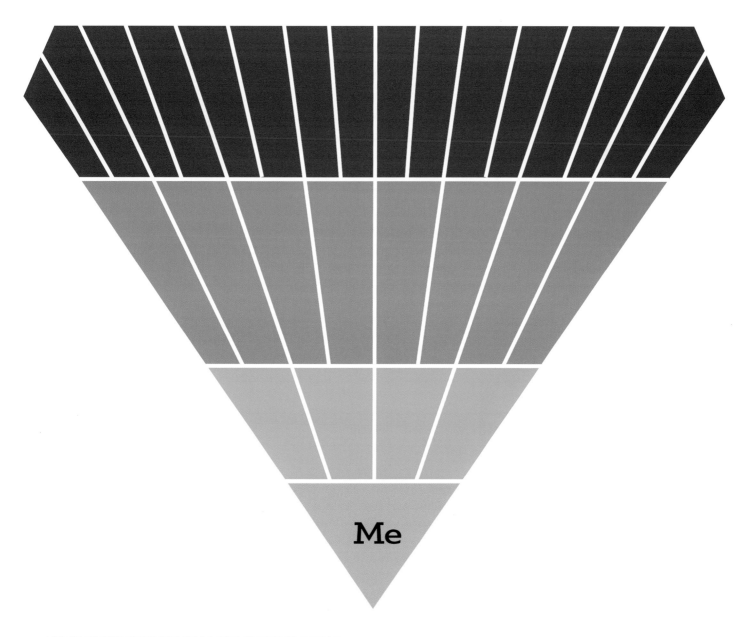

Me

Key

Me

In my household

Close to me

Other important people

Anecdotal Notes

Child   Date   Time

What I observed

Teacher's Name

Appendix C - Temperament Assessment

CHILD'S NAME   DATE

COMPLETED BY

Place an X on the point of the continuum which best describes this child's behavior.

1. Activity level

   ←——————————————————→
   LOW ACTIVITY   HIGH ACTIVITY

2. Regularity of biological rhythms

   (sleeping, eating, and elimination)

   ←——————————————————→
   REGULAR RHYTHMS   IRREGULAR RHYTHMS

3. Approach/withdrawal tendencies

   ←——————————————————→
   FINDS IT EASY TO   FINDS IT DIFFICULT TO

   APPROACH/RARELY   APPROACH/OFTEN

   WITHDRAWS   WITHDRAWS

4. Mood, positive to negative

   ←——————————————————→
   POSITIVE MOOD   NEGATIVE MOOD

5. Intensity of reaction

   ←——————————————————→
   LOW INTENSITY   HIGH INTENSITY

6. Adaptability

   ←——————————————————→
   SLOW TO ADAPT   QUICK TO ADAPT

7. Sensitivity to light, touch, taste,

   sound, and sights

   ←——————————————————→
   LOW SENSITIVITY   HIGH SENSITIVITY

8. Distractibility

   ←——————————————————→
   LOW DISTRACTABILITY   HIGH DISTRACTABILITY

9. Persistence

   ←——————————————————→
   LOW PERSISTENCE   HIGH PERSISTENCE

Adapted from California State Department of Education (1990). Flexible, fearful, or feisty:The different temperaments of infants and toddlers. Videotape. Sacramento, CA: Department of Education.

Notes:

Appendix D - Sample Transition Schedules

For an infant or toddler

Week 1

- Visit the classroom for 30-45 minutes with a family member. During the visit, hold the child and comment on what is going on in the classroom.
- Increase the duration of the visit on subsequent days, implementing routines (feeding, sleeping, diapering) as needed, so the caregiver can see how the child prefers to experience these routines.
- Caregiver or teacher begins to interact with the child after hearing her voice and seeing her in action in the classroom for a while.

Week 2

- Caregiver/teacher begins to interact more frequently with the child, initiating interactions and implementing one or two of the routine activities
- Caregiver/teacher spends time interacting with the child one-on-one while the family member leaves the room for a few minutes and up to 2 hours as the week progresses.

Week 3

- Family member begins to practice and arrival (and then a departure) routine and follows it everyday upon arrival (and before departure).
- Family members stay in the classroom with the child for 15-30 minutes before departing and upon returning.
- Child stays in the classroom for up to 4 hours without a family member. Over the week, the child's day in the classroom is lengthened until it simulates the family's schedule.

For a preschool child

First few days

- Visit the classroom for 30-45 minutes with a family member. During the visit, follow the child's lead about whether to watch or join in
- Increase the duration of the visit on subsequent days, with the family member staying close as needed and observing when not needed.
- Caregiver or teacher begins to interact with the child after hearing her voice and seeing her in action in the classroom for a while.

After a few days

- Caregiver/teacher begins to interact more frequently with the child, initiating interactions and supporting efforts to join in activities and play
- Family member establishes and implements a predictable arrival and departure schedule
- Family member begins to practice and arrival (and then a departure) routine and follows it everyday upon arrival (and before departure).
- Family members stay in the classroom with the child for 15-30 minutes before departing for a short while before upon returning.

Second week

- Child stays in the classroom for up to 4 hours without a family member.
- Over the week, the child's day in the classroom is lengthened until it simulates the family's schedule and additional days are added.
- Over the week, the child's day in the classroom is lengthened until it simulates the family's schedule.

These are sample transition schedules. Some children will transition more quickly; other may need more time to feel comfortable enough to spend the day in the classroom. Make sure to modify schedules to fit children's family situations, family needs, children's temperament, and other individual factors.

Appendix E - PLACES TO FIND GOOD CHILDREN'S BOOKS

You can help ensure that you are choosing good children's books by keeping the following in mind as you make your selections:

Characteristics of Good Children's Books
• interesting and engaging story
• familiar subjects
• inclusive language
• respectful of diversity
• free of biases and stereotypes
• engaging to the imagination
• allow for emotional exploration and reflection
• appropriate for the age and stage of audience

The list that follows includes well-known organizations that offer recommendations for good children's books for children of all ages. Check out these sites for titles to meet specific developmental, emotional, and social experiences that are relevant, helpful, and interesting to the children in your classroom.

Center for Social and Emotional Foundations for Early Learning: csefel.vanderbilt.edu

National Association for the Education for Young Children: www.naeyc.org

Reach Out and Read: www.reachoutandread.org

Scholastic, Inc.: www.scholastic.com/parents

The Book Vine: www.bookvine.com

Zero to Three: www.zerotothree.org

For more resources and book lists, you can also contact your local library's children's branch (both online and in person), child development specialists, or children's mental health care providers.

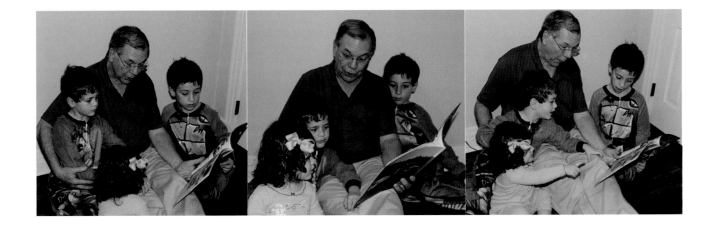

Appendix F - Sample Preschool/Pre-K Block Schedule

Time	Block
	Classroom Opens
	Routines and Relationship Building • Greeting every child upon arrival • Routines(such as breakfast, diapering/toileting, holding after transition to school) • Individual relationship-building activities (such as SET Time, book reading, playing in centers with children during self-selected manipulatives, blocks, arts and crafts, dramatic play, etc.) to fit children's needs as they transition to school
	Language/Vocabulary Development and Intentional Teaching (Literacy, mathematics; science and social studies; dramatic play; creative arts and crafts; writing; sensory play; creative arts and crafts, etc.) • Routines (such as snack, diapering/toileting as needed) • Small group language/vocabulary development activities such as singing songs; repeating rhymes and finger plays; reading books to groups; labeling pictures; listening to children's conversation; asking open-ended questions; etc. • Intentional teaching such as guided reading experiences (reading a story and asking questions); joining a child in a favorite activity and playing side by side; reading a non-fiction book about a topic of interest to a small group of children; helping a child sketch his or her block building or count then number of blocks or label the construction features (arch, buttress, bridge, road, etc.); helping children look around for the letter that begins their name; discussing the art or craft techniques children are using or asking them to tell you about their work; etc. • Group time with small groups of children
	Outdoor Play/Relationship Building, Language Development, and Intentional Teaching • Play games with children; take a walk around the playground and label things you see; play with a child who doesn't have a playmate and invite another child to join with you; make the letters of your name with bodies; jump 1 or 10 times while counting; sing a song to go along with children's play ideas; go on a bear hunt; scout out an ant hill and observe what the ants are doing; paint with water on a fence; etc. • Offer a blanket and a couple of books to read when children get tired of gross motor activities; etc.
	Routines, Lunch, and Nap/Relationship Building and Language/Vocabulary Development • Hand washing before lunch; songs, rhymes, and finger plays while you wait or while you are washing your hands; toileting/diapering; helping with table setting; etc. • Small group activities for children who have finished their routines and are waiting for lunch such as reading books to yourself; etc. • Pat children's backs; etc.
	Outdoor Play/Relationship Building, Language Development, and Intentional Teaching • Play games with children; take a walk around the playground and label things you see; play with a child who doesn't have a playmate and invite another child to join with you; make the letters of your name with bodies; jump 1 or 10 times while counting; sing a song to go along with children's play ideas; go on a bear hunt; scout out an ant hill and observe what the ants are doing; paint with water on a fence; etc. • Offer a blanket and a couple of books to read when children get tired of gross motor activities
	Language/Vocabulary Development and Intentional Teaching (Literacy, mathematics; science and social studies, sensory play, writing; dramatic play, etc.) • Routines (such as snack, diapering/toileting as needed) • Small group language/vocabulary development activities such as singing songs; repeating rhymes and finger plays; reading books to groups; labeling pictures; listing to children's conversation; asking open-ended questions; etc. • Intentional teaching such as guided reading experiences (reading a story and asking questions); joining a child in a favorite activity and playing side by side; reading a non-fiction book about a topic of interest to a small group of children; helping a child sketch his or her block building or count then number of blocks or label the construction features (arch, buttress, bridge, road, etc.); helping children look around for the letter that begins their name; discussing the art or craft techniques children are using or asking them to tell you about their work; etc. • Group time with small groups of children
	Classroom Closes

Appendix G: SET for Life - Helpful Words and Phrases

Helpful Words and Phrases	Skills or Abilities Being Learned or Practiced	Message to the Child
"Who are you talking to?" "Use his/her name."	Reciprocity; mutual relatedness/ engagement; directed communication and verbal skills	Respect for others
"You might be interested."	Mutual relatedness/engagement	Respect for others
"It's not your worry."	Anxiety reduction; responsibility for self/age-appropriate responsibility	Child is only responsible for him/ herself
"After a while, you'll be able to _____."	Competency	Acknowledges child's efforts; instills belief/expectation that she/he will accomplish goal
"What's your idea/plan?"	Organizing; problem-solving; conflict resolution	Doesn't assume wrong-doing
"How come?" (instead of "Why?")	Organizing; problem-solving; conflict resolution	Nonjudgmental interest or concern
"I wonder."	Organizing; problem-solving; conflict resolution	Nonjudgmental; adults don't have all the answers
"That sounds like a wish."	Organizing; problem-solving; conflict resolution	Acknowledges feelings behind the statement
"Yes" before "No"	Organizing; problem-solving; conflict resolution	You are the child's ally
"Let's make a plan."	Delay of gratification; self-regulation/internalized self-control	You are the child's ally
"You can ask _____. She/he might say yes, and she/he might say no."	Autonomy; choice/control	Prepares child for response
"You can _____ or I can/will help."	Control/choice; independence; decision-making	No power struggle; you are a resource for the child
"Shucks!"	Self-control (can feel emotions without needing to act them out physically)	Validates feelings; non-judgmental concern; helps children "feel felt" by others
"Hold on."	Impulse control	Nonjudgmental concern
"Those words are too hard to hear."	Empathy for others	Avoids invalidating feelings behind the words; supports social understanding
"Take a look."	Nonverbal communication	Empowers child to read and respond to non-verbal cues Focuses attention

Helpful Words and Phrases	Skills or Abilities Being Learned or Practiced	Message to the Child
"Look at my eyes." "Let me see your eyes."	Nonverbal communication	Supports reciprocal communication
"I think that makes you _____ (sad, happy, frustrated, bothered, worried, excited, etc.)."	Identifying and understanding feelings; modulation of feelings by expressing them	Validates feelings; helps children "feel felt" by others; supports development of emotional self-regulation
"You may not use those words." "You can say _____."	Boundaries/limits; social understanding (ability to voice concerns, fears, emotions in appropriate ways)	Substitutes appropriate verbal interactions for inappropriate ones
"Tell him/her." "Tell him/her in a regular voice." (vs. loud or whinning voice)	Assertiveness; advocacy	Supports child's ability to handle conflict situations verbally
"An new idea might change my mind, the badgering (nagging, whining, etc.) won't."	Identifying what works and what doesn't	Assists children to reflect and think of alternatives
"It's a challenge." "It's a dilemma."	Labeling	Assists in identifying difficult situations
"It won't happen that way."	Clarifying	Gives child structure and clarifies what they can and cannot expect to happen
"Let's think together, we'll figure it out."	Advocacy	Supports child and confirms adult as child's ally
"Wow! Tell me how you did that!"	Builds self esteem	Assists child in sequencing – by having them verbally tell the steps to what they did, avoids using praise

Appendix H: Preschool/Pre-K Communication Log

CHILD'S NAME

WEEK OF

Day	Sign In	Bed Time	Wake up Time	Behavior Change?	Parent Comments	Snacks/Meals	NAP(S)	Activities/Teacher Comments	Sign Out
M						Snack AM Y N / PM Y N / Lunch	Y N		
T						Snack AM Y N / PM Y N / Lunch	Y N		
W						Snack AM Y N / PM Y N / Lunch	Y N		
Th						Snack AM Y N / PM Y N / Lunch	Y N		
F						Snack AM Y N / PM Y N / Lunch	Y N		

REFERENCES

S·E·T
FOR LIFE
AN EARLY
CHILDHOOD
TEACHER'S GUIDE

Albrecht, K., & Miller, L.G. (2000). Innovations: The comprehensive infant curriculum. Lewisville, NC: Gryphon House.

Albrecht, K., & Miller, L.G. (2000). Innovations: The comprehensive toddler curriculum. Lewisville, NC: Gryphon House.

Albrecht, K., & Miller, L.G. (2004). Innovations: The comprehensive preschool curriculum. Lewisville, NC: Gryphon House.

Albrecht, K., & Miller, L.G. (2001). Innovations: Infant and toddler development. Lewisville, NC: Gryphon House.

American Heritage Dictionary of the English Language (4th ed.). (2009). Boston, MA: Houghton Mifflin Company.

Banghart, P., & Susman-Stillman, A. (2008). Demographics of family, friend, and neighbor child care in the United States National Center for Children in Poverty. Retrieved from http://www.nccp.org/publications/pub_835.html.

Beaty, J.J. (2013). Observing development of the young child (8th ed.). Upper Saddle River, NJ: Pearson.

Berk, L.E. (1994). Vygotsky's theory: The importance of make-believe play. Young Children, 50 (1), 30-39.

Birkmeayer, J., Kennedy, A., & Stonehouse, A. (2008). From lullabies to literature: Stories in the lives of infants and toddlers. Washington, DC: National Association for the Education of Young Children (NAEYC).

Brazelton, T.B. (1992). Touchpoints: The essential reference guide - Your child's emotional and behavioral development. Reading, MA: Addison-Wesley Publishing Co.

Brazelton, T.B., & S.I. Greenspan. (2000). The irreducible needs of children: What every child must have to grow, learn, and flourish. Cambridge, MA: Perseus Publishing.

Bredekamp, S. (2014). Effective practices in early childhood education: Building a foundation. Upper Saddle River, NJ: Pearson.

Bronfenbrenner, U. (1992). Ecological systems theory. Cambridge, MA: Harvard University Press.

Carlson-Paige, N. (2008). Taking back childhood. New York: Hudson Street Press.

Cassidy J., Kirsch, S., Scolton, K.L., & Parke, R.D. (1996). Attachment and representations of peer relationships. Developmental Psychology, 32, 892-904.

Chess, S., & Thomas, A. (1987). Know your child. New York: Basic Books.

Copple, C., & Bredekamp, S. (Eds.). (2009). Developmentally appropriate practice in early childhood programs: Serving children from birth through age 8 (3rd ed). Washington, DC: National Association for the Education of Young Children (NAEYC).

Cox, C., & Galdo, L. (1990). Multicultural literature: Mirrors and windows on a global community. The Reading Teacher, 43(8), 582-589.

Dawson, G., Rogers, S., Munson, J., Smith, M., Winter, J., Greenson, J., Donaldson, A., & Varley, J. (2010). Randomized, controlled trial of an intervention or toddlers with autism: The early start Denver model. Pediatrics, 125(1), 17-23. doi: 10.1542/peds.2009-0958

Edwards, C., Gandini, L., & Forman, G. (Eds.). (2012). The hundred languages of children: The Reggio experience in transformation (3rd ed.). Santa Barbara, CA: Praeger.

Elias, C., & Berk, L. (2002). Self-regulation in young children: Is there a role for sociodramatic play. Early Childhood Research Quarterly, 17, 1-17.

Erickson, E.H. (1963). Childhood and society. New York: Workman.

Fein, G.G., Gariboldi A., & Boni, R. (1993). The adjustment of infants and toddlers to group care: The first six months. Early Childhood Research Quarterly, 8, 1-14.

Gerber, M. (1979). Resources for infant educarers: A manual for parents and professionals. Los Angeles, CA: Resource for Infant Educarers (RIE).

Gerber, M. (1998). Dear parent: Caring for infants with respect. Los Angeles, CA: Resources for Infant Educarers (RIE).

Gerber, M. (1998). Your self-confident baby: How to encourage your child's natural abilities – from the very start. Hoboken, NJ: John Wiley & Sons, Inc.

Gilliam, W. S. (2005). Prekindergarteners left behind: Expulsion rates in state prekindergarten systems. Newhaven, CN: Yale University Child Study Center.

Gordon, I. (1970). Baby learning through baby play. New York: St. Martin's Press.

Greenberg, M.T., Cicchetti, D., & Cummings, E.M. (Eds.). (1990). Attachment in the preschool years: Theory, research, and intervention. Chicago, IL: University of Chicago.

Greenman, J., & Stonehouse, A. (1996). Prime times: A handbook for excellence in infant and toddler programs. St. Paul, MN: Redleaf Press.

Greenspan, S.I. (1989). The essential partnership: How parents and children can meet the emotional challenges of infancy and childhood. New York, NY: Viking Penguin Inc.

Greenspan, S.I. (1993). Infancy and early childhood. Madison, CT: International University Press.

Greenspan, S.I. (1997). The growth of the mind and the endangered origins of intelligence. Reading, MA : Addison-Wesley Publishing Co., Inc.

Greenspan, S.I., & Greenspan, N. T, (1989). First feelings: Milestones in the emotional development of your baby and child. New York, NY: Penguin Group.

Greenspan, S.I., & Lewis, N. (1999). Building healthy minds: The six experiences that create intelligence and emotional growth in babies and young children. Cambridge, MA: Perseus Books.

Greenspan, S.I., & Shanker, S.G. (2004). The first idea: How symbols, language, and intelligence evolved from our primate ancestors to modern humans. Cambridge, MA: De Capo Press.

Greenspan, S.I., & Weider, S. (1998). The child with special needs: Encouraging intellectual and emotional growth. Cambridge, MA: Perseus Books.

Greenspan, S.I., & Wieder. S. (2006). Infant and early childhood mental health: A comprehensive, developmental approach. Arlington, VA: American Psychiatric Publishing Co., Inc.

Hamre, B.K., & Pianta, R. (2005). Can instructional and emotional support in the first-grade classroom make a difference for children at risk of school failure? Child Development, 76(5), 949-967.

Hesse, E. (2008). The adult attachment interview: Protocol, method, of analysis, and empirical studies. In Cassidy, J., & Shaver, P. R. (Eds.), Handbook of attachment: Theory, research, and clinical applications (pp. 552-598), New York, NY: Guilford.

Hart, B., & Risley, T., (1995). Meaningful differences in the everyday experience of young American children. Baltimore, MD: Brookes Publishing.

Holmes, J. (1993). John Bowlby and attachment theory. New York, NY: Routledge.

Honig, A. (2002). Secure relationships: Nurturing infant/toddler attachment in early care settings. Washington, DC: National Association for the Education of Young Children (NAEYC).

Howes, C., & Spieker, S. (2008). Attachment relationships in the context of multiple caregivers. In Cassidy, J., & Shaver, P. (Eds.), Handbook of attachment: Theory, research, and clinical applications (2nd ed.) (pp 317-332). New York, NY: Guilford Press.

Howes, C., Phillips, D.A., & Whitebrook, M. (1992). Thresholds of quality: Implications for the social development of children in center-based care. *Child Development*, 63, 449-460.

Jalongo, M.R. (2004).Young children and picture books. Washington, DC: National Association for the Education of Young Children (NAEYC).

Katz, L., Evangelou, D., & Hartman, J. A. (1990). The case for mixed-age grouping in early childhood education. Washington, DC: National Association for the Education of Young Children (NAEYC).

Keyser, J. (2001, March/April). Creating partnerships with families: Problem-solving through communication. *Child Care Information Exchange*, 138, 44-47.

Keyser, J. (2006). From parents to partners: Building a family-centered early childhood program. St. Paul, MN: Redleaf Press.

Kirsh, S.J., & Cassidy, J. (1997). Preschoolers' attention to and memory for attachment-relevant information. Child Development, 68: 1143-1153.

Klugman, E., & Waite-Stupiansky, S. (1997, November). Play, policy, and practice: The essential connections. *Child Care Information Exchange*, 50-52.

Kovach, B.A., & Da Ros, P.A. (1998). Respectful, individual, and responsive caregiving for infants: The key to successful care in group settings. *Young Children*, 53 (3), 61-64.

Laible, D.J., & Thompson, R.A. (1998). Attachment and emotional understanding in preschool children. *Developmental Psychology*, 34(5), 1038-1045.

Lally, J.R. (1995). The impact of childcare policies and practices on infant/toddler identity formation. *Young Children*, 51 (1), 58-67.

Lally, R. (Ed.). (2008). Caring for infants and toddlers in groups: Developmentally appropriate practice (2nd ed.). Washington, DC: Zero to Three.

Landreth, G. (2012). Play therapy: The art of the relationship. New York, NY: Routledge.

Landy, S., Osofsky, J. (2009). Pathways to competence: Encouraging healthy social and emotional development in young children. Baltimore, MD: Paul H. Brookes Publishing Co.

Leavitt, R. L. (1994). Power and emotion in infant-toddler day care. Albany, NY: State University of New York Press.

Losardo, A.,& Notari-Syverson, A. (2001). Alternative approaches to assessing young children. Baltimore, MD: Brookes.

Marion, M. (2010). Guidance of young children. Upper Saddle River, NJ: Merrill.

Maslow, A. (1954). Motivation and personality. New York: Harper & Row.

Mayer, Mercer. (1968). There's a nightmare in my closet. New York, NY: Penguin Putnam Books for Young Readers.

McAfee, O., Leong, D., & Bodrova, E. (2004). Basics of assessment: A primer for early childhood educators. Washington, DC: National Association for the Education of Young Children (NAEYC).

McMullen, M.B. (1999). Achieving best practices in infant and toddler care and education. *Young Children*, 54 (4), 69-75.

Modessitt, Jeanne. (1992). Sometimes I feel like a mouse. New York, NY: Scholastic, Inc.

National Research Council and Institutes of Medicine. (2000). From neurons to neighborhoods: The science of early childhood development. Washington, DC: National Academy Press.

Nelson, Kadir. (2005). He's got the whole world in his hands. New York, NY: Dial Books for Young Readers.

Nemeth, K. (2009). Many languages, one classroom: Teaching dual and English language learners. Lewisville, NC: Gryphon House

Nemeth, K. (2012). Basics of supporting dual language learners: An introduction for educators of children from birth through age 8. Washington, DC: National Association for the Education of Young Children (NAEYC).

Nemeth, K. (2012). Many languages, building connections: Supporting infant and toddlers who are dual language learners. Lewisville, NC: Gryphon House.

National Scientific Council on the Developing Child. (2004). Children's emotional development is built into the architecture of their brains: Working Paper no. 2. Retrieved from http://developingchild.harvard.edu/index.php/resources/reports_and_working_papers/working_papers/wp2/.

Oliver, S.J., & Klugman, E. (2002, September). What we know about play. *Child Care Information Exchange*, 16-18.

Parten, M.B. (1932). Social participation among preschool children. *Journal of Abnormal Psychology*, 27, 243-269.

Perry, B.D. (2002). Childhood experience and the expression of genetic potential: What childhood neglect tells us about nature and nurture. *Brain and Mind*, 2, 79-100.

Perry, B.D. (2006). Applying principles of neurodevelopment to clinical work with maltreated and traumatized children: The neurosequential model of therapeutics. In Webb, N. B. (Ed.). Working with Traumatized Youth in Child Welfare, (pp 27- 52). New York, NY: Guildford Press.

Perry, B.D., & Hambrick, E. (2008). The neurosequential model of therapeutics. *Reclaiming Children and Youth*, 17 (3), 38-43.

Piaget, J. (1962). Play, dreams, and imitation in childhood. (C. Gattegno & F.M. Hodgson, Trans.). New York: Norton.

Raikes, H. (1996). A secure base for babies: Applying attachment concepts to the infant care setting. *Young Children*, 51 (5), 50-67.

Reisenberg, J. (1995). Reflections on quality infant care. *Young Children*, 50 (6), 23-25.

Schore, A.N. (1994). Affect regulation and the origin of the self: The neurobiology of emotional development. Hillsdale, NJ : Lawrence Erlbaum Associates.

Schweinhart, L. J., Montie, J., Xiang, Z., Barnett, W. S., Belfield, C. R., & Nores, M. (2005). Lifetime effects: The HighScope Perry Preschool study through age 40. (Monographs of the HighScope Educational Research Foundation, 14). Ypsilanti, MI: HighScope Press.

Shonkoff, J.P. et al. (2012).The lifelong effects of early childhood adversity and toxic stress. *Pediatrics*. 129(1), 232-246. doi: 10.1542/peds.2011-2663.

Shore, R. (1997). Rethinking the brain: New insights into early development. New York: Families and Work Institute.

Siegel, D.J. (1999). The developing mind: Toward a neurobiology of interpersonal experience. New York, NY: Guilford Press.

Siegel, D. J. (1999). Relationships and the developing child. *Child Care Information Exchange*, 130, 48-51.

Siegel, D., & Bryson, T. (2012). The whole-brain child: 12 revolutionary strategies to nurture your child's developing mind. New York, NY: Bantam Books.

Simon, N. (1976). All kinds of families. Morton Grove, IL: Albert Whitman & Company.

Sroufe, L.A., & Fleeson, J. (1986). Attachment and the construction of relationships. In Hartup, W.W., & Rubin, A. (Eds.), Relationships and development , (pp.51-71). Hillsdale, NJ: Erlbaum.

Steyer, J. (2002). The other parent: The inside story of the media's effect on our children. New York, NY: Atria Books.

Thompson, J.E., & Thompson, R.A. (2007, November/December). Natural connections—Children, nature, and social-emotional development, *Child Care Information Exchange*, pp 46-49.

Thompson, R. A. (2002). The roots of school readiness in social and emotional development. *The Kauffman Early Childhood Exchange*, 1, 8-29.

Thompson, R.A. (2009). Development of self, relationships, and social emotional competence: Foundations for early school success. In O.A. Barbarin, & B. H. Wasik (Eds.), Handbook of child development and early education: Research to practice (pp. 147-171). New York: Guildford Press.

Thompson, R.A. (2012). Establishing the foundations: Prosocial education in early childhood education. In. A. Higgins-D'Alessandro, M. Corigan, & P.M Brown (Eds.), The handbook of prosocial education: Developing caring, capable citizens, (p. 535-554). New York: Roman & Littlefield.

Vaughan, B.E., Kopp, C.B., & Krakow, J.B. (1984). The emergence and consolidation of self-control from eighteen to thirty months of age: Normative trends and individual differences. *Child Development*, (55) 900-1004.

Vygotsky, L. (1978). Mind in society: The development of higher psychological processes. Cambridge, MA: Harvard University Press.

Wieder, S., & Wachs, H. (2012). Visual/spatial portals to thinking, feeling, and movement: Advancing competencies and emotional development in children with learning and autism spectrum disorders. Mendham, NJ: Profectum Foundation.

INDEX

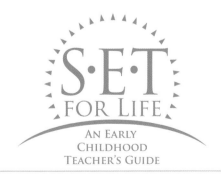

S·E·T
FOR LIFE
AN EARLY
CHILDHOOD
TEACHER'S GUIDE